Ezekiel
From Destruction to Restoration

Tova Ganzel

Ezekiel
From Destruction to Restoration

Translated by Kaeren Fish

Maggid Books

Ezekiel
From Destruction to Restoration

First English Edition, 2020

Maggid Books
An imprint of Koren Publishers Jerusalem Ltd.

POB 8531, New Milford, CT 06776-8531, USA
& POB 4044, Jerusalem 9104001, Israel
www.maggidbooks.com

Original Hebrew Edition © Tova Ganzel, 2012
English Translation © Koren Publishers Jerusalem Ltd., 2020

Cover art: Detail from *The Vision of the Prophet Ezekiel* (1830), Ditlev Blunck
Located at SMK – Statens Museum for Kunst, Copenhagen, Denmark
Photo by Villy Fink Isaksen (public domain)

The publication of this book was made possible through the generous support of *The Jewish Book Trust*.

All rights reserved. No part of this publication may be reproduced, stored in a retrieval system or transmitted in any form or by any means, electronic, mechanical, photocopying, or otherwise, without the prior permission of the publisher, except in the case of brief quotations embedded in critical articles or reviews.

ISBN 978-1-59264-520-6, *hardcover*

A CIP catalogue record for this title is available from the British Library

Printed and bound in the United States

Dedicated in honor of our children and with gratitude to those who have been and continue to be instrumental in their Jewish education and in fostering their love of Tanakh.

Nicole and Raanan Agus

Contents

Preface ix

Introduction: Ezekiel, Prophet of Exile xiii

SECTION I:
PRE-DESTRUCTION PROPHECIES

Chapter 1: The Journeys of God's Glory (Ezekiel 1:1–28) 3

Chapter 2: The Introduction of Individual Accountability
(Ezekiel 2:1–3:21) 15

Chapter 3: Symbolic Acts and Their Meaning (Ezekiel 3:22–5:17) 25

Chapter 4: The Language of the Nation's Sins: Echoes and
Leitmotifs (Ezekiel 6:1–8) 47

Chapter 5: Doom Is Coming (Ezekiel 6:11–7:27) 53

Chapter 6: Ezekiel, Deuteronomy, and Descriptions of the
Nation's Sins (Ezekiel 8:1–18) 63

Chapter 7: God's Glory Departs from the Temple (Ezekiel 9:1–11:25) .. 75

Chapter 8: Zedekiah and the End of the Monarchy
(Ezekiel 12:1–20; 17:1–24; 19:1–14) 85

Chapter 9: "Prophets" and Their Prophecy (Ezekiel 12:21–14:11) 107

Chapter 10: Individual Righteousness and Salvation
(Ezekiel 14:12–23) 119

Chapter 11: Parables: The Vine and the Adulterous Wife
(Ezekiel 15:1–16:63) 129

Chapter 12: Justice and Responsibility (Ezekiel 18:1–32) 137

Chapter 13: The Beginning of the End (Ezekiel 20:1–21:37).......... 147

Chapter 14: The Destruction of Judah and Jerusalem
(Ezekiel 22:1–24:14)................................. 171

SECTION II:
PROPHECIES CONCERNING THE NATIONS

Chapter 15: Brief Prophecies Concerning the Nations (Ezekiel 25:1–17) 183

Chapter 16: Prophecies to Tyre (Ezekiel 26:1–28:26) 191

Chapter 17: Prophecies to Egypt (Ezekiel 29:1–32:32) 201

SECTION III:
POST-DESTRUCTION PROPHECIES

Chapter 18: The People, the Prophet, and God Respond to the
Destruction (Ezekiel 33:1–33)......................... 209

Chapter 19: The Past and Future Shepherds of Israel (Ezekiel 34:1–31) .. 217

Chapter 20: God's Eternal Preference for Israel over Edom
(Ezekiel 35:1–36:15)................................. 221

Chapter 21: The Nation's Purification and Restoration
(Ezekiel 36:16–38) 231

Chapter 22: The Dry Bones and the Future Kingdom (Ezekiel 37:1–28).. 245

Chapter 23: Gog from the Land of Magog (Ezekiel 38:1–39:29)....... 257

Chapter 24: The Temple with God's Glory in Its Midst
(Ezekiel 40:1–43:27)................................. 279

Chapter 25: Temple Functionaries (Ezekiel 44:1–31) 293

Chapter 26: A New Place for God (Ezekiel 45:1–48:35).............. 301

Conclusion: A Unique Prophet, a Unique Prophecy 311

Bibliography 313

Preface

The book of Ezekiel is unique among the books of Tanakh insofar as it describes what is happening to the nation of Israel during the years surrounding the Destruction of the Temple, from an external and internal perspective simultaneously. In the prophecies of Ezekiel, emanating from Babylon, we hear the immediacy of the nation's cry of pain and grief, but also the echo of distance and disconnect. The prophet is not speaking from Jerusalem, the epicenter of these events. From his location in exile he utters a prophecy of revival and relays the divine promise that God will remain in the midst of His people forever. The prophet's title, *tzofeh*, which means observer, is largely a reflection of this reality. He is not located in the midst of the events, but at the same time he is not unaware of them; he observes them. The prophecies, especially in the first part of the book, are harsh, and the study of Ezekiel can leave one with a sense of sorrow and pain. At the same time, however, the very existence of these prophecies conveys the message that the bond between God and His people is an eternal one.

The purpose of this book is to make Ezekiel accessible to those seeking its unique perspective. I have tried to treat the biblical book systematically, with a focus on central subjects in each chapter. When the same topic appears in more than one chapter, the discussion in the latter chapter is meant as a complement to the former. I recommend reviewing the text of the relevant chapter in Ezekiel in its entirety before reading the discussion of it, although I quote the verses that are central to the discussion. In general, I have tried to avoid explaining the meaning of individual words and verses, focusing instead on the themes arising from them. Those interested in a close reading of the verses can consult the traditional commentaries (as presented in the *Mikra'ot Gedolot* editions) as well as more contemporary editions (such as *Daat Mikra*). I have tried to keep footnotes and bibliographical references to a minimum. Still, they appear wherever I wrote a chapter based on an idea that I learned from reading the works of other scholars, or as references for those seeking greater breadth or depth in a subject that I address only briefly, where there are other sources that have discussed the subject in a manner that dovetails with my aim in writing this book.

I embarked on in-depth study of the book of Ezekiel in 2000, when I chose it as the topic of my doctoral thesis at Bar-Ilan University: "The Concept of Holiness in the Book of Ezekiel." Many of the insights that came to me as I wrote my thesis have been incorporated into this book. My thesis was supervised by Prof. Rimon Kasher, and it was he who introduced me to the world of Ezekiel. After I had completed my thesis I gave it to Prof. Baruch Schwartz, and our discussions added another layer to my understanding of the biblical book. I also gained much from my students at Bar-Ilan University (in the Ludwig and Erica Jesselson Institute for Advanced Torah Studies, in the Department of Bible Studies, and in the Basic Jewish Studies program) and at Herzog Academic College. The discourse in the classes in which I taught Ezekiel, and the notes I added to my lesson plans in the wake of those discussions, helped to mold this book. I thank the translator, Kaeren Fish, and editor, Deena Glickman, for ensuring the high standard of the English edition, and the staff at Maggid – Matthew Miller, Rabbi Reuven Ziegler, Ita Olesker, Shira Finson, Caryn Meltz, Rachelle Emanuel, and Carolyn Budow Ben-David – for their professional guidance. I also thank Yeshivat Har Etzion's Israel Koschitzky Virtual Beit Midrash, where an earlier version of this book first appeared.

Preface

I was fortunate enough to study many of the chapters of Ezekiel at the homes of Prof. Moshe Greenberg *z"l* and Prof. Jacob Milgrom *z"l*, in their later years. For me, this was an encounter with two intellectual and spiritual giants. It is to these two venerated scholars, who held the book of Ezekiel so dear to their hearts until their last days, that I dedicate this book.

Finally, I thank my father and my mother for raising me in a home that was centered around Torah. The realization of that early inspiration was made possible thanks to the encouragement, patience, and devotion of my husband, Chezi.

May God reward them.

Tova Ganzel
Jerusalem

Introduction
Ezekiel, Prophet of Exile

The book of Ezekiel covers a fateful period of some twenty-two years in the history of the Jewish people, beginning with year five of King Jehoiachin's exile (593 BCE) and ending fifteen years after the Destruction of the First Temple (571 BCE).[1] It was a momentous age, unprecedented in many ways. The Jewish nation was split between two centers, with each group maintaining a disparate identity. The Destruction of the Temple and the subsequent exile engendered the unprecedented challenge of preserving the nation's identity in the absence of the familiar Temple in Jerusalem and at a distance from its land.

Ezekiel, prophet and priest and one of the exiled in Babylonia, with his prophetic messages and the encouragement he offered, laid new ideological groundwork. The Jewish nation, he declared, could and must exist in two loci – Judah and Babylonia – concurrently, with each group preserving a discrete Jewish identity.

Ezekiel's words are the only clear example of prophecy conveyed in Babylonia during the period that extended from the Destruction until Cyrus's declaration and the return to the land around thirty-five years

---

1. The last explicit date in the book is found in the prophecy to Egypt (Ezek. 29:17); it comes in the twenty-seventh year of the exile of Jehoiachin.

later. The independent status of the Jewish community in Babylonia at that time is discernible in the king of Babylonia's gracious treatment of Jehoiachin (II Kings 25:27–30; Jer. 52:31–34), and the Jews apparently maintained this status throughout the Second Temple period (Est. 2:5–6). The period between the Destruction of the Temple and the Return to Zion is also addressed by prophecies in Jeremiah, Lamentations, Isaiah, and perhaps even Joel and Obadiah. But these prophecies respond to the events of the Destruction from the perspective of the Land of Israel, as distinct from Ezekiel's prophecies, which are conveyed in Babylonia and grapple with the contemporaneous crisis in the land from a Diasporic vantage point. Thus, the prophet Ezekiel possesses a clear and unique ideological perspective. All of these factors make the book of Ezekiel essential to understanding both the Destruction and exile and their lasting influence on the Diaspora Jewish identity to this day.

The book of Ezekiel is organized almost completely chronologically, with chapters 1–24 dating to the years before the Destruction and chapters 33–48 to the years after it. The central chapters (25–32) contain a collection of prophecies directed towards other nations; these are placed together because of their content, rather than due to chronological considerations. The prophecies conveyed after the Destruction complement those dating from before it. Ezekiel's prophecies, then, may be studied both in order of their appearance and by subject. In the current volume, we will conduct an analysis that relates to the book's narrative in the order in which the prophecies appear while simultaneously examining the different subjects that appear in it thematically. We will also address the more general questions that arise from a study of the prophecies.[2]

---

2. Editor's note: All translations of biblical passages in this volume are based on *Tanakh: The Holy Scriptures* (Philadelphia: Jewish Publication Society, 1917), although changes have been made in cases in which my understanding of the language and its nuance differed from that of JPS and emendations have been made for the purposes of style and uniformity. Translations of Rashi's commentary on Tanakh are based on A. J. Rosenberg's *Judaica Books of the Prophets: A New English Translation of the Text and Rashi* (New York: Judaica Press). Translations of talmudic passages are based on Isidore Epstein, ed., *The Babylonian Talmud* (London: Soncino Press, 1961), with emendations.

Introduction

EZEKIEL IN HISTORICAL CONTEXT

Nebuchadnezzar, orchestrator of the Destruction, was a figure with a storied past, and the Destruction itself was part of a greater campaign – a campaign not described in the Babylonian chronicles we currently have, but found in scriptural sources.[3] Sometimes referred to in Tanakh as Nebuchadrezzar, Nebuchadnezzar II (604–562 BCE), son of Nabopolassar, reigned following the death of his father in 605 BCE, during the reign of Jehoiakim (609–597 BCE). A few months after he headed the Babylonian army in the battle of Carchemish against Egypt (Jer. 46:2) his father, Nabopolassar, died, and Nebuchadnezzar hurried back to Babylonia, where he ascended the throne. Immediately upon his coronation Jeremiah described him as "My servant, King Nebuchadrezzar of Babylon" (Jer. 25:9), and expressed opposition to anyone who did not accept the new king's authority (Jer. 25). In the winter of 604 BCE, Nebuchadnezzar's army conquered Ashkelon and took its king into captivity.[4] In 601 BCE Nebuchadnezzar fought against the king of Egypt in a war that depleted both forces, and thereafter Nebuchadnezzar devoted himself to rehabilitating his army. This, it seems, was the moment that Jehoiakim picked to rebel against Nebuchadnezzar (II Kings 24:1). In 597 BCE Nebuchadnezzar laid siege to Jerusalem in response to this rebellion, but it appears that Jehoiakim died before the siege.

After Jehoiakim's death, his son Jehoiachin ascended the throne. Three months later, he surrendered himself to the king of Babylonia (II Kings 24:12; Jer. 22). Nebuchadnezzar exiled him to Babylonia, along with his family and the dignitaries of Jerusalem (including Ezekiel), and made Zedekiah king in his stead. Zedekiah's rebellion against Nebuchadnezzar, against which Ezekiel rails in chapter 17 (see also Jer. 27), appears to have taken place in the year 595 BCE.[5] In response, in 587 BCE,

---

3. The historical information here is taken from Bill T. Arnold, *Who Were the Babylonians?* (Atlanta: Society of Biblical Literature, 2004), 91–99.
4. These events made an impression in Jerusalem, too, and their echo can even be felt in II Kings 24:1 ("King Nebuchadnezzar of Babylon came up, and Jehoiakim became his vassal for three years") and 24:7 ("for the king of Babylon had seized all the land that had belonged to the king of Egypt"). This may also be the reason for the calling of "a fast before the Lord" the following year (Jer. 36:9).
5. Since the Babylonian chronicle breaks off in the eleventh year of Nebuchadnezzar, the exact year of the rebellion is unknown.

Ezekiel

Nebuchadnezzar once again laid siege to Jerusalem, beginning on the tenth of Tevet in the ninth year of Zedekiah (II Kings 25:1; Jer. 39:1; Ezek. 24:1–2) and lasting until the ninth of Av in the eleventh year of his reign (II Kings 25:3–4) in the summer of 586 BCE.

There are various estimates of the number of Judeans exiled at the time of the Destruction of the Temple, but a remnant was left behind. This remnant rebelled once again against Nebuchadnezzar in 582 BCE. Consequently, this remnant too was expelled (described in Jer. 52:30). Nebuchadnezzar's imperialistic aspirations did not end with the conquest of Jerusalem; indications of this are evident in Ezekiel's prophecy to Tyre, and later in the prophecy to Egypt (Ezek. 29:17–21), which is the latest prophecy in the book of Ezekiel (570 BCE).

"Brought to Babylon as Exiles by the King of Babylon" (II Kings 24:16)

The account provided in the book of Kings supplies us with the nation's perspective on the events of Ezekiel's time – despite the fact that Ezekiel himself is not mentioned by name in any biblical book other than his own.

> At that time, the troops of King Nebuchadnezzar of Babylon marched against Jerusalem, and the city came under siege. King Nebuchadnezzar of Babylon advanced against the city while his troops were besieging it. Thereupon King Jehoiachin of Judah, along with his mother, and his courtiers, commanders, and officers, surrendered to the king of Babylon. The king of Babylon took him captive in the eighth year of his reign. He carried off from Jerusalem all the treasures of the House of the Lord and the treasures of the royal palace; he stripped off all the golden decorations in the Temple of the Lord – which King Solomon of Israel had made – as the Lord had warned. He exiled all of Jerusalem: all the commanders and all the warriors – ten thousand exiles – as well as all the craftsmen and smiths; only the poorest people in the land were left. He deported Jehoiachin to Babylon; and the king's wives and officers and the notables of the land were brought as exiles from Jerusalem to Babylon. All the able men,

to the number of seven thousand – all of them warriors, trained for battle – and a thousand craftsmen and smiths were brought to Babylon as exiles by the king of Babylon. And the king of Babylon appointed Mattaniah, Jehoiachin's uncle, king in his place, changing his name to Zedekiah. (II Kings 24:10–17)[6]

The Judean elite, exiled in the year 597 BCE, included Ezekiel son of Buzi, a priest and prophet. Jehoiachin's exile was a pivotal event for Ezekiel. The entire chronology of his book is enumerated according to the years of the exile of Jehoiachin (Ezek. 1:2; 8:1; 20:1; 24:1; 26:1; 30:20; 31:1), as are the date of the prophecy foretelling the Destruction of the Temple (33:41) and the prophecies that are revealed post-Destruction (29:17; 32:1, 17; 40:1). This exile dealt a heavy national blow to the lifestyle and status of the inhabitants of Judah. Without the king and his family, the men of valor, the craftsmen, and all the treasures of God's House and the king's house, the land was left destitute.

Nebuchadnezzar likely considered this exile, in which he removed one king (Jehoiachin) and replaced him with another (Zedekiah), to be more significant in asserting Babylonia's authority over Judah than the exile that followed the Destruction of the Temple eleven years later. The appointment of Gedalia after the conquest of Jerusalem and the Destruction of the Temple indicates that, in Nebuchadnezzar's eyes, the fate of the inhabitants of Jerusalem had been sealed earlier. But the locals saw things differently. To them, as long as the Temple was standing nothing had really changed. The events of the past, in particular the campaign of Sennacherib, still echoed in their ears.[7] They expected that another miracle would save them in the final moments of the siege, firmly believing that the Temple was indestructible.

---

6. See also Jeremiah 27:19–20, 29; II Chronicles 36:9–10.
7. In the year 701 BCE, Sennacherib set out on a campaign to the west that included the Kingdom of Judah, in order to punish Judah for rebelling against the Assyrian Empire. Assyria succeeded in conquering and razing all of the Judah's cities, exiling many of the residents, and even took the Temple's vessels. Miraculously, Jerusalem remained independent, and the Temple remained standing. As a result, from then on the Judeans in Judah believed that Jerusalem was invincible and that the Temple would never be destroyed – contrary to the words of the prophets.

Ezekiel

"Men of Your Kindred" and "Those Who Live in These Ruins": Two Distinct Populations

Ezekiel's prophecy took place at a time when two discrete groups were forming within the nation and thus the historical context is crucial to understanding the book's full significance.[8] His goal in his pre-Destruction prophecies was to impress upon the people the idea that God had departed from the Temple and a new reality had begun. The book abounds with discussions of this new reality of exile and Destruction and the dilemmas it raises. How does divine retribution relate to the individual (ch. 14, 18, 33)? What is the proper attitude towards Babylonia (ch. 17)? What is the status of the covenant between the nation of Israel and God, now that it has been violated by the nation and the Temple is to be destroyed (especially chapters 20, 36)? The prophetic response to these questions lays the foundation for understanding Israel's future restoration (ch. 34–39), the vision of the future Temple (ch. 40–48), and the prophecies to the nations (ch. 25–32).

Although most of the prophecies to the exiles of Jehoiachin relate to events in the Land of Israel at the time, some of the prophecies in the book paint a picture of God's view of the Babylonian exiles, in particular how their identity is distinct from that of the inhabitants of Jerusalem during the same years. Thus in chapter 11 Ezekiel quotes the "inhabitants of Jerusalem,"[9] who say that the exiles have distanced themselves

---

8. See Oded Bustenay, *Galut Yisrael ViYehuda BeAshur UBeBavel (Mei'ot 8–6 Lifnei HaSfira)* (Haifa: Pardes, 2010).
9. The subject of Jerusalem's names as they appear in Ezekiel is of importance. The twenty-six cases in which Jerusalem is called by name are all found in the pre-Destruction chapters (with one exception). They provide a picture of the shift in Jerusalem's status throughout the sections of the book. The pre-Destruction exhortatory chapters highlight divine anger at the city. In chapter 22, idolatry is described as defiling the city's name; Jerusalem is called "impure of name" (v. 5). From this point on, when the city and its name are impure, there is no longer any cause to apply the name Jerusalem to the city in which the Divine Presence resides. Ezekiel uses different designations for the city. The name Jerusalem is found only once in the restoration chapters, in 36:38: "like the flocks of Jerusalem ... so shall the [once] ruined cities be filled with human flocks," but this description relates not to the future, but to the crowds that filled the cities in the past.

Introduction

from God and from His land, and that they are not counted among the inheritors of the land and those close to God:

> Then the word of the Lord came to me: "O mortal, [I will save] your brothers, your brothers, the men of your kindred, all of that very House of Israel to whom the inhabitants of Jerusalem say, **'They are far from the Lord; to us the land has been given as a possession.'"** (11:14–15)[10]

God's response, however, conveyed through the prophet, is that while those taken in captivity are currently in exile, God is with them there, in a "small sanctuary:"

> Say then: Thus said the Lord God: "I have indeed removed them far among the nations and have scattered them among the countries, and I have become to them **a small sanctuary** (*mikdash me'at*) in the countries whither they have gone." (11:16)[11]

This dialogue – featuring both the claim of the inhabitants of Jerusalem and reassurance to the exiles – demonstrates the exiles' uncertainty regarding their identity in relation to the inhabitants of Jerusalem, and their questioning of God's place in their midst. Their concern is unsurprising considering that the ten tribes who had been exiled some 150 years prior (some in 732 BCE, and the majority in the years 722–720 BCE) had lost their identity. Thus, Ezekiel's prophetic message (like that of Jeremiah in Jer. 29:1–9) to the exiles is a new one, requiring a change of historical perspective. For the first time, the prophets affirm

---

10. Portions of this quote have been rendered in English following Koren's new translation (forthcoming), which I find closer to the text's meaning.
11. The Hebrew term *mikdash me'at* is often translated as "diminished sanctity" or "small sanctuary." I prefer the latter translation rendered by Block, as it indicates that God's presence is diminished both in terms of length of time and in terms of strength relative to the past. See D. I. Block, *The Book of Ezekiel Chapter 1–24*, NICOT (Cambridge: William B. Eerdmans, 1997), 349–50. In Jewish tradition, the words *mikdash me'at* have become a term for the synagogue; see Menachem Ben-Yashar, "HaMerkava BeSefer Yeḥezkel VeMikdash Me'at," *Iyunei Mikra VeParshanut* 4 (1997): 9–28.

the Jewish identity of the exiles: They remain part of God's nation – even though the Judeans still living in their homeland have a different view, maintaining that God's place is still in the Temple in their midst.

Surprisingly, this view of the inhabitants of the land does not change even after the Destruction, as we learn from a different dialogue that Ezekiel quotes in his prophecies after the Destruction:

> The word of the Lord came to me: O mortal, those who live in these ruins in the Land of Israel argue, "Abraham was but one man, yet he was granted possession of the land. We are many; surely, the land has been given as a possession to us." (33:23–24)

Even after the Temple is burned down, Jerusalem is devastated, and the captives have been led away by Nebuzaradan (II Kings 25), when only a few of the "poorest people in the land" (II Kings 24:14) are left in Jerusalem, they maintain their view that they are numerous in comparison with the solitary Abraham. Therefore, those who remain in the land will inherit the land, they claim, not those who have been taken into captivity to Babylonia. The prophet dismisses this view:

> Therefore say to them: Thus said the Lord God: "You eat with the blood, you raise your eyes to your fetishes, and you shed blood – yet you expect to possess the land! You have relied on your sword, you have committed abominations, you have all defiled other men's wives – yet you expect to possess the land!" (Ezek. 33:25–26)

Those who have remained in the land have not learned the lessons of the Destruction, indicates the prophet. They continue to sin. Note that the sins Ezekiel lists here are unconnected to the Temple, which has been destroyed. He goes on to reject the claim of those remaining in the land; not only are they not destined to inherit the land, but it will instead become completely desolate – which is indeed what happens after the murder of Gedalia.[12]

---

12. After the Destruction, the Babylonian king designated Gedalia son of Ahikam as leader. His murder at the hands of his fellow Judeans was the final nail in the coffin

> Thus said the Lord God: "As I live, those who are in the ruins shall fall by the sword, and those who are in the open I have allotted as food to the beasts, and those who are in the strongholds and caves shall die by pestilence. I will make the land a desolate waste, and her proud glory shall cease; and the mountains of Israel shall be desolate, with none passing through. And they shall know that I am the Lord, when I make the land a desolate waste on account of all the abominations which they have committed." (33:27–29)

The dwelling places of those remaining in the land described here are typical of a population that remains after the destruction of a city: They live in the open fields, in strongholds, and in caves. But if this prophecy brought some comfort to the captives in Babylonia, Ezekiel concludes that it is not only those remaining in the land who have not changed their deeds, it is also those exiled with Jehoiachin:

> Note well, O mortal: your fellow countrymen who converse about you by the walls and in the doorways of their houses and say to each other and propose to one another, "Come and hear what word has issued from the Lord." They will come to you in crowds and sit before you in throngs and will hear your words, but they will not obey them…. They hear your words, but will not obey them. But when it comes – and come it will – they shall know that a prophet has been among them. (33:30–33)

The Destruction establishes Ezekiel's authenticity as a prophet who bears God's word. But though the people come to hear God's word from him, their behavior remains unchanged even after they find out that the Temple has been burned and Jerusalem destroyed.

Both groups, the inhabitants in the land and those exiled to Babylonia, despite their differences, have this in common: Neither changes its behavior during these years. Perhaps, then, we can see that Ezekiel's

---

for the community, which ceased to be a sovereign entity; the remaining Judeans subsequently fled to Egypt (Jer. 44). Thus, there were three centers of Jewish life: Jerusalem, Babylonia, and Egypt.

prophetic mission at the time was not to call upon the people to mend their ways and repent, but rather to explain the significance of the events in Jerusalem, and thereby to lay the groundwork for the prophecies of rebuilding which came after the Destruction, as well as the vision of the future Temple.

In a time of change, Ezekiel was a novel prophet, the first to function in the Diaspora. His prophecy constituted a significant milestone; it fostered a Jewish presence in the Diaspora and established that God's presence existed there in a "small sanctuary." The ideological infrastructure in Ezekiel's prophecy, it appears, laid the spiritual groundwork upon which Diaspora Jewry has based itself for two thousand years of exile, primarily since the Second Temple's destruction. In effect, it attests to the fact that Jews can live in any place in the world. Even following the establishment of the State of Israel, this infrastructure remains relevant.

Section I
Pre-Destruction Prophecies

The first section of the book of Ezekiel, comprising the first twenty-four chapters, consists of the prophecies expressed by Ezekiel in the years before the Destruction. Located as he was in Babylonia following the exile, Ezekiel was in a novel position: He was prophesying from outside of the Land of Israel about the future of the nation.

The purpose of Ezekiel's prophecies during this period was to inform the people that God had departed from His Temple in Jerusalem. He therefore describes in detail the divine chariot and the journeys of God's glory outside the Temple (especially in chapter 1 and chapters 10–11). Moreover, Ezekiel emphasizes that the Destruction of the Temple is only a matter of time; even in the years leading up to this event, Jerusalem is defiled and God's presence is not found within the city (1:28–3:15; 24:15–27). Ezekiel's symbolic acts (especially in chapters 4–5) reinforce this message, which climaxes in the description of the sins of the people and the corruption of the city (especially in chapters 8–11, 15, 23). The essence of the prophet's role is to be an observer (*tzofeh*) of what is happening (3:17–21; 33:1–9), along with conveying his prophecies to those who visit his house (8:1; 14:1; 20:1). Employing a number of different forms – symbolic acts, language drawn from biblical books, and parables – Ezekiel lends credibility to the dire and disheartening predictions for the nation's future.

Chapter 1

The Journeys of God's Glory

Ezekiel 1:1–28

SETTING THE STAGE: EZEKIEL AND THE SIGNIFICANCE OF "THIRTY YEARS" (1:1–2)

A literalist (*peshat*) reading of the prophecies of Ezekiel raises many difficulties. Rabbi Eliezer of Beaugency,[1] in his commentary on Ezekiel, notes these complexities, explaining the difficulty of interpreting the words of the prophet in his introduction:

> Son of man, see with your own eyes and hear with your own ears and set your heart to the language of this prophet, for it is wondrous, esoteric, and brief. Even to our sages, of blessed memory,

---

1. Rabbi Eliezer of Beaugency lived in the twelfth century and belonged to the second generation of Tosafists. Of his commentary on the Bible the sections on Isaiah, Ezekiel, and the Twelve Minor Prophets are still extant. In his commentary he represents the extreme literalist school in France, emerging from the school of Rabbi Samuel ben Meir (Rashbam). One of the distinguishing features of this school is the almost complete avoidance of reliance on midrash (see Menachem Cohen, ed., *Mikraot Gedolot "HaKeter": Sefer Yeḥezkel* [Jerusalem: Bar-Ilan University Press, 2000], 10).

his words appeared to contradict teachings of the Torah, so esoteric and concise were they.

The first specific problem that arises for Rabbi Eliezer of Beaugency (and many other commentaries) is the date with which the book begins: "In the thirtieth year, on the fifth day of the fourth month" (Ezek. 1:1). First, there is no indication of the point from which the prophet counts these thirty years. Second, the next verse gives a different date, counting from the exile of Jehoiachin, but the relationship between the two counts is unclear: "On the fifth of the month – it was the fifth year of the exile of King Jehoiachin" (v. 2).

Rabbi Eliezer of Beaugency writes in his introduction:

> He does not explain how he calculates "thirty years." And although the words of *Targum* [*Yonatan*] are … that this is [thirty years] since Hilkiah the Priest found the Torah scroll, nevertheless this is not the [customary] way of the Writings…. We might suggest the following: We find no prophet rebuking his own generation about Torah and the commandments the way he does. Most of what he says is like Torah speech; he almost repeats the entire Torah for them…. It was as though he was teaching them a new Torah, for it had been forgotten in the days of Menashe. And since his prophecies and his words concerned the words of the Torah scroll that had been found, therefore he counted [the years] from the time of its discovery, for the whole essence of his book is dependent upon it.

Rabbi Eliezer of Beaugency accepts the solution proposed by *Targum Yonatan* – that the prophet refers in the first verse to the thirty years that had passed since the discovery of the Torah scroll during the reign of Josiah – even while acknowledging that "this is not the [customary] way of the Writings [to count]." But his answer does not simply resolve the question of the dates; it emphasizes a connection to the Torah that is significant. Rabbi Eliezer of Beaugency thus appears to be solving two fundamental difficulties in Ezekiel: First, how is it possible that during such fateful years for the Jewish people, Ezekiel almost entirely avoids any call to the people to repent? Second, why does Ezekiel, unlike all

The Journeys of God's Glory

other prophets, give the people statutes and laws? And some that appear to contradict laws of the Torah, at that? By adopting the explanation of "the thirtieth year" as referring to the discovery of the Torah scroll in the days of Josiah, Rabbi Eliezer of Beaugency emphasizes that despite the discrepancies between the perceptions familiar to us from the Torah and those arising from a study of the book of Ezekiel, the prophecy of Ezekiel in its entirety rests upon the Torah, as emphasized at the very outset when the date of the prophecy is noted in relation to the discovery of the Torah scroll in the days of Josiah.

Other commentators, meanwhile, attribute different significance to the thirty years: Rabbi Menachem ben Shimon[2] views the date as an indication of Ezekiel's age, while Rashi, Radak, Rabbi Joseph Kara,[3] and other commentaries, in light of *Seder Olam Rabba* 24, regard the "thirty years" as placing the date in the context of the Jubilee cycle. Although this view is not supported by the plain text, it does offer another significant message to the inhabitants of Babylonia of that time – and perhaps even future generations. Counting the years in accordance with the Jubilee in the Land of Israel creates a direct link between the prophecy conveyed outside the land and events in the land. Likewise, the book thus alludes, right from the outset, to the fact that Ezekiel's prophecy in its entirety is for the sake of the Land of Israel, as Rabbi Judah HaLevi notes: "Whosoever prophesied did so either in the [Holy] Land, or concerning it… Ezekiel and Daniel on account of it" (*Kuzari* II:14).[4]

---

2. Active in Posquières, Provence, in the twelfth century, Rabbi Menachem ben Shimon served as an example of a purely literalist, or *peshat*-based commentary, eschewing both philosophical and midrashic approaches and focusing on language and style. Of his commentaries, only those on Jeremiah and Ezekiel remain today (see Cohen, *Yeḥezkel*, 11).
3. Rabbi Joseph Kara (1055–1125) was one of the great molders of *peshat* exegesis in his time. He was a disciple and colleague of Rashi, and his commentaries are based on Rashi's commentaries on Tanakh. He devoted himself primarily to teaching Tanakh and its commentary; this would appear to be the reason for his being known as "Kara" (see Cohen, *Yeḥezkel*, 9–10). His extant commentaries cover only some of the books of Tanakh; he may have written commentaries on all the books (see Avraham Grossman, *Ḥakhmei Tzarfat HaRishonim* [Jerusalem: Magnes, 2001], 289).
4. Translator's note: Translations of the *Kuzari* in this volume are taken from Hartwig Hirschfeld, trans., *The Kuzari (Kitab al Khazari): An Argument for the Faith of Israel* (New York: Schocken, 1964).

Ezekiel 1:1–28

Admittedly, this view, too, is far removed from the literal meaning of the text. Perhaps Moshe Greenberg, stating "The date in vs. 1 is explained in vs. 2 in terms of the era of Jehoiachin's exile,"[5] is correct in proposing that the reference is to the thirtieth year of the exile of Jehoiachin, and that the aim of this introduction is to make note of the date of the last prophecy of the book (after the prophecy in the twenty-seventh year, as recorded in 29:17).

THE CHARIOT AND THE JOURNEYS OF GOD'S GLORY (1:3–28)

At the beginning of his book, Ezekiel describes how "the heavens were opened and I saw visions of God." Chapter 1, described by Ḥazal as the working of the divine chariot (*ma'aseh merkava*), is one of the most difficult chapters to understand in the Tanakh.[6] We will address the significance of the divine chariot as the introduction to the book of Ezekiel as a whole. At the beginning of the chapter we are told that Ezekiel receives his prophecy in Babylonia: "When I was in the community of exiles by the Chebar River" (1:1), a point that Rashi and Radak note in their commentaries.

Ezekiel's vivid description of "the visions of God" in chapter 1 expresses the power of the prophet's encounter with the divine vision. He portrays these visions in all their force ("a stormy wind" [v. 4], "they went" [vv. 12–13]; "dashing to and fro" [v.14]); in all their color ("a huge cloud and flashing fire, surrounded by a radiance" [v. 4]; "their sparkle was like the luster of burnished bronze" [v. 7]; "looked like burning coals of fire. This fire, suggestive of torches" [v. 13]; "in appearance

---

5. See Moshe Greenberg, *Ezekiel 1–20*, The Anchor Bible Dictionary (Garden City, NY: Doubleday, 1983), 39.
6. The well-known teaching of our sages on the Mishna (Ḥagiga 2:1) makes this point: "The subject of forbidden relations may not be expounded in the presence of three... nor [the work of] the chariot in the presence of one." "Thus far you have permission to speak, thenceforward you have not permission to speak, for so it is written in the book of Ben Sira: Seek not things that are too hard for thee, and search not things that are hidden from thee" (Ḥagiga 13a). Similarly, Rashi's commentary on Ezekiel 1:27: "No permission was granted to ponder over this verse," and on 8:2, "It is forbidden to reflect on this verse."

like sapphire" [v. 26 and elsewhere]); and in all their sound ("like the sound of mighty waters…a tumult like the din of an army" [v. 24]). As the prophet's description of the vision progresses, he gradually seems to lose his grasp of tangible expression. It grows increasingly difficult for him to describe what he is experiencing. See, for example, the pervasive use of the prepositional *kaf* (like), and the growing number of instances in which he refers to a *demut* (semblance or likeness):

> Above the expanse over their heads was **the semblance of** a throne, **in appearance like** sapphire; and on top, upon **this semblance** of a throne, there was **the semblance** of a human form. From **what appeared as** his loins up, I saw **a gleam as of** amber – **what looked like** a fire encased in a frame…**what looked like** fire. There was a radiance all about him. **Like the appearance of the bow which shines in the clouds on a day of rain, such was the appearance** of the surrounding radiance. That was **the appearance of the semblance** of the presence of the Lord. (vv. 26–28)

This divine vision, which appears at the very outset of the book, holds the key to understanding one of Ezekiel's central prophetic messages.[7] The recollection of this vision and the messages it embodies accompanies Ezekiel's prophecy throughout the rest of the book, as we will see.

The Movement of God's Glory throughout the Book of Ezekiel

Encounters with the divine vision are recorded throughout the book, from this first one, in the fifth year of Jehoiachin' exile, to Ezekiel's vision twenty years later – though no vision includes the level of detail with which the divine vision in the first chapter is described. The prophecies of movement begin in the fifth year, when Ezekiel first sees divine visions upon the river Chebar (Ezek. 1). In these visions, God's glory is borne in a chariot, which indicates motion. Then the prophet is carried upon the wind and hears the sound of the divine vision, and then

---

7. On this divine vision as a sort of prophetic epigraph to the book, and its comparison with Isaiah's prophecy, see Mordechai Breuer, "The Prophecy of Isaiah," in *Pirkei Mo'adot* (Jerusalem: Horev, 1986), 457–75.

arrives at "the exile community that dwelt in Tel Abib by the Chebar River" (3:15). After another prophecy, he sees God's glory as he goes out into the plain, like the glory which he had seen by the river Chebar (3:22–24). A year later, Ezekiel is sitting in his home and he sees a likeness that takes him to Jerusalem "in God's visions" (8:2–3). There, after descriptions of the idolatry being practiced in the Temple, Ezekiel witnesses the departure of God's glory from within the Temple (ch. 10). This description ends with the glory of God "on the hill east of the city" (11:23). The most significant message of all of these visions is that God's glory has departed from the Temple.

The third section of Ezekiel, as noted, consists of restoration prophecies. Here we find that in the twenty-fifth year (40:1), Ezekiel has a vision of the return of God's glory to the future Temple. First, there is a return to the Land of Israel (40:2); then Ezekiel experiences a divine vision like the earlier one and sees the glory of the God of Israel returning to the Temple (43:1–5); finally, God's glory fills the House (44:4).

The movement of God's glory as described in Ezekiel's visions throughout the book, it appears, contains prophetic messages that are the central axis around which his prophecies revolve. What are these messages? Why are they significant?

First, even in Ezekiel's pre-Destruction prophecies (between the fifth and twelfth years of the exile of Jehoiachin), the glory of God has already departed from the Temple. The Divine Presence is no longer within the city of Jerusalem. Therefore, during the six first years of Ezekiel's prophecy – from the time he begins to prophesy until the Destruction of the Temple – there is no call to the nation as a whole to mend its ways and to repent (although there is attention to individual repentance; see the discussion concerning chapters 3, 14, 18, 33). The fate of Jerusalem has already been sealed; the Temple is defiled and desecrated, and the city will not be purified until God has poured out His wrath in its midst. Chapters 1–24 of the book, in which Ezekiel establishes his status as a prophet, should be understood against this backdrop.

Second, the description of the journey of God's glory raises the question of where God's glory was to be found during the years of the Destruction. Ezekiel describes God's glory as returning from the north of Babylonia (1:4); thereafter he describes God's glory atop the mountain that is to the east of the city (11:23); finally, the glory of the God of Israel comes "from the way of the earth" (43:2), to dwell in the midst of Jerusalem in the future.[8] Where, then, is God's glory during the years of Destruction and the exile of the nation? Does God's glory wander with the people to Babylonia? Or does it remain in the Land of Israel, outside Jerusalem, waiting for the people to return? What is meant by God's place specifically in the east? What significance should be attached to Ezekiel seeing the divine visions in the heavens? Is it possible that God's glory is exiled with the people to Babylonia but does not descend to the soil of Babylonia, in order not to dwell on the impure soil outside of the Land of Israel?[9]

Third, the description of God's glory wandering intensifies the gap between the assumption held universally by the people (expressed in the prophecies of Ezekiel and Jeremiah during these years) that God would never abandon His Temple and the prophetic message that the presence of God's glory in the Temple depends on the nation's actions; there is no guarantee. Therefore, the very fact that God's glory appears to Ezekiel in Babylonia strengthens the message that God's glory has indeed departed from the Temple.

"The Divine Presence Undertook Ten Journeys" (Chapters 10–11)

There are a number of sources in which Ḥazal describe the process of God's glory departing from the Temple in "ten journeys"; however, the different descriptions do not all list the same stations.[10] In chapters 10–11, Ezekiel describes the process of God's glory leaving the Temple. The stages listed explicitly include the cherub (10:2), the platform or threshold of the House (v. 4), the courtyard (v. 4), the cherubim (v. 5), the platform or threshold again, apparently referring to an outer doorway (v. 18), the cherubim (v. 19), the east gate (11:1), the cherubim (11:22), and an ascent to the hill east of the city (11:23). A study of the verses suggests

---

8. The direction from which the exiles will return to Jerusalem is also mentioned by other prophets: see, for example, Jeremiah 3:18.
9. A comprehensive discussion of these questions is to be found in Ben-Yashar's article, "HaMerkava BeSefer Yeḥezkel," 9–28.
10. See Shmuel HaKohen, "Eser Masa'ot Nasa Shekhina," *Sinai* 88, no. 3–4 (1981): 104–19.

that it is the cherubim that carry God's glory upon their backs, and as such the repeated mention of them as "stations" in the "journey" should be understood only as the means by which this departure is effected.

Hazal's descriptions of the journeys of the Divine Presence are not identical to those in the book of Ezekiel; the closest source to the journey as described in Ezekiel is found in Lamentations Rabba:

> The Divine Presence undertook ten journeys – from cherub to cherub; from cherub to the threshold of the House; from the threshold of the House to the cherubim; from the cherubim to the eastern gate; from the eastern gate to the courtyard; from the courtyard to the roof; from the roof to the altar; from the altar to the wall; from the wall to the city; from the city to the Mount of Olives.[11]

Regardless, the prophetic message is clear: God's glory has departed from the Temple, even before its physical destruction.

The Return of God's Glory to the Temple (Chapters 43–44)

The importance of these visions throughout the book is evidenced in the description of Ezekiel's vision of God's glory returning from the way of the east back into the Temple: "Then he led me to a gate, the gate that faced east. And there, coming from the east with a roar like the roar of mighty waters, was the presence of the God of Israel, and the earth was lit up by His presence" (43:1–2). The next verse appears, at first glance, to be repetitive: "Like the appearance of the vision which I had seen, like the vision that I had seen when I came to destroy the city, and the visions were like the vision I had seen by the Chebar River" (43:3).

It seems that precisely at the moment when God's glory returns to the Temple in Ezekiel's future vision, he feels a need to emphasize that this is the same vision that accompanied him throughout the years of his prophecy before the Destruction of the Temple, when he was in Babylonia. This emphasis is achieved by repeating each of the stations where Ezekiel saw

---

11. Lamentations Rabba *petiḥta* 25 (Salomon Buber, ed., *Midrash Eikha Rabba al pi Ktav Yad BeOtzar HaSefarim Romi* [Hildesheim: Olms, 1967], 29); similarly, Rosh HaShana 31a.

divine visions in the first part of the book. Thus, "Like the appearance of the vision which I had seen," refers to the vision in chapter 1, with the emphasis on the definite article – "*the* vision." Thereafter, "like the vision that I had seen *when I came to destroy the city*" refers to the vision in chapters 8–11, and matches the description of the ruin of the city in chapter 9 (vv. 4–11). Finally, the prophet concludes that all these visions appeared to him when he was *by the Chebar River* (ch. 1–3). In this way Ezekiel emphasizes that even though this was the first time since the Temple had been built by King Solomon that God's glory departed it – indeed the Temple lies in ruins – nevertheless the same divine vision would return and once again dwell in the future Temple. The nation need not fear that the departure of God's glory from the Temple means the departure of His glory from the nation.

In describing the Temple being filled once again with God's glory, the prophet notes, "I fell upon my face" (43:3), much like the end of chapter 1: "The presence of the Lord entered the Temple by the gate that faced eastward. A spirit carried me into the inner court, and lo, the presence of the Lord filled the Temple." (43:4–5).

This description of the return of God's glory into the Temple represents the climax of Ezekiel's visions of the future, since the aim of the building of the Temple, in all its detail, is that God's glory might dwell within it. The uniqueness of this prophecy is also evident in its description of God's throne and the soles of His feet:

> O mortal, this is the place of My throne and the place for the soles of My feet, where I will dwell in the midst of the people Israel forever. The House of Israel and their kings must not again defile My holy name. (v. 7)

> They would defile My holy name by the abominations that they committed. (v. 8)

> And I will dwell among them forever. (v. 9)

From now on, the place of God's entry ("the gate that faced eastward") will be closed, protected against human entry and thereby against further defilement, as we will discuss in more detail later on: "And the Lord said to me: This gate is to be kept shut and is not to be opened! No one shall enter by it because the Lord, the God of Israel, has entered by it; therefore it shall remain shut" (44:2).

It is in this spirit that Rabbi Avigdor Nebenzahl explains:

> It is therefore important that the eastern gate – the main entranceway – be closed, with no practical use except as a reminder: It is through here that God will return, for it was from here that He departed, when the Divine Presence left in anticipation of the destruction. If you remember that God can also depart the Temple, perhaps He will never again have to leave.[12]

This, it appears, is one of the ways in which the future Temple is protected against the possibility of God once again abandoning His Temple in Ezekiel's prophecy. From now on the people will behave only in accordance with God's command (Ezek. 36:27).

These verses at the beginning of chapter 43 describe the resting of the Divine Presence within the nation (vv. 7, 9, and similarly 37:26–28). The only other source in Tanakh that describes God's glory coming to rest is the Revelation at Sinai: "The presence of the Lord abode on Mount Sinai" (Ex. 24:16).[13]

At the giving of the Torah, as in the resting of the Divine Presence in the book of Ezekiel, there is confirmation of the unbreakable bond between God and Israel, ultimately leading to God's glory coming to rest amongst the nation. The realization of this lofty vision will come when "The House of Israel and their kings does not again defile My holy name" (43:7).

---

12. Rav Avigdor Nebenzahl, "HaShaar HaPoneh Kadim Yihyeh Sagur – Lama?" *Sinai* 123–124 (2000): 369.
13. On the occasion of the inauguration of the *Mishkan* we find, "and the presence of the Lord appeared to all the people" (Lev. 9:23), but the expression "abode" in relation to God's glory is not used there.

    We can further appreciate the uniqueness of this expression by noting that in I Kings, chapter 8 (as well as in the parallel account in II Chronicles, chapter 6) the text describes the ceremony of inauguration of the Temple, but despite the special nature of that occasion, God's glory is not described as coming to rest in the Temple.

Furthermore, note that this is the only place in Tanakh where the words "defiling (T-M-A) God's name" appear in combination. The rare use of this phrase expresses the crisis; "God's name" represents holiness, the opposite of any form of impurity. This extreme contrast between God's name and impurity – that is, God's refusal to dwell in an impure setting – has its source in the Torah. This idea is emphasized in two places. First, it is expressed in the command to send impure individuals out of the camp: "Remove from the camp anyone with an eruption or a discharge and anyone defiled by a corpse. Remove male and female alike; put them outside the camp so that they do not defile the camp of those in whose midst I dwell" (Num. 5:2–3). Second, it is seen in the context of cities of refuge, where unintentional killers are sheltered: "You shall not defile the land in which you live, in which I Myself abide, for I the Lord abide among the Israelite people" (Num. 35:34).

A prophetic message arises from the description of the divine chariot at the beginning of the book and the journeying of God's glory described throughout (especially its departing the Temple in chapters 8–11 and its return in chapters 43–44): God's presence in the Temple cannot be assumed to be unconditional; God will not allow His presence to dwell there if the nation causes the Temple to be defiled. But even though the nation refuses to accept the prophet's message and fails to repent, even after the Destruction of the Temple, God will never abandon His people. Still, in order to maintain His presence amongst the people in the future, the conditions of access to God's dwelling place will differ from those of the past.

It is this message, that the connection between God and His people is irreversible – both in the generation of the Destruction and afterwards – that explains the selection of the first chapter of Ezekiel as the *haftara* for Shavuot, the festival of the giving of the Torah (Megilla 31a). Besides the obvious similarity between the description of God's Revelation at Sinai, in fire and thick cloud, and Ezekiel's description of the divine chariot, when we read the vision of the divine chariot on Shavuot, we internalize the message (also notably articulated by Rabbi Eliezer of Beaugency) that the Torah given to Israel is eternal, and remains valid even in times of profound crisis.

Chapter 2

The Introduction of Individual Accountability
Ezekiel 2:1–3:21

The awesome power of the divine visions that Ezekiel beholds is clear from his reaction: "When I beheld it, I flung myself down on my face" (1:28). Immediately after the vision he hears God's voice speaking to him: "And I heard the voice of someone speaking. And He said to me, 'O mortal, stand up on your feet that I may speak to you'" (1:28–2:1).

The appellation "mortal," or, more literally, "son of man" (*ben adam*), with which God addresses Ezekiel occurs repeatedly (the prophet is addressed this way ninety-three times) and is unique to this prophet. Commentators note that Ezekiel – who experiences divine visions described in great detail in chapter 1 – is called "son of man" in contrast to the "face of a man" which he sees in his divine visions. This description emphasizes that seeing these visions did not change the fact that he was a "son of man" in his own eyes ("so that he should not become haughty on seeing the divine chariot," Rashi, 2:1), or in the eyes of the reader – or perhaps even relative to the angels (Rabbi Eliezer of Beaugency).

Ezekiel 2:1–3:21

In this particular passage, another word is emphasized, underlining a different theme. Ezekiel hears "speech," which is a human faculty, four times in just three verses – nonetheless, he is able stand upon his feet only with supernatural support, with the help of the spirit:

> And I heard **the voice of someone speaking**. And He said to me, "**O mortal**, stand up on your feet that **I may speak to you**." As **He spoke to me**, a spirit entered into me and set me upon my feet; and I heard **what was being spoken to me**. (1:28–2:2)

The powerful visions and words bring with them a message for Ezekiel. Ezekiel is told at the outset that he is being sent to the nation to convey God's word, for them to know that a prophet was among them before the Destruction: "that they should not say, 'God did not warn us'" (Rabbi Eliezer of Beaugency). However, the people dwelling in Jerusalem – like those in Babylon – will not change their ways. The role of the prophet, then, is not to bring about repentance but rather to convey God's word and thereby justify the imminent punishment. He has no illusions that his prophetic messages will affect their behavior. Ezekiel knows that the people are likely to respond aggressively to his words (as we deduce from his being encouraged not to fear them, 2:6). God's appellations for the people, also expressions that are unique to this book, attest to this: "that nation of rebels, who have rebelled against Me;" "brazen of face and stubborn of heart;" "a rebellious breed" (2:3–5). These are repeated throughout the book, in contrast to the prophecies that address God's relationship with the nation in a positive context, where He calls them "My people Israel."[1]

IN PLACE OF A DEDICATION: THE EATING OF THE SCROLL (3:1–15)

Ezekiel's words, ostensibly, do not open with a "prophecy of dedication" or "inauguration," as we find in the case of other prophets (see Is. 6; Jer. 1). But chapters 2–3 can be seen as a replacement for an inaugural prophecy

---

1. See, for example, 34:30: "My people the House of Israel;" 36:8; 39:7: " My people Israel."

The Introduction of Individual Accountability

that, while it differs from Isaiah and Jeremiah's inaugural prophecies, also resembles them in certain ways. It may be that the eating of the scroll, in chapters 2–3, represents a substitute for his formal inauguration.[2]

> "And you, mortal, heed what I say to you: Do not be rebellious like that rebellious breed. Open your mouth and eat what I am giving you." As I looked, there was a hand stretched out to me, holding a written scroll. He unrolled it before me, and it was inscribed on both the front and the back; on it were written lamentations, dirges, and woes. He said to me, "Mortal, eat what is offered you; eat this scroll, and go speak to the House of Israel." So I opened my mouth, and He gave me this scroll to eat, as He said to me, "Mortal, feed your stomach and fill your belly with this scroll that I give you." I ate it, and it tasted as sweet as honey to me. (2:8–3:3) [3]

The prophet's ambivalence here is clear. Despite God's thrice-repeated command to eat the scroll, all the prophet does is open his mouth. God then feeds him the scroll. Perhaps this is an expression of his difficulty in accepting his prophetic mission. The content of the scroll, too, makes it difficult to "swallow." It heralds the content of Ezekiel's prophecy to the people: Just as the scroll contains lamentations, with no hint of redemption, so too Ezekiel's prophecy includes, initially, only the coming of the Destruction. Ezekiel thus receives his prophetic mission by two means: the eating of the scroll and the visions reported in chapter 1.

We may assume that Ezekiel, as a priest, was among those who had visited the Temple in Jerusalem before the exile; the prophetic mission at this time is not an easy one for him to accept. Note God's

---

2. See, for example: Rolf Rendtorff, "Ḥazon HaHakdasha shel Yeḥezkel tokh Hashvaa LeḤazonot Makbilim BaMikra (Prakim 1–3)," in *Iyyunim BeSefer Yeḥezkel*, ed. Yitzhak Avishur (Jerusalem: Kiryat Sefer, 1982), 89–108. It would seem that the eating of the scroll is part of the visions at the beginning of the book, for it is only at the conclusion of this prophecy that Ezekiel takes leave of the divine vision described in chapter 1 (3:12–13).
3. Commentators are divided as to whether the prophet literally ate the scroll, or whether this is a prophetic description of a symbolic act.

repeated insistence that Ezekiel is being chosen here as His emissary: "I am sending you," "speak My words to them;" "go speak to the House of Israel." Perhaps an echo of Ezekiel's difficulty in accepting his mission is alluded to in God's words to him: "Do not be rebellious like that rebellious breed" (2:8).

Ultimately, with the end of the event, Ezekiel accepts his mission: "It tasted as sweet as honey to me" (3:3). Perhaps he does so happily – as suggested by Rabbi Joseph Kara: "I rejoiced at going on Your mission." Perhaps he accepts out of resignation: "I saw God's will and I was not able to hold myself back; out of love I learned it and I overcame myself to perform His mission, even though the people are difficult" (Rabbi Menachem ben Shimon). Just as the prophet has no discretion in eating the scroll and its contents, so too there is no room for private deliberation about his prophetic mission.

Part of Ezekiel's difficulty arises from knowing that the nation will reject his message. Any notions that might have set his mind at ease are explicitly rejected before he even begins to speak (3:5–9). The people understand quite well what the message means: "For you are sent, not to a people of unintelligible speech and difficult language, but to the House of Israel" (v. 5). The nation knows that Ezekiel is operating as God's agent and rejects his words: "But the House of Israel will refuse to listen to you, for they refuse to listen to Me" (v. 7). Furthermore, the opposition is not from some marginal group within the nation, nor is it transient or incidental: "For the whole House of Israel are brazen of forehead and stubborn of heart" (3:7; also 2:6).

Thus, in contrast to the nation, which is referred to as "brazen of forehead," the prophet Ezekiel sets out on his mission strengthened, as his name suggests, by God: "But I will make your face as hard as theirs, and your forehead as brazen as theirs. I will make your forehead like adamant, harder than flint" (3:8–9). All this will buttress him in confronting a nation that openly expresses its displeasure: "Do not fear them, and do not be dismayed by them, though they are a rebellious breed." (v. 9).

After this emphasis on the difficulties entailed in the prophetic mission, Ezekiel responds with reluctance, with a sense of God's strong hand supporting and guiding him, but at the same time intensively forcing God's word upon him: "I went in bitterness, in the fury of my spirit, while the hand of the Lord was strong upon me" (v. 14). The reader thus shares the mixed feelings with which Ezekiel approaches the exiles, to whom his prophecies are addressed: "And I came to the exile community that dwelt in Tel Abib by the Chebar River, and I remained where they dwelt" (v. 15). Yet, after only one week, Ezekiel receives another prophecy from God detailing the nature of his task.

THE PROPHET AS WATCHMAN (3:16–21)

We noted earlier that in Ezekiel's prophecy, the advent of the Destruction and exile is only a matter of time. This is rooted partly in the nation's behavior from its very beginnings before the Exodus from Egypt (ch. 20) and partly in the fact that the nation is not going to change its ways (ch. 8). Still, even though the tragic outcome is known in advance, Ezekiel is not exempt from his prophetic mission, just as no individual is exempt from personal responsibility for his own behavior (ch. 18, 33). The response of the people as quoted by Ezekiel is different: If the Destruction is inevitable, they claim, then their actions are of no consequence, and even their individual fates are sealed: "This is what you have been saying: 'Our transgressions and our sins weigh heavily upon us; we are sick at heart about them. How can we survive?'" (33:10). They even attributed their individual fate to the sins of their forefathers (ch. 18).

It is this basic outlook that is challenged by Ezekiel's prophecies. While the prophecies leave no room to doubt the impending Destruction, they nevertheless do not absolve the individual of responsibility for his actions. Thus, in chapter 14 (vv. 12–20) the prophet emphasizes that the righteous among the nation of Israel will be saved – but they will save only themselves. In chapter 18, too, we are told that "the soul that sins – it shall die" (v. 4 and elsewhere). The conclusion of chapter 18 is:

> "Be assured, O House of Israel, I will judge **each one of you according to his ways**," declares the Lord God. "Repent and turn back from your transgressions; let them not be a stumbling block of guilt for you. Cast away all the transgressions by which you have offended, and get yourselves a new heart and a new spirit, that you may not die, O House of Israel. For it is not My desire that anyone shall die," declares the Lord God. "Repent, therefore, and live!" (18:30–32)

Ezekiel 2:1–3:21

This seems to be the essence of the message that the prophet addresses to each individual in his generation: The Temple will be destroyed, and the nation will be exiled from its land – but each individual bears personal responsibility for his own fate, because even at this most bitter time there will be those who will die and those who will be saved. Every individual is charged with taking responsibility for his own actions.

Ezekiel must therefore carry out his mission even if the nation's fate is already sealed. The prophet's mission to each individual is the subject of chapters 3 and 33, in which the prophet is referred to as an observer or watchman (*tzofeh*), an appellation that expresses his task of announcing and warning of the approaching danger.[4]

Let us first examine the prophecy in the order in which it appears in the book, beginning with chapter 3:

> O mortal, I appoint you watchman for the House of Israel; and when you hear a word from My mouth, you must warn them for Me.
>
> If I say to a wicked man, "You shall die," and you do not warn him – you do not speak to warn the wicked man of his wicked course in order to save his life – he, the wicked man, shall die for his iniquity, but I will require a reckoning for his blood from you. But if you do warn the wicked man, and he does not turn back from his wickedness and his wicked course, he shall die for his iniquity, but you will have saved your own life.
>
> Again, if a righteous man abandons his righteousness and does wrong, when I put a stumbling block before him, he shall die. He shall die for his sins; the righteous deeds that he did shall not be remembered; but because you did not warn him, I

---

4. Jeremiah testifies: "And I raised up watchmen for you: 'Hearken to the sound of the horn!' But they said, 'We will not.'" (Jer. 6:17). There is no explicit textual evidence of any personal acquaintance between Ezekiel and Jeremiah, who were contemporaries but prophesied in different places and under different conditions. However, in this verse Jeremiah may be referring to Ezekiel and other prophets with similar messages.

The Introduction of Individual Accountability

will require a reckoning for his blood from you. If, however, you warn the righteous man not to sin, and he, the righteous, does not sin, he shall live because he took warning, and you will have saved your own life. (3:17–21)

The prophet, the text tells us, must address the wicked man and warn him to repent. If the prophet fails to warn him, then the prophet himself bears responsibility for the actions of that wicked person. Likewise, the righteous man who sins despite being warned is responsible for his actions. But if the prophet fails to warn a person, then "I will require a reckoning of his blood from you." A righteous man who has been warned and (consequently) does not sin, will live – and the soul of the prophet will be saved.

Although a superficial review of these verses suggests that all possibilities for sin and amendment are addressed, in fact only three cases are: a wicked man who continues to sin, a righteous man who changes his ways and commits a sin, and a righteous man who apparently has never sinned.[5] But a wicked person who repents is not explicitly mentioned here. Likewise, the three cases depicted reflect only one generation. There is no discussion of children being punished for the sins of their ancestors, which is significant given the people's justification for their behavior – that they are being punished for the sins of their fathers and not for their own actions, which have no significance.

Along with the prophetic message that every person is responsible for his or her own actions, Ezekiel's words are also describing the inhabitants of Jerusalem at the time of the Destruction: They sin and do not change their behavior. The role of the prophet in this case is merely to warn; his mission has no effect on their actions.[6]

---

5. It is possible that the righteous man mentioned here is the same one who sinned but then repented, having been warned by the prophet.
6. For a different and interesting approach to the order of the prophecies in terms of the perception of divine retribution in this book, see the introduction to Yehiel Zvi Moskowitz's commentary in *Sefer Yeḥezkel, Daat Mikra* (Jerusalem: Mosad HaRav Kook, 1985), 14–17.

As noted, the prophecy in chapter 3 is complemented by another prophecy from the year of the Destruction, appearing in chapter 33. This prophecy clarifies the role of the prophet after the news of the Destruction has been broken to the exiles around him: "O mortal, speak to your fellow countrymen and say to them: When I bring the sword against a country, the citizens of that country take one of their number and appoint him their watchman" (33:2).

It would seem that this prophecy, unlike the one in chapter 3, refers to a reality in which the Destruction has already taken place – yet even now there is a need for a watchman. The "people of the land," belonging to the leadership class,[7] appointing the watchman from "one of their number." Perhaps it is from Ezekiel that we learn what role the prophet is charged with.

> Suppose he sees the sword advancing against the country, and he blows the horn and warns the people. If anybody hears the sound of the horn but ignores the warning, and the sword comes and dispatches him, his blood shall be on his own head. Since he heard the sound of the horn but ignored the warning, his bloodguilt shall be upon himself; had he taken the warning, he would have saved his life. But if the watchman sees the sword advancing and does not blow the horn, so that the people are not warned, and the sword comes and destroys one of them, that person was destroyed for his own sins; however, I will demand a reckoning for his blood from the watchman. (33:3–6)

Chapter 33 begins with the watchman being called upon to warn the people. This is before they learn of the Destruction. Later in chapter 33, a refugee who fled from Jerusalem informs Ezekiel of the Destruction. Perhaps in light of this distinction we can understand the differences between the watchman's role as set out in these verses and his role in chapter 3, at the beginning of his path. In chapter 33, too, the prophet relates first to the wicked man (vv. 7–9) who even now – as

---

7. For instance, we see that the "people of the land" appear as part of the list of significant figures among the nation, in 7:26–27.

The Introduction of Individual Accountability

in the past – fails to change his ways. However, in this later chapter we also see the people's reaction:

> Now, O mortal, say to the House of Israel: "This is what you have been saying: '**Our transgressions and our sins weigh heavily upon us; we are sick at heart about them. How can we survive?**'" Say to them: "As I live – declares the Lord God – it is not My desire that the wicked shall die, but that the wicked turn from his [evil] ways and live. **Turn back, turn back from your evil ways, that you may not die, O House of Israel!**" (vv. 10–11)

Now, as the stench of Destruction wafts in the air, we hear clear sounds that we have not heard until this point. On one hand, we heard the despair of the people; on the other, the impassioned call of the prophet. He calls to all individuals, whoever and wherever they may be – even now, as the Temple stands in ruins and Jerusalem is in foreign hands – to save themselves from death. The prophet now speaks of a righteous person who sins (vv. 12–13) and – for the first time – of a wicked person who repents of his evil ways (vv. 14–16). The sins the people atone for here, we note, are personal sins, the transgressions of the individual, with no connection to the Temple and its ceremonial ritual, to the Land of Israel, to its defilement, or to its purification; these are no longer relevant:

> So, too, when I say to the wicked, "You shall die," and he turns back from his sinfulness and does what is just and right – if the wicked man restores a pledge, makes good what he has taken by robbery, follows the laws of life, and does not commit iniquity – he shall live, he shall not die. None of the sins that he committed shall be remembered against him; since he does what is just and right, he shall live. (vv. 14–16)

The conclusion of this prophecy emphasizes the same prophetic message once again, sharpening the contrast between divine retribution and the commonly held perception amongst the people that God surely does not differentiate between retribution meted out to the individual and the general punishment of the nation. To the contrary: The prophet insists that God judges all people in accordance with their individual actions.

> Your fellow countrymen say, "The way of the Lord is unfair." But it is their way that is unfair! When a righteous man turns away from his righteous deeds and commits iniquity, he shall die for it. And when a wicked man turns back from his wickedness and does what is just and right, it is he who shall live by virtue of these things. And will you say, "The way of the Lord is unfair"? I will judge each one of you according to his ways, O House of Israel! (vv. 17–20)

This comparison between chapter 3 and chapter 33 highlights once again the fact that Ezekiel's mission is not meant to cause the people to change their ways; rather, it comes to convey God's word to His people. Between the lines we glean something of the relationship between the individual and the collective in the generation of the Destruction. In this difficult era for the nation, even though the Destruction is now inevitable, the individual is still able to change his own behavior – a change that will lead to his own deliverance from death. Later on, we will see how Ezekiel's prophecies of rebuilding, in chapters 34–39, also accord with this distinction between individual behavior and the status of the nation as a whole. This idea, that the individual must view himself as responsible for his or her own actions unrelated to the collective, is new, an outgrowth of the nation's new status following the Destruction.

Chapter 3

Symbolic Acts and Their Meaning

Ezekiel 3:22–5:17

Ezekiel is commanded to perform many symbolic acts throughout the book: eating the scroll (ch. 3); shutting himself in his house, bound with cords (ch. 3); limiting his movement and his food for an extended period (ch. 4); shaving his head (ch. 5); wearing chains (ch. 7); and finally, refraining from mourning the death of his wife (ch. 24). The prophecies we examine in this chapter contain a number of these symbolic acts.

A THUNDERING SILENCE (3:22–27)

> Then the hand of the Lord came upon me there, and He said to me, "Arise, go out to the valley, and there I will speak with you." I arose and went out to the valley, and there stood the presence of the Lord, like the presence that I had seen at the Chebar River; and I flung myself down on my face. And a spirit entered into me and set me upon my feet. And He spoke to me, and said to me: "**Go,**

Ezekiel 3:22–5:17

> **shut yourself up in your house. As for you, O mortal, cords have been placed upon you, and you have been bound with them, and you shall not go out among them. And I will make your tongue cleave to your palate, and you shall be dumb; you shall not be a reprover to them, for they are a rebellious breed.** But when I speak with you, I will open your mouth, and you shall say to them, 'Thus says the Lord God!' He who listens will listen, and he who does not will not – for they are a rebellious breed." (3:22–27)[1]

This prophecy raises several questions. In chapters 2–3, the prophet was commanded to go and prophesy to the people. Now it seems that before he has a chance to speak, another prophecy contradicts all that has come before: He must shut himself in his house and refrain from reproving the nation until he is instructed otherwise. Some indication of how long Ezekiel must remain silent is found in chapter 24:

> On that day a fugitive will come to you, to let you hear it with your own ears. On that day your mouth shall be opened to the fugitive, and you shall speak and no longer be dumb. So you shall be a portent for them, and they shall know that I am the Lord. (24:26–27)

This suggests that this silence will end only on the day that a survivor comes from Jerusalem bringing news of the Destruction. And indeed, we see a prophecy ending his term of silence in chapter 33, when the news of the Destruction reaches Babylonia:

> In the twelfth year of our exile, on the fifth day of the tenth month, a fugitive came to me from Jerusalem and reported, "The city has

---

1. Ezekiel is not the only prophet whose prophecy entails personal suffering. Several commentators (such as Abrabanel at the beginning of Hosea) address this issue both conceptually and specifically. Maimonides understands these actions as "in a vision of prophecy in which he saw that he carried out the actions he was ordered to carry out" (Shlomo Pines, trans., *Guide of the Perplexed* [Chicago: University of Chicago Press, 1963], II:46). We will address only one aspect of these symbolic acts, namely, their role in conveying the prophetic messages.

fallen." Now the hand of the Lord had come upon me the evening before the fugitive arrived, and He opened my mouth before he came to me in the morning; thus my mouth was opened and I was no longer speechless. (33:21–22)

Between our chapter, where the prophet is commanded to be silent, and the prophetic directive to end his silence, Ezekiel receives many prophecies which seem directed to the people. If he were actually shut inside his house throughout this period, to whom were these prophecies conveyed? And why, at the end of this period, will Ezekiel be "a portent" to them? Why is it specifically the news of the Destruction, conveyed by word of the survivor from Jerusalem, that concludes Ezekiel's period of silence? These questions can be answered in one of the following ways.

The first possibility interprets the prophecy about silence in a symbolic or metaphoric manner, like the eating of the scroll in chapter 3 and the symbolic acts described in chapters 4–5. This prophecy is thereby integrated into the series of prophetic units which surround it. This possibility is supported by the command given to the prophet after being told to shut himself in the house: "Cords have been placed upon you, and you have been bound with them" (3:25). If indeed the whole image is symbolic, we might assume that the prophet's silence and his symbolic binding are meant to illustrate that although a prophet is living in their midst, his mission has no practical effect during his period of silence – it will only be effective with Jerusalem's destruction. Perhaps this is another way in which the prophet emphasizes the severed relationship between God and His people at this time. An alternate version of this first possibility is that the silence might symbolize not the prophet's silence but God's expected silence over the siege on the city and the Destruction of the Temple. Ezekiel's prophecies upon receiving news of the Destruction continue this message since his prophecies begin to have practical implications from that moment onwards. According to this interpretation, the prophecies in the coming chapters were probably conveyed to the people dwelling with Ezekiel in Babylonia during these years. The prophet was symbolically silent only for a very short time – perhaps only while he was also bound with cords – afterwards, he explained the message that his silence was meant to convey.

A second possibility is that there was an actual period during which Ezekiel was physically shut in his house and did not prophesy. Opinions differ as to how long his silence lasted, ranging from six years (from the date appearing at the beginning of chapter 1 until the Destruction), to more moderate estimates of a portion of this period.[2]

A third possibility is that the prophet's silence represents the fact that his prophecies are only spoken to the elders who come to his house, seeking to hear his words. This interpretation has support in the testimony recorded at the beginning of chapter 8, "I was sitting at home, and the elders of Judah were sitting before me" (8:1), and at the beginning of chapter 14: "Certain elders of Israel came to me and sat down before me" (14:1).

A further possibility, raised by Rabbi Eliezer of Beaugency, also limits the period of silence, but does so in a different manner. He proposes that the imposition of silence on Ezekiel pertains to his role as rebuker – "you shall be dumb; you shall not be a reprover to them of your own accord." This is in contrast to the prophecies he must convey to the people – those spoken by God: "You shall not rebuke them of your own mind, but concerning My words to you [you shall say to them,] 'Thus said the Lord God' – and thereby fulfill your prophetic mission." We may explain this on the basis of Rabbi Menachem ben Shimon's explanation that the silence is the outcome of the nation lacking belief in the prophet's words:

---

2. The commentators who adopt this approach raise different possibilities about the period of silence in this six-year time frame. See, for example, Radak (3:24), who attaches the prophet's silence to the prophecies in chapters 8–11: "So that he would not rebuke them until He had finished conveying all the prophecies to him, up until the verse, 'A spirit carried me away and brought me in a vision by the spirit of God to the exile community in Chaldea' (Ezek. 11:24)." Since the next verse explicitly states, "and I told the exiles all the things that the Lord had shown me" (11:25), it is difficult for Radak to accept the interpretation that Ezekiel remained silent until news of the Destruction arrived. A different possibility, raised in Abrabanel's commentary, is that the command to the prophet to shut himself in his house was to prepare for the symbolic actions that he would undertake.

Symbolic Acts and Their Meaning

> I shall prevent you, at that time, from prophesying to them, because they do not believe in your prophecy…. The exiles thought that they would soon be returning to Jerusalem, and did not believe that the remnant of the people that was still in Jerusalem would be exiled, since this is what their false prophets had prophesied for them.

Perhaps this distinction between a prophet's messages in God's name and those that he gives of his own accord is especially relevant with regard to Ezekiel, since the fate of Jerusalem had already been sealed, and would not be changed regardless. Thus, the prophet is spared the task of calling upon the people – a "rebellious breed" – to change their ways in order to bring about a change in God's plan, or expressing hope that the Temple's destruction might be prevented. The emphasis on the idea that "**you shall not be a reprover** (*ish mokhiaḥ*) to them" (3:26) is amplified in this case because it contradicts the explicit biblical command: "You shall not hate your kinsfolk in your heart. Reprove (*hokhe'aḥ tokhiaḥ*) your kinsman but incur no guilt because of him" (Lev. 19:17).

The people's lack of confidence in Ezekiel changes when the news of the Destruction of the city arrives. His prophecies now verified, he has turned into "a portent," thereby laying the foundation for the prophecies of restoration that he has yet to bring.

Finally, an additional possibility is that because of his divinely-imposed silence, Ezekiel is forced to write down his prophecies, and his messages are conveyed in the form of written texts. Support for this idea is to be found in the "written scroll" that is sent to him (2:9–10) and the inkwell carried by the "man clothed in linen" (9:11). Indeed, the dissemination of written prophecies is particularly relevant for Ezekiel, who prophesied in exile, since the exiles were likely to be dispersed further afield.

In many of Ezekiel's prophecies, such as the case here regarding the prophet's silence, it is difficult to distinguish between actual action and prophetic vision. In many other prophecies he adopts metaphorical language and parables. The parable and the message being symbolized are sometimes interwoven in such a way that it is not correct – nor is it even possible – to distinguish between them. So too here: The line between God's message to the prophet and the concrete reality is deliberately blurred.

In this fashion, each of the possibilities described above might be correct. Rimon Kasher suggests that the episode of silence serves as a kind of rededication of Ezekiel as an emissary of God, since it represents a linking unit between the chapters of dedication and the symbolic actions. In other words, the episode of silence is connected both to the dedication chapters (via the shared motifs and the structure) and to the symbolic acts (especially by means of shared motifs).[3]

All of the possibilities set out above give rise to the same message: Despite the skepticism of the exiles dwelling with Ezekiel ("Go to your people, the exile community, and speak to them". 3:11), the Destruction of the Temple in Jerusalem is imminent, and the prophet's message will have no effect on the people. The mark of the conclusion of this prophetic unit, with this message, is the "enclosure" (*inclusio*) within which it appears: "whether they listen or not, for they are a rebellious breed" – the same statement appears in one formulation or another at the beginning of this unit (2:5), in its middle (3:11), and at its conclusion (3:27).

A SERIES OF SYMBOLIC ACTS (4:1–5:4)

The Later Prophets, unlike the Early Prophets, do not perform miracles (with a single exception, in Isaiah 37:7). Therefore, in order to convey their messages effectively, they must employ both elevated speech and symbolic acts. It is perhaps for this reason that Ezekiel only conveys his prophecies after a series of symbolic acts performed at the beginning of his prophetic career. Indeed, the difficulty of convincing the nation of the authenticity and reliability of God's prophets is clearly demonstrated in Jeremiah's struggle against the false prophets who deny his "credentials" (see, for example, Jer. 26). In the book of Ezekiel, too, even in the

---

3. For a comprehensive discussion on this, see Rimon Kasher, "Parashat HaElem BeSefer Yeḥezkel (unit 3:22–27)," *Beit Mikra* 43, 3–4 (2008): 227–44. In his article, Kasher adds another significant layer which we have not addressed here, namely, a formal comparison between Ezekiel's prophecy of dedication and the command to be silent.

Symbolic Acts and Their Meaning

prophecies that follow the Destruction, the prophet's audience treats his words as bawdy songs – "To them you are just a singer of bawdy songs, who has a sweet voice and plays skillfully; they hear your words, but will not obey them" (33:32) – and they continue to sin.

This motive for performing symbolic acts is shared by all prophets, but in Ezekiel's case there is a further reason: He is prevented by divine command from speaking. Silent by divine mandate, Ezekiel, more than other prophets, needs actions to convey his prophetic messages. These, then, are the substance of chapter 4 and the beginning of chapter 5.

Although there are different ways to enumerate the actions in this unit, we will divide them formally, on the assumption that each symbol is distinguished from its predecessor by the use of the introductory expression *"ve'ata"* (and you). The acts enumerated in chapters 4 and 5 are as follows:

1. Engraving in brick as the introductory symbolic act:

   > And you, O mortal, take a brick and put it in front of you, and incise on it a city, Jerusalem. Set up a siege against it, and build towers against it, and cast a mound against it; pitch camps against it, and bring up battering rams roundabout it. (4:1–2)[4]

   The first act, with independent significance, is the engraving of an impression of the city of Jerusalem upon a brick that is under siege.

2. Along with the representation of a city under siege comes a harsh message, likewise involving the brick: At this desperate time it is futile to turn to God for help. The prophet, in this prophecy, symbolizes God, and the iron pan that he is to place between him and the brick represents an impenetrable barrier between God's

---

4. An illustration of this symbolic act of Ezekiel's may be seen in the clay brick (engraved and then burned in a kiln), upon which is engraved, in cuneiform, a plan of the ancient city of Nippur, which was likewise located on the bank of the Chebar River. See Shmuel Yeivin, "Tokh Kedei Keria BeSefer Yeḥezkel," *Beit Mikra* 18, no. 2 (1973): 164–75.

representative and the besieged city. God's face is not merely turned away from His people; it is hidden from them: "Then take an iron plate and place it as an iron wall between yourself and the city, and set your face against it. Thus it shall be under siege, you shall besiege it. This shall be an omen for the House of Israel" (v. 3).[5]

3. The siege that Jerusalem contends with is represented by the limits placed on Ezekiel's movements. Beyond this, because the nation of Israel persists in its sins, it bears its unbearably heavy iniquity. This too is symbolized by Ezekiel, who lies on his side:

> Then lie on your left side, and let it bear the punishment of the House of Israel; for as many days as you lie on it you shall bear their punishment. For I impose upon you three hundred and ninety days, corresponding to the number of the years of their punishment; and so you shall bear the punishment for the House of Israel. When you have completed these, you shall lie another forty days on your right side, and bear the punishment of the House of Judah. I impose on you one day for each year. Then, with bared arm, set your face toward besieged Jerusalem and prophesy against it. Now I put cords upon you, so that you cannot turn from side to side until you complete your days of siege. (vv. 4–8)

The significance of the period of time that Ezekiel must lie on each side – symbolizing 390 years and then 40 years – is debated by the commentators, who offer various explanations.[6] One understanding of the 390 days that Ezekiel bears the iniquity of the House of Israel is found in *Seder Olam Rabba* 26: "This teaches that Israel had sinned for 390 years, from the time they entered the land until the ten tribes were exiled from it."

---

5. Although the siege appears to be a physical act that is carried out by another nation, Ezekiel (as God's emissary) may be emphasizing that it is God who is laying siege to Jerusalem: "*You* [Ezekiel, God's representative] shall besiege it" (4:3).
6. See the commentaries of Rashi, Radak, Rabbi Menachem ben Shimon, Abrabanel, and Malbim.

Furthermore, and in contrast to the references to the nation elsewhere in the book, there seems to be a distinction here between the expression "House of Israel" and "House of Judah."[7] Thus the 390 days that Ezekiel lies on his left side reflect that the sins of the nation (the "House of Israel" as a whole, not only the inhabitants of Judah, who remained after the exile of the ten tribes) have weighed it down.[8]

The number of years may also refer to the sins of the nation since its very inception, in Egypt (and indeed, Abrabanel understands the total of 430 days as corresponding to the years of bondage in Egypt), rather than to the period since the entry into the land. The prophecy in chapter 20 emphasizes the nation's sins since its formation in Egypt; nowhere in the book is there any explicit mention made of a change in the nation's behavior since entering the land.

Other possibilities include attributing the sins of the House of Israel to the period from the building of the Temple in the days of Solomon up until the Destruction or, alternatively, the period extending from the kingdom of Saul (or David) until the exile of the Kingdom of Israel. But there does not seem to be any clear or exact correlation between these proposed periods and the 390 years.

On the other hand, the period that is devoted to the House of Judah does have some biblical background. See Moses' words to the spies after their sin:

> While your children roam the wilderness for forty years, suffering for your faithlessness, until the last of your carcasses is down in the wilderness. You shall bear your punishment for forty years,

---

7. The most common reference to the nation in the book of Ezekiel is "Israel" (186 appearances), which is almost always as part of the expression "House of Israel," while the name "Judah" appears infrequently (15 times). In Ezekiel the name "Judah" generally seems to refer to the nation as a whole, while elsewhere in Tanakh, the reference is usually to the land (although in many cases it is difficult to distinguish one from the other).
8. Here the meaning of the expression *nasa avon* (to bear iniquity) is that the sinners bear (i.e., they are burdened with) their own iniquity; it is not a transfer of the iniquity to the prophet. See Baruch J. Schwartz, "Mah Bein Munaḥ LeMetafora? Nasa Avon/Pesha/Ḥet BaMikra," *Tarbiz* 63 (1994): 149–71, especially 169.

> corresponding to the number of days – forty days – that you scouted the land: a year for each day. (Num. 14:33–34)

Just as the punishment for the sin of the spies is a year for each day, so too Ezekiel bears the iniquity of Judah for "forty days…a year for each day." The numerical link to the sin of the spies does, possibly, point to a more substantial connection. In the book of Numbers, forty years is the period of time necessary to amend the sin of the spies, following which the Israelites enter the land. Here, the days that Ezekiel lies on his side represent the period extended to Judah to change and mend its ways. With this period over and with nothing changed – in contrast to its biblical past – Israel will now be removed from its land.

Thus far we have examined three of the symbolic acts undertaken by Ezekiel: the engraving of the brick, symbolizing the siege itself; the iron pan, symbolizing the barrier between God's emissary and the people of the city; and lying on his side, symbolizing Israel's sins prior to the Destruction. For his fourth task, the prophet is commanded to perform an action more difficult than its predecessors, which fits in with the general trend of the symbolic acts which express, in gradually intensifying steps, the extent of the crisis which the inhabitants of Jerusalem will face at the time of the Destruction.

4. The famine during the siege is illustrated by a reduction to the bare minimum of Ezekiel's intake of food while he is lying on his side:

> Further, take wheat, barley, beans, lentils, millet, and emmer. Put them into one vessel and bake them into bread. Eat it as many days as you lie on your side: three hundred and ninety. The food that you eat shall be by weight, twenty shekels a day; this you shall eat in the space of a day. And you shall drink water by measure; drink a sixth of a hin in the space of a day. Eat it as a barley cake… (vv. 9–12)

We began our discussion of Ezekiel's symbolic acts by noting that not every act could necessarily be assigned a concrete meaning. But the precise quantities of water and bread enumerated in this prophecy demand our attention. It it at all possible that Ezekiel could subsist on the rations described in these verses? Yehuda Feliks addresses this question:

> With regard to drink, the daily ration of a sixth of a *hin* works out, by our calculations, to 650 g of water. This is a very small amount – especially in the hot climate of Babylonia, but for someone who is not moving about, it is enough to survive on, and indeed, Ezekiel was lying down throughout that time. The prophet's daily portion of bread, however, is much smaller… For more than a year, the prophet ate less than a thousand calories per day… And none of this saved the prophet from the suffering that comes with feeling hungry and thirsty. Lying on one side for three hundred and ninety days likewise entails discomfort. The prophet certainly identified, in body and soul, hungry and thirsty, with the besieged city of Jerusalem.[9]

Concerning the bread that is to be eaten "as a barley cake," the prophet is commanded, "you shall bake it on human excrement before their eyes." Rashi explains, "You shall bake it over coals of dried and burned dung." In other words, the barley cake had to first be baked over human dung that would serve as fuel for the fire. God Himself explains the situation as follows: "So… shall the people of Israel eat their bread, unclean, among the nations to which I will banish them" (v. 13).

But Ezekiel protests, arguing that he has never eaten unclean food: "Then I said, 'Ah, Lord God, my person was never defiled; nor have I eaten anything that died of itself or was torn by beasts from my youth until now, nor has foul flesh entered my mouth'" (v. 14). Radak explains:

> For priests are warned concerning *nevela* (an animal that died of itself) and *trefa* (an animal that was torn by beasts) even more strictly than are Israel, owing to their impurity, as it is written

---

9. Yehuda Feliks, *Teva VaAretz BaTanakh: Prakim BeEkologia Mikrait* (Jerusalem: Reuven Mass, 1992), 217–18.

(concerning the priests), "That which dies of itself, or is torn with beasts, he shall not eat to defile himself with it." (Lev. 22:8)[10]

In other words, Ezekiel's response to the command arises from his identity as a priest, with a special prohibition against eating foods that bring impurity. God acquiesces and permits him instead to bake the cakes upon animal dung: "He answered me, 'See, I allow you cow's dung instead of human excrement; prepare your bread on that'" (v. 15).

The need to bake with dung fuel seems to reflect the food that the inhabitants of Jerusalem were forced to eat under siege conditions,[11] and illustrates the impurity of the people and of the land in a manner that can be appreciated even in the absence of the Temple, and even in exile.

The significance of this act, describing the hunger in the city, is explained at the end of the command:

> And He said to me, "O mortal, I am going to break the staff of bread in Jerusalem, and they shall eat bread by weight, in anxiety, and drink water by measure, in horror, so that, lacking bread and water, they shall stare at each other, heartsick (*venamoku*) over their iniquity. (vv. 16–17)

In other words, the warnings set forth explicitly in *Parashat Beḥukkotai* will be fulfilled: "Those of you who survive ... shall be heartsick (*yimaku*) over the iniquities of their fathers (Lev. 26:39).[12]

5. The final symbolic act, the most distressing of all, describes what awaits the inhabitants of Jerusalem after the siege:

---

10. Further on in the prophecy this limitation on the priests reappears (Ezek. 44:31). The priests' status in Ezekiel's prophecy is covered in chapters 40–48.
11. Among Bedouins and impoverished fellahin it is still acceptable to use dried animal dung for baking. See Feliks, *Teva VaAretz BeTanakh*, 217.
12. Ezekiel's prophetic messages are intensified, in many cases, when we consider their biblical background in general, and Leviticus 26 in particular. We shall devote further discussion to the biblical background of the nation's sins in chapter 4.

> And you, O mortal, take a sharp knife; use it as a barber's razor and pass it over your head and beard. Then take scales and divide the hair. When the days of siege are completed, destroy a third part in fire in the city, take a third and strike it with the sword all around the city, and scatter a third to the wind and I will unsheathe a sword after them. Take also a few [hairs] from there and tie them up in your skirts. And take some more of them and cast them into the fire, and burn them in the fire. From this a fire shall go out upon the whole House of Israel. (5:1–4)

At the very beginning of his prophecy, before even having spoken to the people at all, the shaving of his hair demonstrates what awaits them: a third of the inhabitants of Jerusalem will die by fire; a third will die by the sword; and a third will flee. Of this final third, a small number will be saved and may perhaps even reach Babylonia. These are symbolized by the hairs that are gathered in the skirts of his garment, but even among these, some are burned.

Thus, Ezekiel's symbolic acts are a step-by-step demonstration of what is yet to occur: first the siege with no response from God (or perhaps the siege itself is perpetrated as a divinely guided mission); the unbearable hunger and thirst; and finally – the annihilation of most of the inhabitants of Jerusalem, only a few of whom will escape and be saved.[13]

By means of these actions, Ezekiel demonstrates the deep rift between God and His people and the steadily deteriorating situation of Jerusalem.

---

13. It should be noted that the first two symbolic acts are left unexplained, while the others are explained over the course of their description. The reason for this would seem to be that the drawing of the city on the brick, and the placing of the iron pan, are clear; They speak for themselves – especially since they have a place in the nation's historical memory. This is not the first time that Jerusalem has been besieged (it was previously under siege by Sennacherib). However, the symbolic acts that follow (the concrete outcome of the people's sins, the hunger, and the anticipated suffering) are introduced by Ezekiel for the first time, and so the people cannot be assumed to understand their deeper meaning unless they are explicitly explained.

Ezekiel 3:22–5:17

THE MEANING OF THE METAPHOR: GOD'S ACTIONS (5:5–17)

Assuming that the chapters in the book of Ezekiel follow in chronological order, then Ezekiel's symbolic actions actually represent the first encounter between the prophet, in his divinely appointed role, and the nation. These acts, which introduce Ezekiel's prophecies, serve to focus the aim of his prophecy at the very outset; they leave no room for hope. Indeed, immediately after he performs these actions – which conclude with the haunting message of the fire spreading throughout the House of Israel – we learn of the first verbal message conveyed by the prophet to the people, in which he explains the meaning of the actions:

> Thus said the Lord God: I set this Jerusalem **in the midst of nations**, with countries round about her. But she rebelled against My rules and My laws, acting more wickedly than the nations and **the countries round about her**; she rejected My rules and disobeyed My laws. (5:5–6)

These verses appear to explain that the main cause of the Destruction is the state of Jerusalem as compared to that of the surrounding cities and countries. The comparison seems not only to relate to the city's status; rather, it appears to be about how God Himself is perceived by the pagan nations. Over the hundreds of years preceding the Destruction of the Temple, the Assyrian Empire ruled over Mesopotamia. Nearer the time of the Destruction, the Babylonian Empire arose. Both kingdoms had "temple cities," namely, sacred sites at whose center was the "home" of the local deity, a functioning temple (which also controlled a significant portion of the city's assets).[14] For the surrounding nations, Jerusalem – and the Temple in its midst – represented just another temple city until the Destruction. It was one of many in Mesopotamia.

---

14. This is also reflected in the fact that Babylonian cities from the first millennium BCE have theophoric names; see Ran Zadok, *Geographical Names According to New- and Late-Babylonian Texts* (Wiesbaden: L. Reichert, 1985). For a discussion of the temples, see Hayim Tadmor, *Ashur, Bavel ViYehuda: Meḥkarim BeToldot HaMizraḥ HaKadum* (Jerusalem: Bialik, 2006), 95–121. Models of such temples are on display at the Bible Lands Museum in Jerusalem; some very impressive models can also be found at the British Museum in London.

Symbolic Acts and Their Meaning

Once again, the prophet emphasizes that the nation's actions – rebelling against God's commandments – have brought about catastrophic results. The consequences are enumerated in the following verses introduced by the word, "*lakhen*" ("therefore" or "assuredly"): "Assuredly, thus said the Lord God: Because you have outdone the nations that are round about you – you have not obeyed My laws or followed My rules, nor have you observed the rules of the nations round about you…" (v. 7).

The prophet begins by defining and illuminating the severity of the people's actions. They have not fulfilled God's commandments – but more importantly, they have been less loyal to God than the surrounding nations have been towards their own deities.[15] Accordingly, the consequences will also play out in the sight of the nations:

> Assuredly, thus said the Lord God: I, in turn, am going to deal with you, and I will execute judgments in your midst in the sight of the nations. On account of all your abominations, I will do among you what I have never done, and the like of which I will never do again. (vv. 8–9)

This prophecy signals to the nation the severity of "all [its] abominations" by highlighting the unprecedented actions that God will take in response. This appears to be a reference to the Destruction of the Temple, which had stood since the time it was built by King Solomon.[16]

In light of the above, perhaps we can understand why the nation had not internalized the idea that God might destroy His Temple. They knew that the Destruction of the Temple would be perceived by the nations as weakness on the part of God, reflecting, as it were, God's inability to defend His Temple and ward off its enemies. Thus, the Destruction of the Temple would entail a desecration of God's name

---

15. The use of the word *mishpat* (judgment) rather than *mitzvot* (commandments), or *ḥukkim* (statutes) is of note, given that the most popular deity among the Babylonians was the sun god, their god of justice, whose temple was at Sippar; see Tadmor, *Ashur*, 96.
16. The prophetic message that the imminent divine action is something unrepeatable is understandable, given that the Destruction of the Second Temple (as traumatic as it was) was less terrible than the Destruction of the First Temple.

among the nations. The nations would assume that God had lost His power, so much so that He could not even prevent the downfall of His own Temple. The deliberate divine Destruction of Jerusalem would appear so strange to the nations surrounding Jerusalem that the people of Jerusalem were lulled into believing that this would be enough to prevent the Temple being destroyed despite their severe sins.

The nation also carried the historical memory of the miraculous deliverance of Jerusalem in the year 701, roughly one century earlier, during the campaign of Sennacherib. It was then, against all odds and after a prolonged siege of the city, that the situation was reversed overnight (II Kings 19:35; Is. 37:36; II Chr. 32:21–22). In light of this memory, whose thrice-repeated evocation attests to its tremendous presence in the national consciousness, the inhabitants of Jerusalem held on to their belief that some miracle would occur and the Babylonian army would be defeated. This belief held sway even during the most difficult days of the Babylonian siege, until its final moments. The nation was also aware that the power of the Babylonian Empire was still being consolidated, and that it was far weaker than the Assyrian Empire had been in the days of Sennacherib.[17] So anticipating salvation seemed eminently reasonable to the inhabitants of Jerusalem. This faith, it seems, was shared by the exiles in Babylonia to whom Ezekiel prophesied. Given this assumption of invincibility, it is even more understandable that Ezekiel's prophecy depicts the events of the destruction in Jerusalem in a most painful and piercing way: "Assuredly, parents shall eat their children in your midst, and children shall eat their parents. I will execute judgments against you, and I will scatter all your survivors in every direction" (5:10).

The city's situation is more dire than it has ever been before, or will ever be again – this is the clear message of this portion of the prophecy. The message is communicated in the emphasis that the biblical warnings – "You shall eat the flesh of your sons and the flesh of your daughters" (Lev. 26:29)[18] – will be fulfilled. The situation now, in fact,

---

17. The gap in status between the two empires is clear, inter alia, from the multitude of tablets still extant today describing the might of the kings of Assyria, compared with a dearth of corresponding testimonies from the Babylonian Empire.
18. See also Deuteronomy 28:53–57.

is even worse; not only will parents eat the flesh of their children, but the opposite will occur: Children will eat the flesh of their parents. This description is unparalleled anywhere in Tanakh.

"With all of your Detestable things and all your Abominations" (5:11) – an Analysis of Terms

What actions of the people have brought about this terrible situation? These are stated briefly but harshly: "Assuredly, as I live – said the Lord God – because you defiled My Sanctuary with all your detestable things and all your abominations, I in turn will shear [you] away and show no pity. I in turn will show no compassion" (5:11).

The terse expression "all of your detestable things and all your abominations" refers to the range of sins that the people have committed which are detailed by the prophet in the coming chapters. Appearing more than eighty times over the course of his prophecies, this phrase is Ezekiel's protest of the existence of pagan worship within the nation, referring to idolatry by different terms and names. But until this verse in chapter 5, the actions of the people that caused the Destruction have not been detailed; they will appear only in chapter 6.

The connotations of the different terms that Ezekiel uses for the idolatry practiced by the people must be examined more closely. Some commentators explain the range of terms as an attempt at stylistic variety, breaking the monotony of repetition; such an explanation, however, prevents us from appreciating the precision of the prophetic language. In fact, a terminological (and even etymological) analysis will demonstrate that the particular semantic field[19] employed in a prophecy is important to the full understanding of the differences between Ezekiel's various prophecies of rebuke.

Let us start with a look at the terms "detestable things" (*shikkutzim*) and "abominations" (*to'evot*) which appear in chapter 5.

---

19. Frank Polak notes that apart from the analysis of key words, the *semantic field* can also serve as an organizing feature. While Polack refers specifically to biblical narratives, the same principle applies to the prophecy under discussion. See Frank Polak, *HaSippur BaMikra* (Jerusalem: Bialik, 1994), 91–97.

The root SH-K-TZ is commonly used in Leviticus in reference to impure creatures that are forbidden as food: "You shall not draw abomination upon yourselves (*teshaketzu*) through anything that swarms; you shall not make yourselves unclean therewith and thus become unclean" (Lev. 11:43).[20] In contrast, in Ezekiel this root appears eight times in reference to idolatry, in a manner similar to its use in Deuteronomy: "And you have seen the detestable things (*shikkutzeihem*) and the fetishes of wood and stone, silver and gold, that they keep" (Deut. 29:16).[21] The common term makes it reasonable to assume that the connection between the "detestable thing" that is forbidden as food and the "detestable thing" that is idolatrous expresses the element that they share in common: They both cause impurity. The eating of creeping things brings impurity upon the soul, and perhaps the same result befalls one who loses himself in the pagan worship of the nations.

The term *to'eva* is used far more extensively by Ezekiel than by any other prophet.[22] A *to'eva* is a general term for something that is hateful, disgusting, or worthy of condemnation. It does not allude to any particular type of sin, but rather encompasses and includes many different transgressions and forms of unacceptable behavior. Thus, expressions such as "an abomination unto God" denote the complete opposite of that which is considered to "find favor" in God's eyes.[23] As we shall see, in the book of Ezekiel, this term encompasses the broadest possible range of actions unacceptable to God. These acts ultimately brought about the Temple's destruction and the people's exile from its land. Thus, in chapter 22 alone we find no less than twelve transgressions appearing under the heading of *to'eva*. Moreover, the book of Ezekiel features unique combinations including this term, which are not to be found elsewhere in Tanakh: *to'avot ra'ot* ("vile abominations"; 6:11; 8:9); *to'evot gedolot* ("terrible abominations"; 8:13, 15); and *tzalmei to'avotam shikutzeihem asu* ("their images and their detestable abominations"; 7:20).

---

20. Similarly also Leviticus 20:25.
21. Similarly also Deuteronomy 7:26.
22. The word appears 117 times in the Tanakh, with 45 appearances in the book of Ezekiel alone.
23. According to Baruch J. Schwartz, *Torat HaKedusha* (Jerusalem: Magnes, 1999), 219.

The prophet apparently employs these new combinations in order to upset his listeners, even to shock them. The term *to'evot* thus becomes a catchphrase for the lowly, despicable actions that have defiled all that is holy: the bond between husband and wife (22:11); the land (11:18); the Temple (5:11); Shabbat (23:36–38); and God's name (43:8). Evidence of the power and special significance of this harsh term is the fact that Ezekiel only directs it toward his own people. Although the term is used liberally throughout the book, it is absent from chapters 24–32, where the prophet addresses other nations.

We can thus approach a better understanding of the meaning of the symbolic actions which we discussed earlier. The first verse, which defines the sins that brought about the defilement and the Destruction of the Temple – "because you defiled My Sanctuary with all your detestable things and all your abominations" (5:11) – should be read as a cry. By means of this combination of terms, Ezekiel cries out, as it were, "You have perpetrated the most despicable actions, a mixture of the worst transgressions, and these have caused the Temple to be defiled!" This same cry seems to echo in the second part of the verse: "I in turn will shear [you] away and show no pity. I in turn will show no compassion." Along with the explicit negation – there will be no "pity" or "compassion" – there is a further layer here: the fierceness of the divine response corresponds to the foulness of the deeds perpetrated by the nation.

A Dire Message
This section concludes by interpreting the symbolic act as foretelling annihilation of most of the nation:

> One third of you shall die of pestilence or perish in your midst by famine, one third shall fall by the sword around you, and I will scatter one third in every direction and will unsheathe the sword after them. I will vent all My anger and satisfy My fury upon them and I will find relief; and when I vent all My fury upon them, they shall know that I the Lord have spoken in My passion. (5:12–13)[24]

---

24. Portions of this passage have been translated using Koren's new translation (forthcoming), as it better reflects the meaning I wish to convey.

Ezekiel 3:22–5:17

This language is especially harsh because nowhere else in the book of Ezekiel – not even in the prophecies dating to the years after the Destruction of the Temple – do we find the same terms used as consolation. The expressions "show...pity," "compassion" (v. 11), and "find relief" (v. 13) appear here solely in the negative sense. Perhaps if there were a complementary prophecy which used the same vocabulary but served as a prophecy of consolation, this would soften the message of this prophecy. But the absence of any prophecies in the book of Ezekiel in which God "has compassion" for His people, in which He "shows pity" for them, or in which He "finds relief" for them starkly illustrates the unprecedented, irreversible reality of the Destruction of the Temple. And the consequences will follow shortly:

> I will make you a ruin and a mockery among the nations roundabout you, in the sight of every passerby. And when I execute judgment upon you in anger and rage and furious chastisement, you shall be a mockery and a derision, a warning and a horror, to the nations roundabout you: I the Lord have spoken. (vv. 14–15)

Until now Jerusalem had been seen as one of the region's "sacred cities." Its destruction naturally results – from the nations' polytheistic perspective – in a downgrading of God's status, as it were. In the past, God was perceived as the deity of only the Jewish people in its land. Now, God seems to be sanctifying His name which has been defiled and desecrated in the eyes of the nations; He establishes His status as God, elevated above all other deities, without any dependence on the current state of Judea (see 39:23–24). The fact that the nation that is supposed to represent God in the world has reached such a nadir means that the nations must be brought to understand the new reality in a different light. They must see that God rules the entire world; it is His will that rules all, controlling even other nations and their gods. Thus, the nations will come to understand how God inflicts such devastating damage on His people, as described in the closing verses of this chapter:

> When I loose the deadly arrows of famine against those doomed to destruction, when I loose them against you to destroy you, I

will heap more famine upon you and break your staff of bread. I will let loose against you famine and wild beasts and they shall bereave you; pestilence and bloodshed shall sweep through you, and I will bring the sword upon you. I the Lord have spoken. (5:16–17)

In these verses, the meaning of the starvation in the symbolic act discussed earlier becomes fully clear. The starvation, described as "arrows of famine" sent by God, is accompanied by wild beasts, pestilence, and blood. These verses are somewhat reminiscent of *Parashat Haazinu*: "I will sweep misfortunes on them, use up My arrows on them: wasting famine, ravaging plague, deadly pestilence, and fanged beasts will I let loose against them, with venomous creepers in dust" (Deut. 32:23–24).

Here, too, we find God's "arrows" sowing destruction amongst the people, as well as famine and "fanged beasts" (like the "evil beasts" in Ezekiel). Moses introduces *Parashat Haazinu* with the following declaration:

For I know that, when I am dead, you will act wickedly and turn away from the path that I enjoined upon you, and that in time to come misfortune will befall you for having done evil in the sight of the Lord and vexed Him by your deeds. (Deut. 31:29)

This comparison with the verses from *Haazinu* underlines the fact that Ezekiel's prophecy is actually the realization of Moses' warnings to the people prior to his death.

This prophetic unit (Ezek. 5:5–17) is one of the harshest that is delivered to the nation anywhere in Tanakh. It remains difficult to read, even as we are removed by so many generations. The horror it arouses is highlighted by the fact that seven times (over the course of these thirteen verses) the prophet emphasizes that his prophecy comes entirely from God. Verse 5 begins with the expression, "Thus said the Lord God," and likewise verses 7 and 8. In verse 11, God's name is mentioned in the context of an oath: "As I live – said the Lord God." Then, in verse 13, we find, "they shall know that I the Lord have spoken in My passion;" likewise in verse 15: "I the Lord have spoken." It is not for nothing that this dreadful prophecy needs to resound – both at the time it was conveyed and for all generations – with the explicit, repeated insistence that it all comes from God. And so, perhaps, some slight consolation can be found in God's command to Ezekiel, as His representative, that he "set [his] face against it" (the brick representing Jerusalem) – as if to say, the suffering will be unbearable, but it is not ignored. God watches His people always, even at this most dire time.

Chapter 4

The Language of the Nation's Sins: Echoes and Leitmotifs

Ezekiel 6:1–8

Chapters 6 and 8 of the book of Ezekiel are each devoted in their own way to detailed descriptions of the sins that ultimately led to the Destruction and the exile. In chapter 6, Ezekiel is commanded to prophesy to the mountains of Israel that the places of pagan worship will be destroyed (a complementary prophecy, speaking of restoration for the mountains of Israel, is found in chapter 36). To fully understand the meaning of verses 3–6 and the idolatry that they depict, we will return to their biblical source in Leviticus 26.[1] This method of study, known as intratextual exegesis, is based on the assumption that much can be

---

1. For more detailed discussion of the connection between Leviticus 26 and Ezekiel, see Jacob Milgrom, *Leviticus*, The Anchor Yale Bible Commentaries (New York: Doubleday, 2000), 23–27.

Ezekiel 6:1–8

learnt from "the light that one biblical text shines on another."[2] In our case, the prophet consciously evokes the text in Leviticus in order to indicate that it is being actualized in his own time. As such, the full picture is clarified by looking at chapter 26 in its entirety, including the blessings promised to those who observe God's commandments at the beginning of that chapter (Lev. 26:3–13, which can be compared with Ezek. 34:24–28).

Chapter 26 of Leviticus opens with the prohibition of serving idols, and continues with the reward for those who follow God's path and the punishment awaiting those who violate God's covenant with His people. The retribution for these sinners is described in detail in verses 16–41.

The prophetic message in Ezekiel chapter 6 is that at this point, the nation is being punished for the deeds depicted in Leviticus 26. What they are suffering now is what was defined in Leviticus as the punishment for those sins. The verses of rebuke in Leviticus are linked to the situation in Ezekiel's prophecy which describes the people's sins using the same expressions that appear in the book of Leviticus. These expressions are not common in Tanakh; therefore, their very mention causes the warnings and punishments set down in the book of Leviticus to echo in the ears of Ezekiel's listeners (as well as in the consciousness of later readers).

Let us start by presenting the similarity between the two descriptions:

---

2. Yair Zakovitch, *Mavo LeParshanut Penim Mikra'it* (Even Yehuda: Rekhes, 1992), 9, and see also pp. 126–28, although Zakovitch does not address Ezekiel at all. Adopting his terminology, we could say that "the exegetical endeavors in this case are an 'aspiration for concretization' as well as for 'actualization.'" In our instance, the language in Ezekiel provides chapter 26 of Leviticus with "concrete anchorage and illustration" along with "reconciling it with the present reality: bringing the text written in the past closer to its reader in the present."

Leviticus 26:30–33	Ezekiel 6:3–8
I will destroy **your shrines** and cut down **your incense stands**, and I will heap your **carcasses** upon your **lifeless fetishes**. I will spurn you. I will lay your cities in ruin and make your sanctuaries **devastated**, and I will not savor your pleasing odors. I will make the land **devastated**, so that your enemies who settle in it shall be appalled by it. **And you I will scatter** among the nations, and I will unsheath the sword against you. Your land shall become **a desolation and your cities a ruin.**	I will bring a sword against you and destroy **your shrines**. Your altars shall be **devastated** and your **incense stands** smashed, and I will hurl down your slain in front of your **fetishes**. I will cast the **carcasses** of the people of Israel in front of their fetishes, and **scatter** your bones around your altars in all your settlements. The towns shall be **ruined** and the shrines shall be **devastated**. Thus your altars shall be **ruined** and bear their punishment; your fetishes shall be smashed and annihilated, **your incense stands** cut down, and your handiwork wiped out; and the slain shall fall in your midst. Then you shall know that I am the Lord. Yet I will leave a remnant, in that some of you shall escape the sword among the nations and be **scattered through the lands**.

The connection between these two chapters is especially pronounced through the use of the unusual expression "incense stands" (*ḥamaneikhem*) and the description of the corpses of the nation of Israel being placed before, or upon, their idols – likewise a striking image. Let us examine the significance of these two expressions more closely.

Ḥamanim, "incense stands" or "sun images," were a type of idolatry; the term appears only once in the Torah (Lev. 26:30) and rarely in the Prophets. Rashi explains that the *ḥaman* was "a sort of idolatrous image that was placed on roofs, for the sun (*ḥama*)."[3] At the same time, it is possible that *ḥaman* denotes a structure for idolatrous worship, at

---

3. See also the careful distinction made by Rabbi Menachem ben Shimon in his commentary on this verse.

the center of which there stood a great square stone, sometimes with indentations, or a room in which to exhibit idols. The stone was surrounded by pillars, and had a flat roof over it. An altar was built in front of the stone.[4]

The term *gilulim*, "fetishes," is used extensively by Ezekiel, and it is important to distinguish it from other similar terms (*shikkutzim, elilim, atzabim*). The root of the word, however, is not self-evident. There are several possible roots: *Galal*, a stone (for covering a well), may be the source.[5] It may be referring to *gelel*, dung (as in the plural, *gelalim*); Rashi adopts this interpretation. The root G-L-L might also be employed to create a deliberate ambiguity (considering the similarity among a circle, a pile of stones, and dung), resting in the same semantic field. In this case the basic meaning of the term is something rolled up (round), with the connotation of round dung.

The power of such terms in the book of Ezekiel is also evident from a comparison with Leviticus 26:30, where both *ḥamanim* and *gilulim* are mentioned. In Leviticus, these terms appear at the climax of the list of curses that will befall the nation between a verse describing parents eating their children's flesh and a verse describing the destruction of the land and the Temple. Perhaps the purpose of this verse in Leviticus is to emphasize that the people will be killed because they attached themselves to places of idol worship (Ibn Ezra, Rashbam). In other words, the carcasses of the people will be left in the place where they served idols.[6] The expression in Leviticus, "lifeless fetishes" (*pigrei giluleikhem*), thus refers to the carcasses of the animals offered to idols. *Pigrei giluleikhem* could also be interpreted as the monuments where

---

4. This reflects the view of Rimon Kasher, *Yeḥezkel 1–24, Mikra LeYisrael* (Tel Aviv: Am Oved/Magnes, 2004), 217. Kasher cites proof for his interpretation from verses in Isaiah and in Chronicles. In Isaiah (17:8; 27:9) the *ḥamanim* are mentioned together with *asherim* (trees used for idolatrous worship), along with "altars." In Chronicles (II Chr. 14:4), *ḥamanim* are mentioned together with shrines used for idolatry, and according to II Chronicles 34:4, *ḥamanim* are found above the altars. (The only other mention is in verse 7 of our chapter.)
5. Both in the Aramaic and Greek translations and in a similar form in Akkadian (galālu), the term refers to a stone that is engraved with inscriptions and pictures.
6. See I Kings 13:1–2 – "The man of God...cried out against the altar: 'O altar, altar! Thus said the Lord: A son shall be born to the House of David, Josiah by name; and

idolatry was performed. This recalls *pigrei malkheihem*, "the corpses of their kings" (Ezek. 43:7–8), which might be understood as an allusion to the fact that the pagan kings were buried at their places of pagan worship (in contrast to the prohibition on any burial at the Temple site).

Aside from this verse in Leviticus, *gilulim* are mentioned in the Torah only in Deuteronomy 29:16 – "You have seen their [the Egyptians'] detestable things [idols] and the fetishes of wood and stone, silver and gold, that they kept." Rashi comments (ad loc.): "You have seen their *shikkutzim* [their idols,] so called because they are as loathsome as impure things (*sheketz*); *giluleihem'* – [fetishes so called because they are] as foul and abominable as dung (*gelel*)."

The word *gilulim* as defined above, and its frequent appearance in the book of Ezekiel with the term "abominations" (*to'evot*), show that the deeds of the nation are described harshly and frankly in Ezekiel's prophecies. These connotations of the words used to describe the nation's idol worship should be kept in mind by the contemporary reader, too. Only then can he or she understand the full significance of God's fierce anger at His people.

Thus, we see the effect of the use of shared terminology in prophecy. The prophet describes the actions of the people in detail, so the obvious ramifications of their acts, with which they are familiar from the book of Leviticus, echo in their ears by association, without the prophet having to describe them with the same level of detail.

However, there is another, more optimistic, link between our prophecy and the book of Leviticus. Leviticus 26 makes mention of God's covenant with His people right after the rebuke for their unspeakable deeds. This covenant is absent from the prophecy of harsh rebuke in chapter 6 of Ezekiel. The technique employed here by the prophet generates an important complementary message that, although not explicitly mentioned, hovers, implicitly, in the background. Leviticus 26 begins by setting down the blessings that awaits the nation of Israel if it follows God's ways. The text states:

---

he shall slaughter upon you the priests of the shrines who bring offerings upon you. And human bones shall be burned upon you." Further evidence of this is found in II Kings 23:14, 20.

> If you follow My laws... I will establish My abode in your midst, and I will not spurn you. I will be ever present in your midst: I will be your God, and you shall be My people. I the Lord am your God who brought you out from the land of the Egyptians to be their slaves no more, who broke the bars of your yoke and made you walk erect. (Lev. 26:3–13)[7]

Admittedly, the phrase "I will not spurn you" expresses the extent of loathing that may arise if the people do not walk in God's ways. But this extreme expression is also accompanied by a formulation of the covenant that attests to the depth of the connection between God and His people ("I will be your God"). This message is even repeated at the end of Leviticus 26, where the Torah emphasizes that even when the nation's actions cause a rift between itself and God, the covenant forged between them will stand the people in good stead and protect them, even in the most difficult times:

> Then will I remember My covenant with Jacob; I will remember also My covenant with Isaac, and also My covenant with Abraham; and I will remember the land. For the land shall be forsaken of them, making up for its sabbath years by being desolate of them, while they atone for their iniquity; for the abundant reason that they rejected My rules and spurned My laws. Yet, even then, when they are in the land of their enemies, I will not reject them or spurn them so as to destroy them, annulling My covenant with them: for I the Lord am their God. I will remember in their favor the covenant with the ancients, whom I freed from the land of Egypt in the sight of the nations to be their God: I, the Lord. (Lev. 26:42–45)

---

7. This connection between the people's sins and the formulation of the covenant is already hinted at in the commentary of Hizkuni (Hezekiah ben Manoah; thirteenth century, France) on Leviticus 26:30 – "'I will cast the carcasses of the people of Israel in front of their fetishes,' – this is the opposite of: 'I will be your God, and you will be My people.'"

Chapter 5

Doom Is Coming
Ezekiel 6:11–7:27

JEREMIAH'S PROPHECY TO THE EXILES IN BABYLON

Ezekiel's prophecies follow chronological order: Chapter 1 is dated the fifth year of the exile of Jehoiachin, while the date at the beginning of chapter 8 is the sixth year of the exile. We can therefore conclude that the symbolic acts and prophecies of Destruction in chapters 6–7 were uttered approximately five years before the Destruction (592 or 591 BCE), and about three years before the Babylonians laid siege to Jerusalem. The exiles in Babylonia, we saw earlier, also assumed that their situation was a temporary one, and that they would be returning to Jerusalem soon. An echo of their impressions can be heard in a prophecy of Jeremiah that relates to their future:

> As I live – declares the Lord – if you, O King Coniah [Jehoiachin], son of Jehoiakim, of Judah, were a signet on my right hand, I would tear you off even from there. I will deliver you into the hands of those who seek your life, into the hands of those you dread, into the hands of King Nebuchadrezzar of Babylon and into the hands of the Chaldeans. I will hurl you and the mother who bore you into another land, where you were not born; there

you shall both die. They shall not return to the land that they yearn to come back to. (Jer. 22:24–27)

In this prophecy, Jeremiah addresses a question that occupied Jerusalem's residents: the status and role of Jehoiachin, who was exiled to Babylonia just a few months after his coronation in Jerusalem. This issue seems to have plagued the inhabitants of Jerusalem, who wondered about the status of the king who had ruled over them for such a short time. The kings of Babylonia treated him with respect, and Jehoiachin's special status in exile exacerbated the exiles' difficulty in resolving this question.[1]

We must distinguish between the short term and the long term in respect to Jehoiachin. In the short term, he seems to have been cast aside like an unwanted object: "Is this man Coniah a wretched broken pot, a vessel no one wants? Why are he and his offspring hurled out, and cast away in a land they knew not?" (Jer. 22:28). Jeremiah's response contains a prophetic message to the inhabitants of the land, a message which will stay with the exiles for as long as they are in Babylonia: Although they cannot understand it now, Jehoiachin's importance lies precisely in his exile:

> O land, land, land, Hear the word of the Lord! Thus said the Lord: Record this man as without succession, one who shall never be found acceptable; for no man of his offspring shall be accepted to sit on the throne of David and to rule again in Judah. (Jer. 22:29–30)

In his own days in Judah he is childless; in his own days he is "one who shall never be found acceptable." In Judah's years of desolation, none of his progeny will prosper as king or ruler. But in the long term, Jehoiachin's exile serves as the people's salvation. This is evident in Jeremiah's prophecy about Jehoiachin's exile:

---

1. Note the difference between the description of his exile (II Kings 24:12–16; 25:27–30) and that of Zedekiah (II Kings 25:6–7).

The Lord showed me two baskets of figs, placed in front of the Temple of the Lord. This was after King Nebuchadrezzar of Babylon had exiled King Jeconiah [Jehoiachin] son of Jehoiakim of Judah, and the officials of Judah, and the craftsmen and smiths, from Jerusalem, and had brought them to Babylon. One basket contained very good figs, like first-ripened figs, and the other basket contained very bad figs, so bad that they could not be eaten.

And the Lord said to me, "What do you see, Jeremiah?" I answered, "Figs – the good ones are very good, and the bad ones very bad, so bad that they cannot be eaten."

Then the word of the Lord came to me: Thus said the Lord, the God of Israel: As with these good figs, so will I single out for good the Judean exiles whom I have driven out from this place to the land of the Chaldeans. I will look upon them favorably, and I will bring them back to this land; I will build them and not overthrow them; I will plant them and not uproot them. And I will give them the understanding to acknowledge Me, for I am the Lord. And they shall be My people and I will be their God, when they turn back to Me with all their heart.

And like the bad figs, which are so bad that they cannot be eaten – thus said the Lord – so will I treat King Zedekiah of Judah and his officials and the remnant of Jerusalem that is left in this land, and those who are living in the land of Egypt: I will make them a horror – an evil – to all the kingdoms of the earth, a disgrace and a proverb, a byword and a curse in all the places to which I banish them. I will send the sword, famine, and pestilence against them until they are exterminated from the land that I gave to them and their fathers. (Jer. 24:1–10)

Even after the exile of Jehoiachin, Jeremiah reports, the inhabitants of Jerusalem do not grasp that the exiles in Babylonia – Jehoiachin first and foremost among them – are the remnant that has been saved from destruction. It is these exiles who will return one day to rebuild the land which was about to be destroyed.

Perhaps the need to confirm this prophecy about Jehoiachin prompts the prophet Haggai to use the same phrase about the signet ring in his own prophecies about Zerubbabel, grandson of Jehoiachin, at the start of the Return to Zion. This gives encouragement to the returnees, who fear that God's presence is no longer with them. He declares: "On that day – declares the Lord of Hosts – I will take you, O My servant Zerubbabel son of Shealtiel – declares the Lord – and make you as a signet; for I have chosen you – declares the Lord of Hosts" (Hag. 2:23). In so doing, he is also promising the fulfillment of Jeremiah's promise: "As I live – declares the Lord – if you, O King Coniah, son of Jehoiakim, of Judah, were a signet on my right hand, I would tear you off even from there" (Jer. 22:24).

The prophetic message that the end of Jerusalem is imminent is also important for the exiles in Babylonia. They, too, believe that somehow God will save Jerusalem's inhabitants, allowing them to survive this crisis. The exiles themselves might – in a best-case scenario – return to the land; otherwise, they will assimilate and disappear among the nations.

This is arguably the most important "news" in the prophecy found in Jeremiah 29, when Jeremiah sends a letter from Jerusalem to the exiles. He instructs them to settle in Babylonia; they will not be returning soon. It does not occur to them that it may be their children who will return to the land, not them – or that they can settle in Babylonia without assimilating. The idea that the Jewish people can survive or thrive in exile is foreign to them. While our generation recognizes this as part of the nation's history, at that time, for the exiles in Babylonia, it was unthinkable. These circumstances were the backdrop for the symbolic acts performed by Ezekiel, through which he describes the imminent reality awaiting the inhabitants of Jerusalem. This is also why the sins of the nation, set forth explicitly by Ezekiel, make the exile both necessary and inevitable.

THE DEATH OF JERUSALEM'S INHABITANTS (6:11–14)

At the end of chapter 6 the punishment of death described at the end of chapter 5 appears once again. The emphases in these verses seem to highlight the immediate historical context of the events; these verses thereby complement Jeremiah's prophecy to the inhabitants of the land. First, those who manage to escape the Destruction are mentioned. Upon reaching Jehoiachin and the exiles, they will tell of the people's actions and of the Destruction they witnessed. This will be accompanied by clapping of hands, stamping of feet, and a cry of sorrow on the part of the prophet: "Strike your hands together and stamp your feet and cry: Aha!" (6:11), expressing lamentation over the fate of the House of Israel. The descriptions of death here are no longer general in nature; they depict with accuracy the fate of the city's inhabitants: "He who is far away shall die of pestilence, and he who is near shall fall by the sword, and he who survives and is protected shall die of famine" (v. 12).[2]

Finally, the nation's sins and God's actions against the nation are set forth: "When your slain lie among the fetishes round about their altars, on every high hill, on all the mountaintops, under every green tree, and under every leafy oak – wherever they presented pleasing odors to all their fetishes" (v. 13); and the fate of the entire land is sealed: "I will ... lay the land waste and desolate in all their settlements, from the wilderness as far as Diblah" (v. 14).

The exiles, like those who remained in Jerusalem, seized upon the Temple and Jerusalem, still standing, as proof that all was under control. For this reason, the prophecies of chapters 4 and 5 deal specifically with Jerusalem. Now, after detailed attention has been paid to the city, the prophecy removes any doubt by addressing what will happen throughout the land. Each of these emphases concludes with a statement of the purpose of all of these events: "Then they shall realize it was not without cause that I the Lord resolved to bring this evil upon them.... And you shall know that I am the Lord.... Then they shall know that I am the Lord" (vv. 10–14).

But even after these prophecies, neither the inhabitants of Jerusalem nor the exiles in Babylonia were convinced. The Temple was still standing; Jerusalem's inhabitants remained steadfast despite the crises they had faced since the time of Solomon. These facts made a stronger

---

2. That this prophecy of Ezekiel and the previously quoted prophecies of Jeremiah complement each other is also evident in the descriptions of punishment in the verses here. Compare Ezekiel 6:12; 7:15; Jeremiah 24:10; 27:13.

Ezekiel 6:11–7:27

impression on them than did the prophecies of Jeremiah and Ezekiel. Perhaps physical distance from Judah also contributed to the denial in Babylonia; the exiles could not see the deteriorating situation for themselves and considered their own exile the worst possible situation. So the struggle waged by Jeremiah and Ezekiel against the nation's preconceived notions, reinforced by false prophets, was not over. Jeremiah's prophecies dating to this period emphasize the futility of Zedekiah rebelling against Nebuchadnezzar, king of Babylonia, since the exile of the remnant of Judah was only a matter of time (Jer. 27:12–22).[3]

In contrast to Jeremiah, Ezekiel (in his prophecies in the coming chapters) addresses the two flawed assumptions held by the exiles that caused them to brush off his warnings: First, many prophets over the generations had spoken of the Temple's destruction. The people had become accustomed to this; even if the possibility was contemplated seriously, it was regarded at most as something that was theoretically possible, but not in the foreseeable future. This assumption is addressed by the prophet in chapter 7. Second, despite the nation's sins, the Temple still stood. And how could it be otherwise, lest God's name be desecrated in the eyes of the nations? It is this view that is confronted in the end of Ezekiel's prophecy in chapter 7, as well as in chapters 8–11.

DOOM IS UPON YOU (7:1–12)

We have noted the greatest challenge facing the prophet: convincing the people that the Destruction of the Temple was imminent. This is the focus of chapter 7. To convey his messages (which appear to have been stated verbally in addition to being committed to writing), Ezekiel enlists all possible means. Thus far we have noted two of them: the use of symbolic acts and the borrowing of expressions familiar from the Torah. Now, another means is adopted: a key word or leitmotif aimed

---

3. Admittedly, in this context Jeremiah also prophesies the imminent downfall of the king of Babylonia (Jer. 51:49–53). The prophecies about subjugation to Babylonia, sounded along with the prophecies describing its imminent destruction, strengthen the prophetic message that Babylonia's ascendancy was for a short time only in order to allow Babylonia to serve as God's emissary in destroying His Temple, when the nation's deeds made this inevitable.

at emphasizing the subject of the prophecy as a whole. We see here the repeated use of the word "*ketz*" ("end" or "doom"):

> You, O mortal, [say:] Thus said the Lord God to the Land of Israel: "Doom! Doom is coming upon the four corners of the land. Now doom is upon you! I will let loose My anger against you.... A singular disaster; a disaster is coming. Doom is coming! The hour of doom is coming! It stirs against you; there it comes! The cycle has come around for you, O inhabitants of the land; the time has come; the day is near. There is panic on the mountains, not joy. Very soon I will pour out My wrath upon you and spend My anger on you.... Here is the day! See, the cycle has come round; it has appeared. The rod has blossomed; arrogance has budded.... The time has come, the day has arrived." (Ezek. 7:2–12)

The word "doom" stands out in these verses both because it is repeated six times and because it is accompanied by a verb – "comes" – which also appears six times. In addition, we find the expressions "the time has come," "it is near," and "the day has arrived," all belonging to the same semantic field.[4]

The fact that imminent doom features so prominently is because it is precisely the crux of the prophecy. This is the difference between what the audience is accustomed to hearing from its prophets – i.e., threats and warnings about the Destruction of the Temple – and what Ezekiel is telling them: that the Destruction is already underway.

Despite the similarity between parts of this prophecy and those that have been uttered in the past, the repetition and emphasis of this semantic field serves to highlight the prophecy's revolutionary message. Perhaps with a view to emphasizing that the fate awaiting Jerusalem is drawing near, Ezekiel enlists another technique: deliberate allusion to the story of the Flood. He achieves this by using the word *ketz* in conjunction with the expression "full of lawlessness [*ḥamas*]" (7:23), just as they

---

4. In other words, beyond the use of the key word, the prophecy contains many words that have the same general meaning.

Ezekiel 6:11–7:27

occur in close proximity in Genesis (Gen. 6:11–13).[5] Indeed, it appears that the link to the deeds that brought about the Flood is intentional; it emphasizes the chapter's prophetic message: The sins of the generation of the Flood – the violence and corruption – led to God declaring, "I have decided to put an end [*ketz*] to all flesh, for the earth is filled with lawlessness [*ḥamas*]" (Gen. 6:13).

God's method of bringing the end upon Jerusalem is described succinctly with the same words used in chapter 5, recalling what was already said there in detail:

> Now doom is upon you! I will let loose My anger against you and judge you according to your ways; I will requite you for all your abominations. I will show you no pity and no compassion; but I will requite you for your ways and for the abominations in your midst. And you shall know that I am the Lord. (Ezek. 7:3–4)

In the second part of the chapter, Ezekiel illustrates for the exiles the inhabitants of Jerusalem's reaction to the impending end, using increasingly intense language. He starts by evoking scenes of buying and selling, seemingly mundane activities, but ones that bring no cause for rejoicing for those about to go into exile (7:12–13). He goes on to declare that there is no point in preparing for war, since death is near (vv. 14–15), and concludes with a description of the very difficult circumstances that will face the escapees and the mourners (vv. 16–19). It is painful to imagine the scenes described in verses 16–18 – survivors fleeing to the mountains, crying out in pain, fearful, dressed in mourning, defeated and shamed – but it seems that this is an accurate portrayal of the aftermath of the Destruction.[6]

---

5. See Kasher, *Yeḥezkel 1–24*, 223.
6. In verse 17, "and all knees shall turn to water," the water expresses their fear. According to Rabbi Isaiah di Trani (thirteenth–fourteenth century, Italy), this refers to "the urine that they pass in their great fear," while Rabbi Menachem ben Shimon interprets it as "perspiration – for a person perspires when he is afraid, owing to his great toil and sorrow."

THE END AND ITS RAMIFICATIONS (7:20–27)

In the chapter's final section, Ezekiel prophesies for the first time that the Temple will be desecrated by outsiders, and then points to the main culprits. The prophecies that follow, beginning with verses 20–24, are devoted to this idea – despite the fact that exiles and inhabitants of Jerusalem alike view it as an impossibility:

> For out of their beautiful adornments, in which they took pride, they made their images and their detestable abominations – therefore I will make them an unclean thing to them. I will give them as spoil to strangers, and as plunder to the wicked of the earth; and they shall defile them. I will turn My face from them, and they shall defile My treasures; ruffians shall invade it and defile it....[7] I will bring in the worst of the nations to take possession of their houses; so shall I turn to naught the pride of the powerful, and their sanctuaries shall be defiled. (7:20–24)

Here again, as at the beginning of the chapter, Ezekiel emphasizes his prophetic message by using different appellations for each of its elements: the Temple ("their beautiful adornments," "My treasures," "the pride of the powerful"); the fate that will befall it ("unclean," "as spoil," "as plunder"); God's emissaries who will carry out this punishment ("the strangers," "the wicked of the earth," "ruffians," "the worst of the nations"), and finally, the terrible outcome ("they shall defile them," "shall be defiled," "and defile it," "to take possession" – all indicating the defilement of the Temple). To those who heard Ezekiel, defilement of the Temple seemed

---

7. The subject of the phrase "and they shall defile My treasures" is not clear. One possibility is to connect it to the first part of the verse, "I will turn My face from them," so that the subject is Israel. God turns His face away from the nation, after their sins have caused the Temple to be profaned, and the end of the verse explains how this profanation comes about: "ruffians shall invade it and defile it." Alternatively, only the first part of the verse – "I will turn My face from them" – refers to Israel, while the other nations are the subject of the rest of the verse: "and they shall defile My treasures; ruffians shall invade it and defile it." Either way, the actual desecration of the Temple is carried out by the nations who are sent by God to the Temple, and their very presence defiles it.

to be an impossibility, a contradiction in terms. Yet defilement of the Temple through the presence of strangers is also mentioned elsewhere as the cause of its profanation: "Admitting aliens, uncircumcised of spirit and uncircumcised of flesh, to be in My Sanctuary and profane My very Temple…." (44:7). Perhaps this is why, later in the book, strangers are removed from the Temple in the vision of the future Temple ("Let no alien, uncircumcised in spirit and flesh, enter My Sanctuary"; 44:9).[8]

In conclusion, Ezekiel points to all the leaders and authorities amongst the nation as helpless in preventing the Destruction:

> Horror comes, and they shall seek safety, but there shall be none. Calamity shall follow calamity, and rumor follow rumor. Then they shall seek vision from the **prophet** in vain; instruction shall perish from the **priest**, and counsel from the **elders**. The **king** shall mourn, the *nasi* shall clothe himself with desolation, and the hands of **the people** of the land shall tremble. I will treat them in accordance with their own ways and judge them according to their deserts. And they shall know that I am the Lord. (7:25–27)

Ezekiel's use of imagery and language is designed to convince the nation – in exile and in Jerusalem – that the end is a fait accompli and no hope remains. In the following chapters, Ezekiel experiences a divine vision in which he sees, from close proximity, how the Temple has been defiled. This, too, might be explained in terms of the principle outlined at the beginning of this chapter: Within Ezekiel's attempts to concretize the Destruction, the description of the Temple as defiled (even though in reality it is still standing) is meant to persuade the exiles that there is no longer any point in hoping to return to Jerusalem.

---

8. Aside from defilement of the Temple by strangers, Ezekiel also mentions a specific act whose severity in and of itself causes the Temple to be defiled: "On the very day that they slaughtered their children to their fetishes, they entered My Sanctuary to desecrate it. That is what they did in My House" (23:39).

Chapter 6

Ezekiel, Deuteronomy, and Descriptions of the Nation's Sins

Ezekiel 8:1–18

THE DIVINE VISION

Having prophesied to the people about the defilement of the Temple, Ezekiel now sees a divine vision with a different theme: Although the Temple is still standing, it is effectively empty and insignificant.[1] This message extends throughout chapters 8–11, which together form a single prophetic unit. In this unit, Ezekiel is transported in a vision to Jerusalem, after which he returns to the elders of Judah sitting before him. Chapter 8, the first part of this vision, is devoted to enumerating the reasons for God's glory leaving the Temple. This is a more detailed depiction than those the prophet has offered so far (5:11; 6:7, 20) and its purpose is "to show him the actions for which the Temple is destroyed and God's glory departed" (Radak).

---

1. Verses 1–3, which introduce this prophecy, relate to subjects that we have already discussed: the time and place in which the prophet speaks and his target audience, as well as the divine vision that he saw at the start of his prophetic mission.

Ezekiel 8:1–18

These verses, depicting idolatry, emphasize that Ezekiel is seeing these visions as God's representative.[2] This impression is achieved through the repeated use of the root R-A-H (to see), along with mention made of eyes.[3] This is in contrast to the people's perception that God's abandonment of the land means that He does not see (8:12, and also further on, 9:9). This message is also emphasized in verse 18: "I in turn will act with fury; I will show no pity, nor will I show compassion."

This chapter is divided into four parts, each focusing on a different type of idolatry, and each concluding with God telling the prophet, "You shall see even more terrible abominations than these" (8:6, 13, 15, and a variation in v. 17).[4] It is not necessary to assert that these forms of idolatry occurred simultaneously in all parts of the Temple. Rather Ezekiel sees, by means of a divine vision, four symbolic sins (which might in fact have actually been committed over the course of earlier years): the "infuriating image" (vv. 5–6); the engravings on the walls and offering of incense (vv. 7–13); the "women bewailing Tammuz" (vv. 14–15); and the prostration to the sun (vv. 16–17).[5]

In each section, Ezekiel encounters a sight worse than the one before in a new location.[6] In the second vision, Ezekiel even identifies "the elders of the House of Israel" offering incense, and notes Jaazaniah

---

2. As the Talmud teaches (Yoma 9b): "Why was the first Sanctuary destroyed? Because of three [evil] things which prevailed there: idolatry, immorality, bloodshed." Sexual immorality and bloodshed are addressed in later chapters.
3. Expressions here include: "As I looked," "visions of God," "like the vision that I had seen," "turn your eyes," "I turned my eyes," "Do you see," "you shall yet see," "And I looked," "enter and see," "I entered and looked," "have you seen," "the Lord does not see us," "you shall see," "Have you seen," and "Do you see" as well as what we have translated as "I will show no pity," which can be more literally rendered as "my eye will not spare."
4. For discussion of the literary structure of this unit, see Kasher, *Yeḥezkel 1–24*, 241–43.
5. For one presentation of this argument, see Moskowitz's introduction to this chapter in *Sefer Yeḥezkel*, 49.
6. Some scholars view the progression as a move inwards into the inner parts of the Temple. But if this is the case, the words "the entrance of the Penimith (lit. 'inner') Gate" (8:3) must be understood as referring to an outer gate, or alternatively disregarded for the purposes of the progression.

the son of Shafan by name.[7] This group of elders contrasts with the "elders of Judah" who are sitting before Ezekiel in Babylonia as he experiences this vision. This seems to highlight the difference between the "elders of Judah" (exiled during the exile of Jehoiachin, together with Ezekiel), and those who remained in Jerusalem. The latter, no longer part of "Judah," are referred to as "Israel." By means of the appellation "Israel" the prophet emphasizes that the inhabitants of Jerusalem represent the nation's continuity. But this situation changes after the destruction of Judah, when it becomes clear that the people's continuity is represented instead by the exiles of Jehoiachin. This opens the door to Ezekiel's prophecy that the nation will be rebuilt, after its destruction, specifically by Judean exiles (Ezek. 37).

DESCRIPTIONS OF IDOLATRY

Ezekiel 8 and Deuteronomy 4

Ezekiel, as we have seen, uses a variety of terms to describe the Jewish people's idolatry. Sometimes he suffices with a general reference, while elsewhere he is more detailed and provides examples – such as in the terms used in Ezekiel 6 (which is clearly based on Leviticus 26, as explained above in chapter 4).

We will now take a closer look at the very detailed description of the nation's sins in chapter 8, which evokes chapter 4 of Deuteronomy (especially Deut. 4:15–19). A review of the language in Deuteronomy can contribute to our understanding of the full significance of Ezekiel's prophecy in chapter 8. The expressions common to the two sources include "image" (*semel*; in our chapter, *semel hakina*, "infuriating image"), engravings of *remes* and abominable beasts, and prostration to the sun. To these the prophet adds the *gilulim*, which also appear in Leviticus

---

7. The identity of this person is unknown. He might have been related to the Shafan family, who were loyal to God and did not sin (see, for example, Jer. 26:24). If this hypothesis is correct, then the message of this vision is that even leaders whose families had followed God for generations had become sinners. For more on the Shafan family, see Benzion Lurie, "Shafan – Sofer HaMelekh," *Beit Mikra* 34, no. 3 (1989): 261–64.

Ezekiel 8:1–18

(discussed previously), and the "women bewailing Tammuz," which is not mentioned elsewhere.[8]

1. The "image" (*semel*) is the first vision of idolatry that Ezekiel encounters in chapter 8, and it is mentioned twice as part of the expression, "infuriating image:" "that was the site of the infuriating image that provokes fury" (v. 3); "and there, north of the gate of the altar, was that infuriating image on the approach" (v. 5).

   In the Torah, the word "*semel*" occurs only once: "not to act wickedly and make for yourselves a sculptured image (*semel*) in any likeness whatever: the form of a man or a woman" (Deut. 4:16).[9]

2. Like the first vision, the second (including the expression "*kol tavnit remes*," "all detestable forms of creeping things") is also directly connected to Deuteronomy 4 and describes another form of idolatry. The biblical background to this second description of idolatry in the Temple is found in the verses in Deuteronomy warning against the fashioning of different forms:

   > For your own sake, therefore, be most careful – since you saw no shape when the Lord your God spoke to you at Horeb out of the fire – not to act wickedly and make for yourselves a sculptured image in any likeness whatever... the form of anything that creeps on the ground (*tavnit kol remes*). (Deut. 4:15–18)[10]

---

[8]. It should be noted that throughout the book of Ezekiel mention is made of other types of idolatry (in addition to the engravings of *remes* and prostration to the sun) that are also mentioned in Deuteronomy: "detestable things (*shikkutzim*)," "wood and stone," passing children through fire, "on lofty mountains and on hills or under any luxuriant tree." The command to cut these down is also common to both sources. See more at the end of this chapter.

[9]. The word "*semel*" occurs five times in Tanakh: once in Deuteronomy 4, twice in Ezekiel 8, and twice more in II Chronicles 33 (vv. 7, 15), as part of the description of the idolatry that Manasseh introduced into the Temple. (Some scholars view Ezekiel 8 as a reflection of the period of Manasseh; see Greenberg, Ezekiel 1–20, 202.)

[10]. It should be noted that the terms "*tavnit*" and "*remes*" also occur in the book of Leviticus, the latter being used in the sense of "creeping things" forbidden for consumption.

3. The third vision, in which "there sat the women bewailing Tammuz," has no parallel in Tanakh. Nevertheless, there are other sources attesting to its nature. Yaakov Klein writes the following about this worship:

> "Tammuz" is the name of the Sumerian shepherd god, Dumuzi (the name means "the faithful son" or "the legal son"). Dumuzi was also viewed in Mesopotamia as the god of vegetation and played a central role in fertility rites...alongside his partner, Inanna-Ishtar. In Sumerian literature, Dumuzi is also depicted as the tragic figure: he is a god who dies, goes down to Sheol, and is resurrected each year. While in Sheol, ceremonies of lamentation and other magical, sympathetic ceremonies are held for him...
>
> The legends of the tragic death of Dumuzi and his descent to Sheol are the subject of many Sumerian lamentations...
>
> The popular "weeping for Tammuz" was unquestionably a women's form of worship.... We can deduce this from the Sumerian lamentations...which always attributed the lament to female figures. Furthermore, most of Sumerian lamentations for Tammuz are composed in language that is characteristic of women; and the priest-lamenters apparently imitated women in their voices and accents....[11]

The prophet's succinct description of women sitting and weeping for Tammuz in the Temple thus reflects a form of pagan worship that is familiar to us from inscriptions from the Ancient East.

4. Ezekiel describes his fourth vision as follows:

> And there, at the entrance to the Temple of the Lord, between the portico and the altar, were about twenty-five men, their backs

---

11. Taken from Klein's explanation as cited in Gershon Brin, ed., *Yeḥezkel*, Olam HaTanakh (Tel Aviv: Revivim, 1993), 48–51. See also Greenberg, *Ezekiel 1–20*, 171, for a discussion of "wailing for Tammuz."

Ezekiel 8:1–18

to the Temple of the Lord and their faces to the east; they were bowing low to the sun in the east. (8:16)[12]

This scene, too, relates to a warning that appears only in Deuteronomy: "And when you look up to the sky and behold the sun and the moon and the stars, the whole heavenly host, you must not be lured into bowing down to them or serving them" (Deut. 4:19).[13]

Ezekiel's prophecy about the sins the people committed in the Temple, then, recalls phrases that are known to us only from chapter 4 of Deuteronomy. This is no coincidence. Note the context within which the prohibitions on idolatry in Deuteronomy are found: a command to the nation to fulfill God's word. This command is repeated several times at the beginning of the chapter:

> And now, O Israel, give heed to the laws and rules that I am instructing you to observe, so that you may live to enter and occupy the land that the Lord, the God of your fathers, is giving you. You shall not add anything to what I command you or take anything away from it, but keep the commandments of the Lord your God that I enjoin upon you.... You, who hold fast to the Lord your God, are all alive today.
>
> See, I have imparted to you laws and rules, as the Lord my God has commanded me, for you to abide by in the land that you are about to enter and occupy. Observe them faithfully, for that will be proof of your wisdom and discernment to other peoples....

---

12. The same sort of worship was practiced during the reign of Manasseh (II Kings 21:5), until Josiah's revolution (23:5). If we assume that this form of idolatry did not reappear, this could be proof that the visions Ezekiel experiences in our chapter reflect forms of idolatry that were practiced at different times over the years, and not necessarily worship that occurred in his lifetime when his prophecy took place.
13. Other than Deuteronomy 4, the warning appears again in Deuteronomy 17:3 – "turning to the worship of other gods and bowing down to them, to the sun or the moon or any of the heavenly host, something I never commanded...."

> But take utmost care and watch yourselves scrupulously, so that you do not forget the things that you saw with your own eyes and so that they do not fade from your mind as long as you live. And make them known to your children and to your children's children.... For your own sake, therefore, be most careful – since you saw no shape when the Lord your God spoke to you at Horeb out of the fire. (Deut. 4:1–15)

Ezekiel's repeated allusion to chapter 4, which contains these warnings, emphasizes the nation's sins to God during Ezekiel's time.

Later in Deuteronomy 4, following the warnings not to engage in idolatry, mention is made of the covenant between God and the nation, followed by a description of what will happen to those who "forget the covenant:"

> When you have begotten children and children's children and are long established in the land, should you act wickedly and make for yourselves a sculptured image in any likeness, causing the Lord your God displeasure and vexation, I call heaven and earth this day to witness against you that you shall soon perish from the land that you are crossing the Jordan to possess; you shall not long endure in it, but shall be utterly wiped out. The Lord will scatter you among the peoples, and only a scant few of you shall be left among the nations to which the Lord will drive you. There you will serve manmade gods of wood and stone that can neither see, nor hear, nor eat, nor smell. (Deut. 4:25–28)[14]

To reinforce his prophecy, Ezekiel emphasizes the causes that have led to the Destruction of Jerusalem and the exile of the people. He does this not only explicitly – through the words of the prophecy itself – but

---

14. The importance of this comparison between Deuteronomy 4:1–40 and the book of Ezekiel goes beyond the descriptions of idolatry. In fact *all* of Ezekiel's prophecies maintain an indirect dialogue with other parts of the chapter. Other elements of comparison include: the importance of the way in which Israel's situation is perceived by the nations; the place of the Exodus in the bond between God and the nation; the dispersion of Israel among the nations; and the forging of the covenant between God and His people.

Ezekiel 8:1–18

also indirectly, by drawing a parallel between the people's deeds (as he views them in his own time) and the repeated warnings to the people not to act in this way – borrowed, in this case, from Deuteronomy 4.

Ḥamas

> And He said to me, "Do you see, O mortal? Is it not enough for the House of Judah to practice the abominations that they have committed here, that they must fill the country with lawlessness [*ḥamas*] and provoke Me still further and thrust the branch to their nostrils? I in turn will act with fury, I will show no pity or compassion; though they call loudly in My hearing, I will not listen to them." (Ezek. 8:17–18)

The meaning of the word "*ḥamas*" in these verses is very significant. Most commentators fail to note the meaning here, but Rimon Kasher explains:

> Ḥamas is violent social injustice…. The expression occurs in the story of the Flood, so what we have here is more than merely a hint of the punishment that awaits Judah. What the verse means is that God's anger towards Israel arises not only from their religious abominations, but also from their sins in the moral and social sphere.[15]

While this is one possible explanation, it seems that *ḥamas* in this verse is still related to religious sins. The end of the verse, for example, describes those who "thrust the branch to their nostrils," which appears to be a form of pagan worship.[16] This being so, we must view this chapter in its entirety as an introduction to chapters 9–11, where Ezekiel sees God's glory leaving the Temple. (We will look more closely at the meaning of *ḥamas* in the appendix to chapter 12.)

---

15. Kasher, *Yeḥezkel 1–24*, 253–54. See also previous chapter for a discussion on *ḥamas* and the allusion to the Flood.
16. "Their nose" (*apam*) is one of the eighteen instances of *kina hakatuv*, in which a reading is changed to protect God's honor (see Mekhilta DeRabbi Yishmael, *Massekhta DeShira Beshalach* 6 [see H. Saul Horowitz and Israel Abraham Rabin, eds., *Mekhilta DeRabbi Ishmael* (Jerusalem: Bamburger at Wahrman, 1970), 135]). For the literal interpretation of the expression, see Rashi, Radak, Rabbi Joseph Kara, Rabbi Eliezer of Beaugency, Rabbi Jospeh ibn Caspi, Rabbi Menachem ben Shimon, and modern scholars ad loc.

Ezekiel, Deuteronomy, and Descriptions of the Nation's Sins

Idolatry in Ezekiel and Deuteronomy: A Broader Perspective
While our focus in this discussion is on Ezekiel 8, the descriptions of idolatry serve as a central topic in the book. Along with our assertion that Ezekiel, in his prophecy in chapter 8, deliberately alludes to the prophecy in Deuteronomy 4 to describe the idolatry in which the people are engaged, we can also take note of other terms used by Ezekiel to describe idolatry – which are found only in Deuteronomy. Ezekiel seems to have had these terms, and the contexts in which they appear, in mind when speaking of idolatry as a cause of the Destruction.

1. *Shekketz, shikkutzim* ("detestable things"): The term, discussed earlier (in chapter 3), appears in Deuteronomy in the framework of the covenant on the plains of Moab (Deut. 29:16). Moses emphasizes that the covenant between God and the nation – as well as its conditions, and the penalties for its violation – applies to the future generations as well. Here, too, Ezekiel emphasizes that it is the sins of the people that have evoked the punishment set down in Deuteronomy, including destruction and exile.

2. **The warning not to pass children through fire**: "Let no one be found among you who consigns his son or daughter to the fire, or who is an augur, a soothsayer, a diviner, a sorcerer" (Deut. 18:10). This warning appears as one of the prohibitions of adopting the abominations of the other nations, and includes the emphasis: "For anyone who does such things is abhorrent to the Lord, and it is because of these abhorrent things that the Lord your God is dispossessing them before you" (Deut. 18:12). Therefore, the consequence of these actions, as described by Ezekiel is, once again, inevitable: "And if to this very day you defile yourselves in the presentation of your gifts by making your children pass through the fire to all your fetishes, shall I respond to your inquiry, O House of Israel? As I live – declares the Lord God – I will not respond to you" (20:31).

3. **The location of the sites of worship**: The Torah mentions "on lofty mountains and on hills or under any luxuriant tree" only once in Deuteronomy, as part of the command that the *bamot* be destroyed:

"You must destroy all the sites at which the nations you are to dispossess worshipped their gods, whether on lofty mountains and on hills or under any luxuriant tree" (Deut. 12:2). In Ezekiel, the lofty mountains and luxuriant trees are mentioned as places where God will carry out His verdict upon all those who have not only failed to destroy such places (as they were commanded to, in Deuteronomy), but who went so far as to engage in the idolatrous worship there themselves:

> And you shall know that I am the Lord, when your slain lie among the fetishes round about their altars, on every high hill, on all the mountaintops, under every green tree, and under every leafy oak – wherever they presented pleasing odors to all their fetishes. (Ezek. 6:13)

4. **The command to uproot idolatry:** Like the command concerning the destruction of the places and altars where the nations served their gods, this directive is common to both books. Ezekiel describes the future destruction:

> The towns shall be laid waste and the shrines shall be devastated. Thus your altars shall be laid waste and bear their punishment; your fetishes shall be smashed and annihilated, your incense stands cut down, and your handiwork wiped out. (6:6)

With these words he states that the Destruction might have been avoided, had the nation observed the command appearing in Deuteronomy, which uses the same terms:

> Instead, this is what you shall do to them: you shall tear down their altars, smash their pillars, cut down their sacred posts, and consign their images to the fire. (Deut. 7:5)

> Tear down their altars, smash their pillars, put their sacred posts to the fire, and cut down the images of their gods, obliterating their name from that site. (Deut. 12:3)

Ezekiel, Deuteronomy, and Descriptions of the Nation's Sins

The Outcome of Idolatry: Defilement of the Nation

The consequence foretold in Deuteronomy for idolatry is exile. This, then, is another way in which the prophecy highlights the reason for the exiles' plight. Along with this message, Ezekiel's prophecy again emphasizes that the people's acts have caused the defilement of the nation, the land, and the Temple – a result not mentioned in Deuteronomy.[17] In Leviticus, though, we do find two different contexts in which defilement is caused by engaging in idolatry. The first is: "Do not turn to ghosts and do not inquire of familiar spirits, to be defiled by them: I the Lord am your God" (Lev. 19:31). In other words, consulting mediums and wizards has the effect of defiling the nation. In the next chapter we read: "And I will set My face against that man and will cut him off from among his people, because he gave of his offspring to Molech and so defiled My sanctuary and profaned My holy name" (Lev. 20:3). Sacrificing to Molech, the text tells us, defiles the Sanctuary.

As in the verses in Leviticus, Ezekiel also states that the nation and the Temple have been defiled. But he adds the defilement of the land, not mentioned explicitly in the Torah, as a direct result of idolatry. There is also a quantitative difference: in Leviticus, only two verses speak of idolatry causing the defilement of the people and of the Temple;[18] in the book of Ezekiel this issue appears in no less than thirty verses.[19]

The necessity of repeatedly emphasizing this matter during Ezekiel's time is understandable; false prophets were constantly present, insisting that the Temple would not be destroyed. These false prophets also claimed that the Temple vessels that had been carried into captivity would be

---

17. In comparison, it is worth noting that in Deuteronomy, *tuma* ("defilement" or "impurity") is associated with the following situations: ritually impure meat, animals, disposal of tithes, reuniting with an ex-wife who married another man in the meantime, and delay in burying a corpse.
18. This is in addition to many other verses in Leviticus which mention defilement in other contexts (menstruation, seminal issue, *tzaraat*, etc.) that are unrelated to idolatry.
19. The defilement of the Temple is mentioned for the first time in Ezekiel 5:11, and then in 9:7 and 23:38. Defilement of the people first occurs in 4:13–14 (in the prophet's symbolic act), then in 14:11, and afterwards mainly in chapters 20 and 23. Defilement of the land is mentioned for the first time in chapter 22. This defilement also has its own special purification, as we shall see in our discussion of chapters 36–39.

returned to the Temple in Jerusalem (Jer. 27:16), and that within a short time the exiles, too, would return to their land (Jer. 28:3–4).

Ezekiel's descriptions of the varieties of idolatry committed by the people appears to deliberately follow the style employed in Deuteronomy, in the instructions and warnings not to follow the other nations' deeds and not to serve their gods. This technique lends additional validity to Ezekiel's prophecies about the sins – particularly about the punishment that God will bring. The nation's sin, moreover, is amplified through a broad generalization of all the different types of idolatry and their enumeration together in chapter 8. In this way the prophet underlines the prophetic message that he is conveying: The sins of the people have included idolatry, and this represents justification for the imminent Destruction and exile.[20]

---

20. The terms discussed in this section appear along with the *maskit* (a form of sculpted idol) in Ezekiel 8:12 (mentioned in the Torah in Leviticus 26:1 and in Numbers 33:52) and the *tzelem* (image). Ezekiel mentions three kinds of *tzelem*: "…their images and their detestable abominations (*tzalmei to'evotam*)" (7:20), "phallic images (*tzalmei zakhar*)" (16:17), and "figures of Chaldeans (*tzalmei Kasdim*)" (23:14); cf. also Numbers 33:52.

The root N-T-TZ (to destroy, overthrow) appears in Leviticus 11:35; 14:45; Deuteronomy 7:5; 12:3; and Ezekiel 16:39 (in reference to Jerusalem; it appears later on in chapter 26:9 and 12 in relation to Tyre). The command not to eat meat with its blood appears several times in Leviticus and in Deuteronomy, and Ezekiel emphasizes that in this matter the people also have sinned – see Ezekiel 33:25; 36:13–14.

Chapter 7

God's Glory Departs from the Temple

Ezekiel 9:1–11:25

Chapters 9–11 contain a divine vision in which God's glory leaves the Temple. This is a continuation of the Divine Presence's journey at the beginning of the book of Ezekiel. The core element of the vision here is the final verse of chapter 8: "I in turn will act with fury, I will show no pity or compassion…."[1] In these chapters the prophet refers perhaps not only to the outcome, but also to the manner in which the destruction will be carried out – "with fury" and with "no pity."

---

1. This is the last time we will discuss this phrase, which recurs frequently in the early part of the book (see 5:11; 7:4, 9). Here, it occurs relating to God's response to the nation's deeds, which the prophet observed in chapters 8–11. This verse appears three more times (8:18; 9:5, 10) but after chapter 9, the prophet does not use it again.

Ezekiel 9:1–11:25

SLAUGHTER IN THE TEMPLE (9:1–11)

An interesting juxtaposition appears at the end of chapter 8 and the beginning of chapter 9:

> Though they call loudly in My hearing, I will not listen to them. (8:18)

> Then He called loudly in my hearing, saying, "Approach, you men in charge of the city, each bearing his weapons of destruction." (9:1)[2]

The people cry out loudly – but they remain unanswered. Moreover, Ezekiel hears a loud voice calling upon those who have charge over the city to destroy it. This contrast highlights the chasm separating the nation from God. Ezekiel then sees: "And six men entered by way of the upper gate that faces north, each with his club in his hand; and among them was another, clothed in linen, with a writing case at his waist. They came forward and stopped at the bronze altar" (v. 2).

Six men holding weapons of slaughter arrive from the north (familiar to us already as the origin of punishment). One is there to document proceedings. The detailed and graphic description, including the garb of the scribe and the exact location of the group, alongside the bronze altar, is meant to convey the message that this is not a theoretical depiction. And as the men appear, the glory of the God of Israel begins its journey out of the Temple. Again God cries out, this time to the scribe: "He called to the man clothed in linen with the writing case at his waist" (v. 3).

Now it now becomes clear that the scribe's role is to draw a sign on the forehead of those who express sorrow over the abominations committed in the city: "the men who moan and groan because of all the abominations that are committed in it" (v. 4), marking them so that they will be passed over. As for the rest, the command is to slay them without mercy.

---

2. This verse can be understood in two ways. One is as punctuated above. Alternatively, the voice cries, "Cause those that have charge over the city to draw near," and Ezekiel himself describes how they each hold a weapon of destruction.

This image further reinforces the idea of personal retribution (3:16–21, as discussed previously). We see clearly – even in this generation, even when the decree of Destruction is irreversible – that divine justice is evident. The righteous person will live in his righteousness; only the wicked will die for their sins. But at the same time, it is emphasized that all sinners will indeed be slain: "Kill off graybeard, youth and maiden, women and children" (9:6).

The description in verses 6–7 of old men being slain in the courts of the Temple is horrifying. Whereas the Torah portrays the defilement of the Temple as the result of the nation's sins, Ezekiel's depiction has the defilement caused by a divine command that people be killed in its courtyards. This is a situation unparalleled in all of Tanakh. How can God order an act that will result in the Temple's defilement, contravening the command that its sanctity be strictly preserved? Furthermore, who are these "elders who were in front of the House" (9:6)?

To address the first question, we must recall that the Temple is already defiled because of the deeds of the nation – foremost among them, its leaders. This slaughter, then, demonstrates once again that God's glory is no longer present; the responsibility for this situation rests principally with the officials. The Temple's defilement by God's own command serves as proof that by the month of Elul in the sixth year of Jehoiachin's exile, almost five years before the Destruction, God's glory was no longer there.

Ezekiel is not unmoved by this sight: "When they were out killing, and I remained alone, I flung myself on my face and cried out, 'Ah, Lord God! Are you going to annihilate all that is left of Israel, pouring out Your fury upon Jerusalem?'" (v. 8).

Ezekiel's reaction is instructive on a number of levels. First, in his divine vision he does not see those people being passed over thanks to the mark on their forehead. We can infer, then, that by the time of the Destruction there were no righteous people worthy of being saved (likewise in 14:12–23). Next, the expression "all that is left of Israel" shows that Ezekiel regards the inhabitants of Jerusalem as the remnant of the nation. This sense of national doom – the fear that not a single survivor will remain in Jerusalem – is compounded by the prophet's personal involvement in the situation, by his fright at witnessing the fulfillment of his prophecy. This very real vision leaves even the prophet himself shaken, and may perhaps indicate to us the message that he conveyed to the elders sitting before him.

God's response to the prophet's broken cry: "He answered me, 'The iniquity of the Houses of Judah and Israel is very very great, the land is full of crime and the city is full of corruption'" (9:9) explains the reason for this terrible event. We hear another iteration of the nation's sins: the bloodshed and the injustice perpetrated in Jerusalem. Finally, we see the people's rationalization that has led to all this evil: "For they say, 'The Lord has forsaken the land, and the Lord does not see.'" This verse (like 38:12) informs us that the corruption and idolatry that have overtaken Jerusalem have been caused by a feeling on the part of the leaders that God no longer has His eye on what is happening in the land. Moshe Greenberg proposes:

> The general picture arising here is better suited to the first chapter of Zephaniah before the reforms of Josiah. Besides the various types of idolatry, Zephaniah mentions those "who say to themselves, 'The Lord will do nothing, good or bad'" (Zeph. 1:12 – a parallel to Ezekiel's formulation "the Lord does not see"). This mood seems to belong to the period preceding the reforms of Josiah, because following those great acts the nation relied greatly upon their God and had tremendous faith in Him; they were encouraged in this by the prophets of peace and salvation who multiplied during the generation of Jehoiakim and Zedekiah.... Therefore [Ezekiel] mentions the lawless mood of times gone by to describe the way Jerusalem now appears in God's eyes.[3]

Against this backdrop, it is once again emphasized that the divine response will be devoid of compassion: "I, in turn, will show no pity or compassion; I will give them their deserts" (9:10). Finally, the report of the man clothed in linen – "I have done as You commanded me" (v. 11) – answers Ezekiel's question as to how it was that the entire remnant of the

---

3. Moshe Greenberg, "HaMuva'ot BeSefer Yeḥezkel KeReka LaNevuot," *Beit Mikra* 17, no. 3 (1972): 273–78.

God's Glory Departs from the Temple

people in Jerusalem could be condemned to die. The reply is that none were found who sighed and wept over the state of the city.

FIRE IN THE TEMPLE (10:1–22)

In chapter 10 the prophet describes the divine vision he encountered at the start of his prophetic mission. Here there is an additional dimension which allows us to deduce that not only does the defilement of the city have its source inside the Temple, but it is a fire originating in the Temple that causes the burning of the city. This fire is brought out of the Temple by the same man who indicated that no one in the city was worthy of rescue from the impending disaster. First, we encounter the command: "He spoke to the man clothed in linen and said, 'Step inside the wheelwork, under the cherubim, and fill your hands with glowing coals from among the cherubim, and scatter them over the city.' And he went in as I looked on" (10:2).

This is followed by a description of the departure of God's glory from the Temple and the implementation of this command:

> When He commanded the man dressed in linen: "Take fire from among the cherubim within the wheelwork," he went in and stood beside a wheel. And a cherub stretched out his hand among the cherubim to the fire that was among the cherubim; he took some and put it into the hands of him who was clothed in linen, who took it and went out.... The cherubim ascended; those were the creatures that I had seen by the Chebar River.... Then the presence of the Lord left the platform of the House and stopped above the cherubim ... and they stopped at the entrance of the eastern gate of the House of the Lord, with the presence of the God of Israel above them. They were the same creatures that I had seen below the God of Israel at the Chebar River; so now I knew that they were cherubim.... As for the form of their faces, they were the very faces that I had seen by the Chebar River. (10:6–22)

MEN AT THE TEMPLE GATES (11:1–16)

Having completed this part of his description of the departure of God's glory from the Temple, borne by the cherubim, Ezekiel continues on the subject of the nation's actions in the present. This time, the overall

Ezekiel 9:1–11:25

situation is presented by focusing on the deeds and thoughts of twenty-five men at the entrance to the Temple, two of whom Ezekiel identifies by name:

> Then a spirit lifted me up and brought me to the east gate of the House of the Lord, which faces eastward; and there, at the entrance of the gate, were twenty-five men, among whom I saw Jaazaniah son of Azzur and Pelatiah son of Benaiah, leaders of the people. (11:1)

Ezekiel identifies two noblemen by name, and, in doing so, indicates that the leadership bears responsibility for events at the time.[4] Ezekiel then quotes the people, which gives us an idea of their perspective on the city: . "[The Lord] said to me, 'O mortal, these are the men who plan iniquity and plot wickedness in this city, who say: "There is no need now to build houses; this [city] is the pot, and we are the meat"'" (vv. 2–3).

There is no need to build houses, concede the people – acknowledging that difficult times are on their way. But the people nevertheless maintain that even if they "cook" in the fire of the troubles that await them, they will be saved from annihilation, just as meat in a cauldron is saved from burning. Thus the statement depicts these rebels as preparing themselves for the siege, certain however that they will prevail, since they are important to God.[5]

But their statement can be understood in a way that portrays the speakers as even more arrogant and certain of themselves. They may be referring, not to building houses in Jerusalem, but to building houses in exile. In that case, the assertion that the inhabitants of Jerusalem will not be building houses in the near future is not an expression of coming to terms with the imminent challenges but rather a rejection of Jeremiah's advice to the exiles to build houses in exile (Jer. 29:5). If this is so, their words express their confidence that the city will not be destroyed,

---

4. It also provides some insight into Ezekiel's status before being exiled. Perhaps this familiarity with the nobility (as well as his being exiled with the skilled workers and artisans) suggests that Ezekiel belonged to the aristocracy. He may even have been a Jerusalemite priest, unlike Jeremiah, who, located in provincial Anatot (Jer. 1:1), seems to have lived in the peripheral border region.
5. As Greenberg proposes in "HaMuva'ot BeSefer Yeḥezkel," 275.

nor will they be exiled or build (new) houses (in exile). Following this reading, the metaphor of the "pot" and the "meat" describes them as protected within this city surrounded by a wall, like meat is protected from the fire by the cauldron.

Either way, God's response is: "Many have you slain in this city; you have filled its streets with corpses" (11:6). God places the responsibility for the slain corpses (mentioned in 9:7) on the people of Jerusalem, even though they are killed by a divinely ordained campaign.

> The corpses that you have piled up in it are the meat for which it is the pot; but you shall be taken out of it. You feared the sword, and the sword I will bring upon you – declares the Lord God. I will take you out of it and deliver you into the hands of strangers, and I will execute judgments upon you. You shall fall by the sword; I will punish you at the border of Israel. And you shall know that I am the Lord. This [city] shall not be a pot for you, nor you the meat in it; I will punish you at the border of Israel. (11:7–11)

So, despite their brave words, we see that Jerusalem's inhabitants are in fact afraid. God's response confirms their fears, and emphasizes that despite their claim that they are like meat in a cauldron, they are destined to be brought out of Jerusalem – for even its wall will not protect them – and to be judged on the border of Israel.

The prophecy concludes with Ezekiel's own response to this: "I threw myself upon my face and cried out aloud, 'Ah, Lord God! You are wiping out the remnant of Israel!'" (v. 13). As part of his vision, Ezekiel sees Pelatiah son of Benaiah – one of the two leaders in the group – fall dead. He sees before his eyes that no one in the city will remain alive, and then he expresses his fright – perhaps also his protest – in a cry: Will there truly be no one at all left? This time the prophet receives only a partial response to his cry, and to his falling upon his face. We have previously discussed God's response, concluding that the essence of the message is that God remains with the exiles in a "small sanctuary," and that it is they who represent the remnant of Israel. This is yet another echo of the debate that the exiles in Babylonia maintained with the remnant in

Jerusalem about their status – a debate that reaches its climax after word of the Destruction reaches Babylonia in chapter 33.

RESTORATION! (11:17–21)

For the first time in the book, Ezekiel addresses the future of the exiles following the harsh, painful prophecies to the remnant in Jerusalem. While one might expect a prophecy of consolation, some words of comfort and empathy, this is not to be. Chapters 1–24, which cover the prophecies from the years preceding the Destruction, contain only three prophetic units devoted to the nation's future restoration: in chapter 11 (in the sixth year; see 8:1), chapter 16 (undated), and chapter 20 (in the seventh year; 20:1).[6]

Now we come to the promise that the exiles are destined to return to their land: "I will gather you from the peoples and assemble you out of the countries where you have been scattered, and I will give you the Land of Israel." (11:17). This prophecy is not dependent on the people changing their ways. To the contrary: In the future, God will gather them, assemble them, and give them the Land of Israel. Only after they arrive there ("and they shall return there") do we find that they will "do away with all its detestable things and all its abominations" (v. 18). Are we to deduce from this verse that although the nation does not mend its ways prior to its return to the land, it will repent afterwards? Apparently not. At the end of this prophetic unit it turns out that the people have kept up their evil ways: "But as for them whose heart is set upon their detestable things and their abominations, I will repay them for their conduct" (v. 21).[7]

Admittedly, this is a problematic verse. It is not clear who the prophet is describing. Is he referring to the exiles in the present? The exiles in the future? Or perhaps the inhabitants of Jerusalem?[8] It seems correct to interpret verse 21 as also talking about the exiles who return in the future. This being so, we must assume that the prophet's aim is to

---

6. To these we might perhaps add 17:22–24, which mentions God's future renewal of the monarchy.
7. Concerning the use of the phrase "detestable things and their abominations", see above, chapter 3.
8. This difficulty has led some commentators to suggest that this verse starts with a new subject: While Ezekiel 11:18 describes the deeds of the exiles when they return in the future, verse 21 describes the sins of the inhabitants of Jerusalem in the present.

emphasize that the sins of the people will still exist in their heart ("them whose heart is set upon their detestable things and their abominations") even when they return to the land, and this is why God will give them a new heart: "I will give them one heart and put a new spirit in them; I will remove the heart of stone from their bodies and give them a heart of flesh that they may follow My laws and faithfully observe My rules. They shall be My people, and I will be their God" (vv. 19–20).

It is only in this way, and only at that time, that worship of the "detestable things" and "abominations" will cease. Only then will the covenant between God and His people be fulfilled: "They shall be My people, and I will be their God." This emphasizes that ultimately, the people returning to their land will not remove the detestable things and abominations from their hearts, as is proper. This is also what is unique about this particular prophecy: It expresses God's approach to the people as a result of their decision not to change their ways either before the Destruction or, as we now discover, even afterwards.

It would have been fitting for the exiles returning to their land to cease their idolatrous practices. But they do not; their actions are so much part of them, it is as if they were inscribed in their hearts. So God Himself will have to give them a new heart. This heart of flesh will ensure that henceforth they will follow God's laws and observe His statutes. This prophecy thus complements the response that the book of Ezekiel offers to the claim of Jerusalem's inhabitants (verses 16 and 17 both begin with the word *lakhen*, often translated as "therefore"), and emphasizes (contrary to the claim of the Jerusalemites) that the exiles will return to their land, even though they still adhere to their sinful ways.

A review of these verses shows that while superficially this appears to be a prophecy of consolation, in fact it actually offers little comfort: God will bring back His people to the land in the future, but without the people having repented. Therefore, the prophet concludes with harsh words: "I will repay them for their conduct" (11:21).

PARTING (11:22–25)

> Then the cherubim, with the wheels beside them, lifted their wings, while the presence of the God of Israel rested above them. The presence of the Lord ascended from the midst of the city and

Ezekiel 9:1–11:25

> stood on the hill east of the city. A spirit carried me away and brought me in a vision by the spirit of God to the exile community in Chaldea. Then the vision that I had seen left me. (11:22–24)

The chapter concludes with God's glory departing not only from the Temple, but also from the city of Jerusalem. The same spirit which had brought Ezekiel to see the divine vision (8:3) now delivers him back to Babylonia. The prophet returns to the exiles seated around him and shares what he has seen with them (11:25). But any hope of the people finally internalizing the message of his prophecy is shattered in the very next verses, the beginning of the book's next chapter: "The word of the Lord came to me: O mortal, you dwell among the rebellious breed. They have eyes to see but see not, ears to hear but hear not; for they are a rebellious breed" (12:1–2).

Chapter 8

Zedekiah and the End of the Monarchy

Ezekiel 12:1–20; 17:1–24; 19:1–14

Ezekiel's next prophecy deals with an obscure figure referred to as the *nasi*,[1] whose identity is not revealed even in the divine communication which explains Ezekiel's symbolic actions. The prevailing assumption is that this man is Zedekiah: The description of his exile in the book of Kings and in Jeremiah conforms to the symbolic act presented in our chapter. To understand the full significance of this prophecy, we will broaden our discussion here and review other prophecies of

---

1. The biblical meaning of *nasi* commonly denotes leader or ruler, usually a tribal head or local leader, although the *nasi* is occasionally placed in a royal role, as in Solomon's case (I Kings 11:34). In Ezekiel, in the chapters of the vision of the future Temple (40–48), the term *nasi* frequently refers to the leader of the people and the prophet delineates his functions. In addition, the *nasi* is mentioned in various contexts in chapters 1 to 39, where the use of this honorific – as opposed to king – is ambiguous. I have therefore left the word untranslated, as *nasi* (*nesi'im*) when it refers to Judeans. For further discussion of the term, see the end of this chapter.

Ezekiel that relate to Zedekiah in chapters 17 and 19, as well as a passage in 21:23–32, along with that found here, in chapter 12.

Zedekiah is not mentioned by name in the book of Ezekiel, not even in the passage interpreting the symbolic acts that address his deeds. Furthermore, the kingdom of Babylonia is likewise only mentioned in these chapters indirectly; no prophecy within the prophecies to the nations (ch. 25–32) deals with the future of Babylonia and its destruction.[2] In fact, Babylonia is only mentioned here in the context of its failed war against Tyre (26:7ff.) and the fact that Babylonia is God's emissary in its war against Egypt (29:18–19; 30:10, 24–25; 32:11).[3]

The reason that no prophecy against Babylonia appears in the book of Ezekiel, ostensibly, relates to the indirect manner in which Ezekiel mentions Zedekiah. This connection can be interpreted in one of two ways. First, Babylonia, at the time of the Destruction, functions as God's emissary. Thus, while it fulfills this function, no damaging prophecies are made about its future. Second, because Ezekiel is based in Babylonia, he is unable to denounce the empire in which he dwells. This interpretation also explains the obscure description of Zedekiah who remains anonymous throughout. For the kings of Babylonia, Zedekiah's coronation in Jerusalem had the effect of creating an artificial calm, while in effect discontinuing the monarchy of David's dynasty in Jerusalem. This is evident from the fact that we have no information about Zedekiah after his exile to Babylonia – in contrast to Jehoiachin, who was exiled before him, and was shown honor, even relative to other exiled kings there with him (II Kings 25:27–30). Paying explicit attention to Zedekiah as king, then, may have aroused the ire of the Babylonians – especially because Zedekiah did not fulfill their expectations, instead rebelling against Nebuchadnezzar.

---

2. Jeremiah 59 contains a prophecy of the future destruction of Babylonia and a review of that chapter offers an important complement to Ezekiel's prophecies. That discussion, however, lies beyond the scope of our present study.
3. In addition to its mention in the parable in Ezekiel 23:14ff., and the noting of the length of the siege on Jerusalem by the Babylonians in 24:2.

Zedekiah and the End of the Monarchy

A SYMBOLIC ACT AND ITS MEANING (12:1–16)

Immediately after sharing his divine vision with his fellow exiles (ch. 11), Ezekiel again hears – as at the beginning of his prophetic career (ch. 2) – that the people around him were and remain a "rebellious breed. They have eyes to see but see not, ears to hear but hear not" (12:2). In that sense, they resemble the idols they worship: "Their idols are silver and gold, the work of men's hands. They have mouths, but cannot speak, eyes, but cannot see; they have ears, but cannot hear…" (Ps. 115:4–6).

So Ezekiel is commanded to continue prophesying. But for the first time, his prophecy concerns the future of the inhabitants of Jerusalem who will be exiled – rather than killed – at the time of the Destruction. He demonstrates their fate through another symbolic act. His use of this device may reflect the hope that by describing those who are destined to join the present exiles in Babylonia, the latter will understand the reality of the Destruction's outcome. This prophecy also emphasizes the performance of this act before the exiles, so that those who "have eyes to see but see not" will, finally, see and understand.[4]

> Get yourself gear for exile, and go into exile by day before their eyes. Go into exile from your home to another place before their very eyes; perhaps they will take note, even though they are a rebellious breed. Carry out your gear as gear for exile by day before their very eyes; and go out again in the evening before their eyes, as one who goes out into exile. Before their eyes, break through the wall and carry [the gear] out through it; before their eyes, carry it on your shoulder. Take it out in the dark, and cover your face that you may not see the land; for I make you a portent to the House of Israel. I did just as I was ordered: I took out my gear by day as gear for exile, and in the

---

4. The word "*le'eneyhem*" (in their sight) is repeated seven times in verses 3–7. Other expressions related to sight also occur: "perhaps they will take note" (lit. "perhaps they will see"; v. 3); "you may not see the land" (v. 6), and "carrying it before their eyes" (v. 7). This is a continuation of the motif of sight and eyes used in the book, as we saw earlier (see ch. 6, n. 3).

evening I broke through the wall with my own hands. In the darkness I carried [the gear] out on my shoulder, carrying it before their eyes. (12:3–7)

Through this symbolic act, Ezekiel is commanded to "exile" himself, carrying his "gear for exile." The departure into exile is undertaken in the evening, in the dark, with his face covered, through a hole he digs in the wall. Ezekiel, it seems, repeats this act for a number of days ("by day"). Each morning, a divine explanation of what his act meant follows, in response to the people's question: "Did not the House of Israel, that rebellious breed, ask you, 'What are you doing?'" (v. 9).

God explains the symbolic act:

> This pronouncement concerns the *nasi* in Jerusalem and all the House of Israel who are in it. Say: "I am a portent for you: As I have done, so shall it be done to them; they shall go into exile, into captivity. And the *nasi* among them shall carry his gear on his shoulder as he goes out in the dark. He shall break through the wall in order to carry [his gear] out through it; he shall cover his face, because he himself shall not see the land with his eyes." I will spread My net over him, and he shall be caught in My snare. I will bring him to Babylon, the land of the Chaldeans, but he shall not see it; and there he shall die. And all those around him, his helpers and all his troops, I will scatter in every direction; and I will unsheathe the sword after them. (vv. 10–14)

The language of the prophecy creates a close connection with what we find written later in chapter 17:

> I will spread My net over him and he shall be caught in My snare; I will carry him to Babylon and enter with him into judgment there for the trespass which he committed against Me. And all the fugitives of all his battalions shall fall by the sword, and those who remain shall scatter in every direction. (17:20–21)

Zedekiah and the End of the Monarchy

This prophecy, as we shall see, is God's response to Zedekiah's rebellion against Babylonia – a rebellion that contravenes God's order, conveyed to him by the prophet.

When explaining the symbol in chapter 12, the prophet first relates to the entire "House of Israel," which will be exiled and taken in captivity, and then connects the parable to its interpretation by means of a description of "the *nasi* among them":

> And the *nasi* among them shall carry his gear on his shoulder as he goes out in the dark. He shall break through the wall in order to carry [his gear] out through it; he shall cover his face, because he himself shall not see the land with his eyes. (12:12)

The parallel prophecy in chapter 17 has at its center the figure of "the seed royal" (17:13). Both titles ("*nasi*" and "the seed royal") seem to refer to Zedekiah. In the book of Kings we read:

> The city continued in a state of siege until the eleventh year of King Zedekiah. By the ninth day [of the fourth month] the famine had become acute in the city; there was no food left for the common people. Then [the wall of] the city was breached. All the soldiers [left the city] by night through the gate between the double walls, which is near the king's garden – the Chaldeans were all around the city; and [the king] set out for the Arabah. But the Chaldean troops pursued the king, and they overtook him in the steppes of Jericho as his entire force left him and scattered. They captured the king and brought him before the king of Babylon at Riblah; and they put him on trial. They slaughtered Zedekiah's sons before his eyes; then Zedekiah's eyes were put out. He was chained in bronze fetters and he was brought to Babylon. (II Kings 25:2–7)

The parallel text in Jeremiah reads:

> When King Zedekiah of Judah saw them, he and all the soldiers fled. They left the city at night, by way of the king's garden, through the gate between the double walls; and he set out toward the

Arabah. But the Chaldean troops pursued them, and they overtook Zedekiah in the steppes of Jericho. They captured him and brought him before King Nebuchadrezzar of Babylon at Riblah in the region of Hamath; and he put him on trial. The king of Babylon had Zedekiah's children slaughtered at Riblah before his eyes; the king of Babylon had all the nobles of Judah slaughtered. Then the eyes of Zedekiah were put out and he was chained in bronze fetters, that he might be brought to Babylon. (Jer. 39:4–7; see also 52:7–11)

These descriptions of Zedekiah's exile match the details of Ezekiel's prophecy: the capture of the king, his conveyance to Babylon, and the fate of his company. In chapter 12 we also find mention of the dark (apparently symbolizing night) and the covering of the face (apparently symbolizing Zedekiah's blindness). The prophecy in chapter 17 in which the king will be judged "with God" for having trespassed against Him may also be fulfilled with the king of Babylonia (representing God) "putting him on trial" after he is brought there.

The next few verses in chapter 12 of Ezekiel describe another symbolic act that the prophet must carry out:

> O mortal, eat your bread in trembling and drink your water in fear and anxiety. And say to the people of the land: Thus said the Lord God concerning the inhabitants of Jerusalem in the Land of Israel: They shall eat their bread in anxiety and drink their water in desolation, because their land will be desolate of its multitudes on account of the lawlessness of all its inhabitants. (Ezek. 12:18–19)

These verses, recalling the prophet's restricted eating and drinking in chapter 4, complement the symbolic act described at the beginning of our chapter. Thus Ezekiel connects the beginning of the chapter to the events about which he prophesied at the beginning of the book. The prophet's departure does not occur in a vacuum; it is the result of the situation in the city.

This link is also manifest in the description in the book of Kings, where – similar to the description in Ezekiel – the severity of the famine is expressed in the fact that it reaches even the "people of the land" (the leadership of the people; see Ezek. 7:26–27): "The famine had become acute in the city; there was no food left for the common people" (II Kings 25:3).

Ezekiel also details the reason for the prophecy. Its aim, as we learn from chapter 12, is as follows:

> Then, when I have scattered them among the nations and dispersed them through the countries, they shall know that I am the Lord. But I will spare a few of them from the sword, from famine, and from pestilence, that they may recount all their abominable deeds among the nations to which they come; and they shall know that I am the Lord! (Ezek. 12:15–16)

Indeed, this message is emphasized once again as the conclusion of this prophetic unit: "The inhabited towns shall be laid waste and the land shall become a desolation; then you shall know that I am the Lord" (12:20).

In contrast with the conditions that have prevailed thus far, from now on "knowledge of God" will be attained by those who remain, in order that they testify that it was God who scattered His people among the nations. This diverges from the formulation familiar to us from the Torah:

> Let not the Egyptians say, "It was with evil intent that He delivered them, only to kill them off in the mountains and annihilate them from the face of the earth." Turn from Your blazing anger, and renounce the plan to punish Your people. (Ex. 32:12)

The lesson of knowledge of God will now be learned – even though the exile will involve a desecration of God's name amongst the nations: "But when they came to those nations, they caused My holy name to be profaned, in that it was said of them, 'These are the people of the Lord, yet they had to leave His land'" (Ezek. 36:20).

ZEDEKIAH'S REBELLION AGAINST NEBUCHADNEZZAR (CHAPTER 17)

Chapter 17 begins with Ezekiel posing a riddle and a parable; Zedekiah's death is one part of their interpretation. Owing to the people's

Ezekiel 12:1–20; 17:1–24; 19:1–14

stubbornness in refusing to accept the message of Ezekiel's prophecies, the prophet employs a range of devices aimed at convincing them; at this point, he adds the riddle to his earlier devices. Chapter 17 is divided into three parts: it begins with the riddle and parable (vv. 1–10); it is followed by the explanation (vv. 11–21); and it concludes by intertwining the riddle and its explanation (vv. 22–24).

The Great Eagle: A Riddle and Parable (17:1–10)

The parable begins by describing an impressive eagle that comes from Lebanon, which seizes the top of a cedar and brings it to the "land of traders" (17:4). It then takes "some of the seed of the land," planting it in a fertile field containing plenty of water ("he planted and set it like a willow"; v. 5). A low, wild vine begins to grow. Thereafter a fruitful relationship develops between that vine in its fertile habitat and "another great eagle" (v. 7). But the vine cuts itself off from its field, even though it is well planted and flourishing; in fact, it has no need for the favors of this eagle. The parable concludes with Ezekiel addressing two rhetorical questions to his audience. First, can the vine, cut off from its roots, possibly flourish? Surely it will wither! Second, even while the vine is still planted in the ground, how can it flourish? It will wither when the east wind comes.

The Kingdom: An Explanation (17:11–21)

The parable is indeed a riddle, concealing more than it reveals. Its explanation therefore follows immediately:

> Do you not know what these things mean? Say: The king of Babylon came to Jerusalem, and carried away its king and its officers and brought them back with him to Babylon. He took one of the seed royal and made a covenant with him and imposed an oath on him, and he carried away the nobles of the land – so that it might be a humble kingdom and not exalt itself, but keep his covenant and so endure. But [that *nasi*] rebelled against him and sent his envoys to Egypt to get horses and a large army. Will he succeed? Will he who does such things escape? Shall he break a covenant and escape? (vv. 12–15)

The prophet explains that the great eagle is the king of Babylonia (Nebuchadnezzar), who comes to Jerusalem and then exiles the top of the cedar – the king (Jehoiachin) and his ministers – to Babylonia.[5]

If we assume that "the top of the cedar" is indeed a reference to the exiled Jehoiachin, then the phrases "the land of traders" (*eretz Kena'an*) and "a city of merchants" (v. 4) must refer to Babylonia.[6] Indeed, during this period the Babylonian Empire flourished and was the economic hub of the Ancient East. It is natural, then, for it to be described as "a city of merchants." Later in the parable, we are told that the eagle took "some of the seed of the land and planted it in a fertile field; he planted and set it like a willow beside abundant waters" (v. 5). This seems to refer to Zedekiah, who was of the Land of Israel's royal seed, and was chosen by Nebuchadnezzar to be "in a fertile field" – in other words, in his place in the Land of Israel. According to this explanation, we must interpret the second part of the verse – "he planted and set it like a willow beside abundant waters" – as a description of the good conditions under which Zedekiah embarked on his role leading the inhabitants of the land. This explanation also accords with the continuation of the interpretation:

> He took one of the seed royal and made a covenant with him and imposed an oath on him, and he carried away the nobles of the land – so that it might be a humble kingdom and not exalt itself, but keep his covenant and so endure. (vv. 13–14)

This describes the covenant between the king of Babylonia and Zedekiah following the exile of Jehoiachin ("the nobles of the land"). Their agreement stipulated that Zedekiah would keep the kingdom for

---

5. The difficulties with the interpretation of the parable are apparent at the outset. We shall propose an explanation for the parable as a whole, although various alternatives might be substituted for many of the details over the course of the chapter.
6. The term "*eretz Kena'an*" is used in the Torah and in the Early Prophets as a reference to the Land of Israel, but the commentators suggest here that in the Later Prophets it is sometimes also used as a reference to Babylonia. In our verse, this would seem to be the case – as in 16:29. See also Isaiah 23:11, where *Kena'an* – Babylonia – is commanded to wage war against Tyre, in the same way as in Ezekiel's prophecy to Tyre (Ezek. 26:7ff.).

which he was responsible a "humble," subservient one. Later in the parable, the "seed royal" becomes a vine which, instead of remaining a lowly plant with its tendrils turned inwards and its roots gathered under it, sprouts boughs and grows wild. The uncontrolled spread of this seed turned vine is explained as a reference to Zedekiah's rebellion against Nebuchadnezzar, with the aid of the king of Egypt. The king of Egypt is a great eagle, "with great wings and full plumage," and the vine – Zedekiah – turns to it for help,[7] instead of recognizing that it is planted in good soil by many waters, with the ability to "grow branches and produce boughs and be a noble vine" (v. 8). There is no justification for his rebellion.

The result of Zedekiah's actions is presented, both in the parable and in its interpretation, in the form of a rhetorical question whose outcome is inescapable. How, asks the parable, could the vine have imagined that it would flourish with the help of the eagle, when this meant cutting itself off from its roots and withering? In the interpretation, the formulation is, "Will he succeed? Will he who does such things escape? Shall he break a covenant and escape?" (v. 15). Reaching out to Egypt, in other words, represents the violation of a covenant with unavoidable consequences.

The parable also poses another rhetorical question, raising an additional point to ponder. Even when the vine was planted in the ground, it had no future; if an eastern wind were to blow, the vine would dry up. Perhaps with this image Ezekiel alludes to Zedekiah's reign being temporary in any event – but his rebellion against Babylon has hastened its end.

The explanation of the parable concludes with God's vow:

> As I live – declares the Lord God – in the very homeland of the king who made him king, whose oath he flouted and whose covenant he broke – right there, in Babylon, he shall die. Pharaoh will not fight at his side with a great army and with numerous troops in the war, when mounds are thrown up and siege towers

---

7. Zedekiah's reliance on Pharaoh, king of Egypt, and his army opposes the position adopted explicitly by Jeremiah; see Jer. 37:1–11.

erected to destroy many lives. He flouted a pact and broke a covenant; he gave his promise and did all these things – he shall not escape. (vv. 16–18)

By rebelling against Nebuchadnezzar, we learn, Zedekiah decreed his own death in Babylonia. This violation was a grave breach of trust. The reliance on the king of Egypt to aid him in fighting against Babylonia likewise led to the deaths of the partners.

Verses 19–21 go beyond the national level, which has been discussed thus far, to the divine perspective on these events. The divine perspective is based on earthly events, and illuminates the full force of the disgrace by comparing the violation of the covenant with Nebuchadnezzar to violation of the covenant with God:

> Assuredly, thus said the Lord God: As I live, I will pay him back for flouting My pact and breaking My covenant. I will spread My net over him and he shall be caught in My snare; I will carry him to Babylon and enter with him into judgment there for the trespass which he committed against Me. And all the fugitives of all his battalions shall fall by the sword, and those who remain shall scatter in every direction; then you will know that I the Lord have spoken. (vv. 19–21)

RENEWAL: THE CONCLUSION (17:22–24)

Thus far we have noted that in Ezekiel's prophecy the Destruction is inevitable; the remnant from which salvation will spring is the group of exiles now in Babylonia, along with lone survivors from among the inhabitants of Jerusalem whose role will be to recount what occurred there. To this the prophet now adds a hostile attitude towards Zedekiah, in the wake of his betrayal of Nebuchadnezzar, who is God's agent in his actions against Israel.[8] The parable and its explanation seem to conclude with this message. But the end of the prophecy introduces

---

8. A prophecy complementing this one and clearly suggesting that the Babylonian king is God's agent in his actions, and that Zedekiah should remain subservient to him, is found in Jeremiah 27 and 28:14.

another element, imbuing God's perspective on what has happened with an echo of consolation. Concluding his prophecies in this manner is characteristic of Ezekiel, whose central message often takes a new twist in its closing verses:

> Thus said the Lord God: Then I in turn will take and set [in the ground a slip] from the lofty top of the cedar; I will pluck a tender twig from the tip of its crown, and I will plant it on a tall, towering mountain. I will plant it in Israel's lofty highlands, and it shall bring forth boughs and produce branches and grow into a noble cedar. Every bird of every feather shall take shelter under it, shelter in the shade of its boughs. Then shall all the trees of the field know that it is I the Lord who have abased the lofty tree and exalted the lowly tree, who have dried up the green tree and made the withered tree bud. I the Lord have spoken, and I will act. (vv. 22–24)

Now it emerges that the top of the cedar, as mentioned in the parable, which was taken to Babylonia, will in the future be brought back to a "tall, towering mountain" – "Israel's lofty highlands." There it is destined to grow and bring forth new branches, and even fruit. Its tendrils, which were earlier described as part of the wild branches of the vine, will once again be part of that cedar tree and will give shade to the birds. At that time, it will become clear to all the other "trees of the field" (representing the other nations) that it is God who brought down the cedar, representing His people, and that it is He who determines the nations' statuses, raising them, drying them up, or causing them to flourish.

The prophecy's conclusion indicates that the potential for renewal of the monarchy in Israel rests with Jehoiachin, who is in exile. This conclusion once again emphasizes the unique status of Jehoiachin throughout the book of Ezekiel;[9] and, indeed, it is Zerubbabel – the grandson

---

9. We have already noted that the book illustrates Jehoiachin's importance by enumerating years according to the years of Jehoiachin's exile.

of Jehoiachin[10] – who will eventually lead the nation at the beginning of the Second Temple period.

THE FATE OF THE KINGS OF JUDAH (CHAPTER 19)

We have examined the central elements of the criticism leveled against Zedekiah. Now, in order to round off Ezekiel's prophecies on the subject, we must deviate again from the order of the chapters and turn our attention to the lamentation in chapter 19 and the symbolic act described in the second part of chapter 21.

Our focus has thus far been on Ezekiel's description of the decline of the institution of Israelite monarchy. Now another element is introduced to explain the parable in chapter 17, which depicts historical processes such as the coronation of a man of royal ancestry, Zedekiah, in place of Jehoiachin (17:13), and the obligation of the king of Judah to be loyal to the king of Babylonia, to obey him and act in accordance with his wishes, as well as a demand that the Kingdom of Judah be a "humble kingdom and not exalt itself" (17:14). The king of Judah, we noted, forged a covenant with the king of Egypt, thereby violating both the pledge of loyalty to the king of Babylonia (Nebuchadnezzar) and the oath and covenant with God. The consequence of this act of rebellion was the king's exile to Babylonian and subjsequent judgment (17:15–21). This prophecy concludes the story of the monarchy of Judah, and emphasizes that its last king, too, violated his covenant with God, and thereby failed in his role. And with the end of his reign, the entire institution of the monarchy ends.

The prophecy of chapter 19 shares some stylistic and thematic links with the prophecy about Zedekiah's fate. It returns to the previous generation, the days of Jehoahaz and Jehoiakim. The lamentation seems to have been uttered after the events it describes have transpired, and thereby complements the prophetic perspective that relates to Jerusalem's fate being sealed: "And you are to intone a dirge over the *nasi* of Israel" (19:1).

---

10. From the verses, the reader cannot definitively determine whether Zerubbabel's father was Shealtiel, eldest son of Jehoiachin (Ezra 3:2, 8; Neh. 12:1; Hag. 1:1) or Pedaiah, his third son (I Chr. 3:19).

Ezekiel 12:1–20; 17:1–24; 19:1–14

Ezekiel uses the term "dirge" (*kina*) more often than any other prophet.[11] He mentions it at the beginning and at the end of our chapter (19:1, 14); previously, the content of his prophecies has been described as "lamentations, dirges, and woes" (2:10); it appears four times in his prophecy to Tyre (26:17; 27:2, 32; 28:12) and twice in his prophecy to Egypt (32:2, 16). It seems that just as the term "lament" reveals much about Ezekiel's attitude towards the imminent destruction of Judah, its use in the context of Tyre and Egypt demonstrates the special status of these locations in the book of Ezekiel, as expressed in different ways.

THE *NASI* OF ISRAEL (19:1)

The title "*nasi*" in Tanakh usually means a ruler or governor. In most instances it refers to the head of a tribe or a regional leader, but in some places *nasi* is used in the monarchal sense (for example, Solomon is referred to in this way in I Kings 11:34). The origin of the title – referring to a regional or tribal leader – indicates a status lower than that of a king, with accordingly fewer rights and obligations. The "*nasi* (prince) of Israel" appears in a number of different contexts in chapters 1–39 of the book of Ezekiel, but the use of this title in these chapters, as opposed to the "king," is somewhat ambiguous. At the beginning of chapter 12 the prophet is commanded to exile himself symbolically from his place, and Ezekiel explains this act by describing the departure of the *nasi* into exile (Ezek. 12:1–11). In chapter 19, the prophet takes up a lament for the final kings of Judah, referring to them as the "*nesi'ei Yisrael*" (19:1). Chapter 21 mentions punishment by the sword for the *nasi* and for the people as a result of their evil actions (21:17), and the prophet notes that the day of the *nasi* of Israel has come: "And to you, O dishonored wicked *nasi* of Israel, whose day has come..." (21:30). At the same time, there is no explicit description of the sins of the *nesi'im*, other than the prophecy in chapter 22, which includes the deeds of the *nasi* of Israel:

---

11. The term "*kina*" is not a common one in Tanakh. It first appears when David laments the death of Saul and Jonathan (II Sam. 1:17). Thereafter it occurs in the book of Amos (Amos 5:1; 8:10), and when Jeremiah uses the term to describe the reactions to the Destruction (Jer. 7:29; 9:9, 19). A description of Jeremiah and "all the singers, male and female" lamenting (over Josiah) is found in II Chronicles 35:25.

"Every one of the *nesi'im* of Israel in your midst used his strength for the shedding of blood" (22:6).[12]

The leadership of the people by the *nesi'im*, which included the use of force, has led to acts of bloodshed; but the *nesi'im*, by virtue of their role as leaders, were responsible for preventing such a situation.

In each of the contexts mentioned here in which Ezekiel uses the term *nasi*, the title *melekh* – king – could have been used instead. Ezekiel does indeed use the term *melekh* when speaking of the kings of Israel in the past and of the kings of the other nations in the present, and he deliberately uses the title *nasi* (prince), for the future leader of Israel in chapters 40–48. However, he chooses to refer to the contemporary kings of Judah using the title *nasi* instead of *melekh* (king) in order to indicate that while the *melekh* who is called a *nasi* did have dominion over his kingdom, it was already a truncated, doomed kingdom. Thus, in chapters 12 and 19 the prophecy concerns the *nasi* who is about to be exiled; chapters 21–22 describe the sins of the *nasi* before being removed from his position.

THE USE OF PARABLES

Ezekiel's prophecy to the kings of Judah in chapter 19 is conveyed through two parables: In the first, the royal family of Judah is compared to a family of lions; in the second, to a vine. It would appear that the basis of these parables, along with the connection between them, extends far back in history, when the journey of the tribe of Judah began – in Jacob's blessing to his sons:

> You, O Judah, your brothers shall praise.... Judah is a lion's whelp; On prey, my son, have you grown. He crouches, lies down like a lion, Like the king of beasts – who dare rouse him? The scepter shall not depart from Judah, nor the ruler's staff from between

---

12. The text in chapter 45 also allows us to identify the sin of the *nesi'im*: "And My *nesi'im* shall no more defraud My people, but shall leave the rest of the land to the several tribes of the House of Israel.... Enough, *nesi'im* of Israel! Make an end of lawlessness and rapine, and do what is right and just! Put a stop to your evictions of My people..." (45:8–9). In addition to resorting to force (which leads to bloodshed), the *nasiim* are also guilty of deception and are responsible for the "lawlessness and rapine" that occurs under their leadership, and for the lack of judgment and justice.

Ezekiel 12:1–20; 17:1–24; 19:1–14

his feet; so that tribute shall come to him and the homage of peoples be his. He tethers his ass to a vine, his ass's foal to a choice vine; he washes his garment in wine, his robe in blood of grapes. His eyes are darker than wine; his teeth are whiter than milk. (Gen. 49:8–12)[13]

"What a Lioness Was Your Mother among the Lions!" (19:2–9)

The parable describes two young lions. The conventional interpretation regards the first as symbolizing Jehoahaz (son of Josiah). Opinions are divided as to the symbolism of the second young lion: It might refer to Jehoiakim (according to Rashi, Radak, Rabbi Joseph Kara, and others), to Jehoiachin, to Zedekiah (which would be appropriate since he was the brother of Jehoahaz, from the same mother/"lioness:" both were sons of Hamutal daughter of Jeremiah of Libnah, according to II Kings 23:31 and 24:18),[14] or to all of them (see Rabbi Eliezer of Beaugency).[15]

In prophesying about the fate of the kings of Judah, Ezekiel leaves out only Jehoiachin. This aligns with his prophetic messages concerning the special status of those who were exiled while under his leadership.

To understand the significance of Ezekiel's parable, the prophecy should be compared with the historical events to which it refers, as documented in Chronicles (following the lamentation for Josiah) and the book of Kings.[16] The following table identifies the second young lion as Jehoiakim.

---

13. The significance of the elements common to Jacob's blessing to Judah and to our chapter as well as the prophecy against Zedekiah in chapter 21 is also fascinating, but lies beyond the scope of this discussion.
14. See Greenberg, *Ezekiel 1–20*, 355–56.
15. Substantiation for each of these possibilities is found among traditional and modern commentators on the relevant verses.
16. While the verses below from Ezekiel are cited fully and in the proper order, verses from Chronicles and from Kings are presented only partially, with Jehoahaz's arrival in Egypt brought earlier in order to align with the order of the text in Ezekiel.

Zedekiah and the End of the Monarchy

Ezekiel 19:2–9	II Chronicles 36:1–6	II Kings 23–24
She raised up one of her cubs, He became a great beast	The people of the land took Jehoahaz son of Josiah	Then the people of the land took Jehoahaz (23:30)
He learned to hunt prey – He devoured men.		He did what was displeasing to the Lord… (23:32)
Nations heeded [the call] against him; He was caught in their snare.	The king of Egypt deposed him in Jerusalem and laid a fine on the land of one hundred silver talents and one gold talent.	Pharaoh Neco imprisoned him in Riblah in the region of Hamath, to keep him from reigning in Jerusalem. And he imposed on the land an indemnity of one hundred talents of silver and a talent of gold (23:33).
They dragged him off with hooks to the land of Egypt.	Neco took his brother Joahaz and brought him to Egypt.	He took Jehoahaz and brought him to Egypt, where he died (23:34).
When she saw herself frustrated, her hope defeated, she took another of her cubs and set him up as a great beast.	The king of Egypt made his brother Eliakim king over Judah and Jerusalem, and changed his name to Jehoiakim.	Then Pharaoh Neco appointed Eliakim son of Josiah king in place of his father Josiah, changing his name to Jehoiakim (23:34).

Ezekiel 12:1–20; 17:1–24; 19:1–14

Ezekiel 19:2–9	II Chronicles 36:1–6	II Kings 23–24
He stalked among the lions, he was a great beast; he learned to hunt prey – he devoured men.	He did what was displeasing to the Lord his God.	He did what was displeasing to the Lord…. In his days, King Nebuchadnezzar of Babylon came up, and Jehoiakim became his vassal for three years. Then he turned and rebelled against him (23:37–24:1).
He ravished their widows, laid waste their cities; the land and all in it were appalled at the sound of his roaring.		The Lord let loose against him the raiding bands of the Chaldeans… (24:2)
Nations from the countries roundabout arrayed themselves against him. They spread their net over him, he was caught in their snare.		Arameans, Moabites, and Ammonites; He let them loose against Judah to destroy it, in accordance with the word that the Lord had spoken through His servants the prophets. All this befell Judah at the command of the Lord, who banished [them] from His presence… and the Lord would not forgive (24:2–4).

Zedekiah and the End of the Monarchy

Ezekiel 19:2–9	II Chronicles 36:1–6	II Kings 23–24
With hooks he was put in a cage, they carried him off to the king of Babylon and confined him in a fortress, so that never again should his roar be heard on the hills of Israel.	King Nebuchadnezzar of Babylon marched against him; he bound him in fetters to convey him to Babylon. Nebuchadnezzar also brought some vessels of the House of the Lord to Babylon, and set them in his palace in Babylon.	

This comparison provides insight into Ezekiel's meaning. In addition to the identity of the second young lion, the description of what the young lions do – "He learned to hunt prey – he devoured men" – should also be interpreted as an image from the world of the parable, symbolizing displeasing behavior committed by both kings (despite the brief duration – just three months – of the reign of Jehoahaz). The "nations" mentioned by Ezekiel in verse 4 refer to the king of Egypt, who increases Jehoahaz's financial burdens as a preliminary stage before exiling him to Egypt.

The identity of the lioness (who is described in the introduction to the parable and again in verse 5) is not clear. This image may represent the earthly personalities and functionaries who coronate a king (and unwittingly serve as God's emissaries): first, the people of the land who coronate Jehoahaz, and later, the king of Egypt, who appoints Jehoiakim king.

The comparison with the parallel texts reveals that in the final passage of his parable, Ezekiel is referring to the actions of the king of Babylonia, who has meanwhile risen to greatness. But perhaps – as we have noted previously – circumstances do not allow the prophet to state this explicitly. This seems to explain why much of the concluding part of the parable is obscure, with the only explicit words made in reference to the cessation of the monarchy in Israel being "never again should his roar be heard on the hills of Israel."[17]

"Your Mother Was Like a Vine" (19:10–14)

The prophet now reinforces his message with another parable. This new parable does not appear to be directed at any specific king of Judah; rather, it marks the end of the monarchy of the kings of Judah collectively. First the prophet describes the potential embodied in the vine:

> Your mother was like a vine in your blood,[18] planted beside streams, with luxuriant boughs and branches thanks to abundant waters. And she had mighty rods fit for a ruler's scepter. It towered highest among the leafy trees, it was conspicuous by its height, by the abundance of its boughs. (19:10–11)

Thereafter, the prophet describes the vine being cast down to the ground, dried up, and burned. Eventually, it is cut off from its source of nourishment until it is utterly destroyed by fire. This parable is noticeably harsher than the previous one. The outcome in the first parable is the capture of the lions (that is, kings) live, with hooks; in the second parable, nothing remains of the vine at all: At first it dries up completely, and then, to compound matters, it is burned. Only the conclusion of the parable reveals that the expression "mighty rods fit for a ruler's scepter" (*shivtei moshlim*, which appears at the beginning, v. 11) is a reference to those leaders who are now prevented from carrying out their role: "She is left without a mighty rod, a scepter to rule with" (v. 14). Had the nation been led properly by its leadership, perhaps it could have prevented the results of the fire (v. 12).

Ezekiel concludes in the same spirit with which he began: "This is a dirge, and it has become a [familiar] dirge" (v. 14). This dirge, in

---

17. To complete the picture concerning the death of Jehoiakim and the prophetic messages surrounding his death in Egypt, see Jeremiah 22.
18. This word – *bedamkha* – seems to be deliberately ambiguous. On one hand it is related to "likeness" (*dama*) or "parable" (as Rashi understands it); on the other hand, it recalls "blood" (*dam*; as Rabbi Eliezer of Beaugency understands it), alluding to the reason for the burning of the vine (bloodshed).

Zedekiah and the End of the Monarchy

which the prophet mourns the events of the past, will be a dirge both in the present and in the future. The description of the fate awaiting Jehoahaz and Jehoiakim now turns out as the end of the monarchy of Judah.

A Parable with No Conclusion

This prophetic unit is entirely devoid of any mention of God's name and – unlike the other parables that Ezekiel uses to convey his messages – no interpretation is supplied at its conclusion. This omission is especially glaring given the many instances in which Ezekiel's prophecy is attributed to God ("Thus said the Lord…") throughout the book. Perhaps this is another device to emphasize the prophetic message that God is exiled; He is no longer present. On the revealed level, in the text before us, He is – quite literally – "gone." But it also seems that His presence is indeed hinted at in this chapter, in the form of the "east wind" that dries up the vine (v. 12) – the same force that dries up the vine in chapter 17: "Will it thrive? When the east wind strikes it, it shall wither" (17:10). This possibility is supported by the other appearances of the east wind in Tanakh, where it serves as the vehicle that executes God's judgment. Examples include the plague of locusts (Ex. 10:13), the splitting of the Reed Sea (Ex. 14:21), Jeremiah's prophecy to the people (Jer. 18:17), Jonah's fainting (Jonah 4:8), the wreckage of the Tarshish fleet (Ps. 48:8), and the destruction of Ephraim (Hos. 13:15).[19]

ZEDEKIAH'S FATE (21:23–32)

The fate of the last king of Judah, Zedekiah, is described within a series of prophecies in chapter 21 that depict the end of the Kingdom of Judah. All appear to have been uttered close to the imposition of the siege on Jerusalem on the tenth of Tevet. In verses 23–32, the prophet describes the military campaign of Nebuchadnezzar, king of Babylonia, which will ultimately lead to the conquest of Jerusalem. Zedekiah is described in this prophetic unit as follows: "And to you, O dishonored wicked *nasi* of Israel (*ḥalal rasha nesi yisrael*), whose day has come – the time set for your punishment." (Ezek. 21:30).

---

19. See also Rashi on Psalms 48:8: "'With an east wind': That is an expression of retribution, with which the Holy One, blessed be He, recompenses the wicked."

The expression "ḥalal rasha" has a dual meaning with regard to Zedekiah's fate. On one hand, the prophet calls him "wicked" (rasha – the opposite of the trait inherent in his name, tzaddik), whose sanctity has been profaned (ḥulal) and who has reached his end. On the other hand, he is depicted as a wicked person who has been put to death, or is deserving of death (ḥalal; see II Kings 21). Hence, the time has come for him to be divested of his royal insignia: "Thus said the Lord God: Remove the turban and lift off the crown! This shall not remain as it is; exalt the low and abase the high" (Ezek. 21:31).

The language with which the prophet concludes his message concerning the kings of Judah hints at their sins over the course of generations. Other than this verse, the turban (mitznefet) only appears as one of the priestly garments. The implicit message is that the kings of Judah have been arrogant. In their role as kings, they have not maintained their subjugation to God and His charge. They have not upheld God's sanctity. They have thus brought about the Destruction of Jerusalem and of the Temple: "Ruin, an utter ruin I will make it. It shall be no more until he comes to whom it rightfully belongs; and I will give it to him" (v. 32).[20]

---

20. The Destruction is described here in very obscure language that has no parallel elsewhere in Tanakh. Perhaps the meaning here is that what is about to happen has never happened before.

Chapter 9

"Prophets" and Their Prophecy

Ezekiel 12:21–14:11

Having completed our discussion of the kings of Judah, we return to our study of Ezekiel's prophecies proceeding in order, from 12:21. In this series of prophetic units, Ezekiel responds to prophecies conveyed by speakers who falsely attribute their messages to God. The great diversity of "prophetic" messages that Ezekiel addresses offers us an indication both of the scope of the challenge Ezekiel faces and of the power of the prophets who do not speak in God's name.[1] Based on their location in the book and their content, it is clear that this series of prophetic units preceded the Destruction; the units are arranged consecutively because of the content they share (as in the collection of prophecies to the nations in chapters 25–32).

---

1. This problem is addressed directly in Jeremiah's struggle with the false prophets in his own environment, in Jerusalem (for example, Jer. 28).

Ezekiel's determined struggle in these prophecies is apparent in the repeated emphasis that his message comes from God ("thus said the Lord…"/"…declares the Lord God" [2]) in marked contrast with those who have no authority to convey God's word. The proliferation of false prophets at so difficult a time for the nation is unsurprising. Seeking comfort and consolation at any price, hoping to counter the dark prophecies of Ezekiel in Babylon and Jeremiah in Jerusalem, the people are ready to accept these "prophets" and their message.

The prophets whose words run counter to those of Ezekiel are divided into different groups, whose order in the text may reflect their respective popularity. Ezekiel first addresses their prophetic content – which, it appears, was disseminated widely both in the land and among the exiles. Then he addresses the false male prophets, who appear to have been the largest group both in the Diaspora and in Judah. Thereafter he addresses the false female prophets and then those around him who seek God's word. Finally, he addresses true prophets who have been tempted by God not to spread His word; they are a rarity.

"THE DAYS GROW MANY AND EVERY VISION COMES TO NAUGHT" (12:21–28)

The first argument that was commonly used against Ezekiel's prophecy was that with time his words would lose their relevance. Here Ezekiel addresses himself not to the bearers of this argument, but rather to their audience, and he emphasizes – twice – that this claim is unsound. Perhaps the reason for the widespread popularity of this idea was that it required no effort to undermine Ezekiel's authority as a prophet and the veracity of his arguments. It was enough for these opponents to remind their listeners that warnings as to the Destruction had also been voiced in the past, and the passage of time showed that that which was would ever be so: Jerusalem would not be destroyed, and perhaps – as Rabbi Isaiah di Trani comments – "all the prophets would be gone before their prophecies would be realized."

This prophetic message is conveyed twice:

---

2. This occurs in 12:23, 25 (twice), 28 (twice); 13:2, 3, 8 (twice), 9, 13, 14, 16, 18, 20, 21, 23; 14:4, 6, 8, 11.

"Prophets" and Their Prophecy

	First Prophecy: 12:21–25	*Second Prophecy:* 12:26–28
The people's statement	O mortal, what is this proverb that you have in the Land of Israel, saying, "The days grow many and every vision comes to naught"?	The word of the Lord came to me: See, O mortal, the House of Israel says, "The vision that he sees is far ahead, and he prophesies for the distant future."
God's response via the prophet	Assuredly, say to them, Thus said the Lord God: I will put an end to this proverb; it shall not be used in Israel any more. Speak rather to them: The days draw near, and the fulfillment of every vision. For there shall no longer be any false vision or soothing divination in the House of Israel. But whenever I the Lord speak what I speak, that word shall be fulfilled without any delay; in your days, O rebellious breed, I will fulfill every word I speak – declares the Lord God.	Assuredly, say to them: Thus said the Lord God: There shall be no more delay; whenever I speak a word, that word shall be fulfilled – declares the Lord God.

The first prophecy is placed in the mouth of those still living in the land; they argue that the prophet's words will no longer be relevant with the passage of time. God's response is that before long their own claim will lose its relevance. The prophecies of the Destruction of Jerusalem will be realized soon, in their own days. In the face of the people's claim, "The days grow many and every vision comes to naught," the prophet responds, "The days draw near, and the fulfillment of every vision."

Ezekiel 12:21–14:11

The second prophecy quotes a more specific argument raised by "the House of Israel" against Ezekiel. Their argument is a more moderate one: Not that nothing will come of his prophecies, but rather that they concern matters that are "far ahead," that he prophesies "for the distant future." It is perhaps for this reason that God's response in this second prophecy is also shorter. The Destruction is imminent: "Whenever I speak a word, that word shall be fulfilled." In this unit there is no mention of punishment for those who raise the claims against the prophet, because the focus here is on the content of the rebellious message rather than on its bearers. The bearers will be addressed by the prophet in the next unit.

"THOSE WHO PROPHESY OUT OF THEIR OWN IMAGINATION" (13:1–16)

The second group that Ezekiel targets consists of those who claim that their message is prophecy, while in fact they "prophesy out of their own imagination" (13:2), those "who follow their own fancy, without having had a vision" (v. 3); "They prophesied falsehood and lying divination" (v. 7). Here, too, the prophetic message is given twice. The first time, Ezekiel addresses himself to the false prophets around him in exile; the second time, he speaks to the false prophets who are in Judah.[3]

Note that Ezekiel calls them "prophets" ("the prophets of Israel who prophesy" [v. 2]; "your prophets, O Israel" [v. 4]). Perhaps they were in fact real prophets who had strayed from the proper path. As individuals with the capability and potential of receiving prophecy from God, they were able to mislead the people. This shows even more clearly how complicated Ezekiel's prophetic mission was. The difficulty in differentiating between true prophets and false ones arose, inter alia, from the fact that these were not two completely distinct and separate groups; they were not easily distinguishable from each another.

---

3. I have interpreted the repetition in these prophecies as indicating an orientation to two different audiences, following the example of Kasher, *Yeḥezkel 1–24*, 295.

"Prophets" and Their Prophecy

THE FALSE PROPHETS IN EXILE: "THEY SHALL NOT COME BACK TO THE LAND OF ISRAEL" (13:3–9)

In this prophecy Ezekiel compares the false prophets to jackals: "Your prophets, O Israel, have been like jackals among ruins. You did not enter the breaches and repair the walls for the House of Israel, that they might stand up in battle in the day of the Lord." (4–5).

Shu'alim – translated here as jackals but often rendered as foxes – are only rarely mentioned in Tanakh (Judges 15:4; Song. 2:15). This very unusual comparison between a jackal or a fox, predators that live in the desert, and the false prophets, intensifies the prophetic message.

The lamentation that follows the Destruction includes the words, "Because of Mount Zion, which lies desolate; jackals prowl over it" (Lam. 5:18). There is a link between this description and Ezekiel's words before the Destruction about the false prophets. Through their misleading words, the prophets have made themselves like the jackals that would soon wander among the ruins of the Temple. Ezekiel thereby connects the false prophecies with their consequences.[4] The imagery of the false prophet as a *shu'al* adds a significant dimension to the sight of the jackal amongst the ruins that was seared into the Jewish historical memory as the symbol of destruction and of the hoped-for redemption, in the wake of the teaching of Rabbi Akiva.[5]

Judging from Ezekiel's rebuke, it seems that these prophets could have acted otherwise and helped in the struggle against the lies being disseminated to the people: "You did not enter the breaches and repair the walls for the House of Israel, that they might stand up in battle in the day of the Lord" (13:5). This condemnation supports the explanation that

---

4. There are only two more places in Tanakh that mention the *shu'al*: Psalms 63:11, in which being a desert animal reinforces the meaning of the psalm, and Neh. 3:35, where an analogy similar to the one in Ezekiel is made.
5. "Once again they were coming up to Jerusalem together, and just as they came to Mount Scopus they tore their garments. When they reached the Temple Mount, they saw a jackal emerging from the place of the Holy of Holies. They fell weeping and R. Akiva laughed." (Makkot 24b). R. Akiva explains that just as the jackal now prowling on the Temple Mount represents the fulfillment of the prophecy that Jerusalem would be destroyed, so the prophecies of its rebuilding would now surely be fulfilled, too. His companions respond, "Akiva, you have comforted us."

these prophets actually had the potential to convey true prophecy from God to the people. The severity of their lapse lay in that they prophesied falsely while in the land – and even continued to mislead the people after the exile of Jehoiachin. This is clear from the description of their punishment, which includes languishing in exile:

> My hand will be against the prophets who prophesy falsehood and utter lying divination. They shall not remain in the assembly of My people, they shall not be inscribed in the lists of the House of Israel, and they shall not come back to the Land of Israel. Thus shall you know that I am the Lord God. (v. 9)

FALSE PROPHETS IN JUDAH AND THEIR ANNIHILATION (13:10–16)

In addressing the false prophets in Judah ("Inasmuch as they have misled My people"; 13:10), Ezekiel emphasizes the ramifications of their actions, and his accusation seems to be directed towards the false prophets in exile, too. Here Ezekiel uses a parable of a wall to depict them leading the people astray. These prophets build a wall, as it were, and beautify it on the outside. But, in fact, the wall is built without foundations, and will therefore crumble in a storm.[6] Then those who seek the wall will not find it. Furthermore, its builders will be buried under the ruins. This image depicts those who create false expectations among the people, and Ezekiel goes on to describe the punishment that awaits them: "I will throw down the wall that you daubed with plaster, and I will raze it to the ground so that its foundation is exposed; and when it falls, you shall perish in its midst; then you shall know that I am the Lord" (v. 14).

"THE WOMEN...WHO PROPHESY OUT OF THEIR OWN IMAGINATION (13:17–23)

The third group that Ezekiel addresses in this series of prophecies consists of "the women of your people, who prophesy out of their own

---

6. The wording of these verses is complicated. The commentators understand the literal text in a range of different ways, but the underlying prophetic message remains the same.

"Prophets" and Their Prophecy

imagination" (v. 17). From this prophecy we learn how the women operated and their motivation:

> Woe to those who sew pads on all arm joints and make bonnets for the head of every person, in order to entrap! Can you hunt down lives among My people, while you preserve your own lives? You have profaned My name among My people in return for handfuls of barley and morsels of bread; you have announced the death of persons who will not die and the survival of persons who will not live – lying to My people, who listen to your lies. (vv. 18–19)

The false prophetesses beautify themselves in order to "hunt down lives." They "sell" people their future – life or death – in exchange for "handfuls of barley and morsels of bread." This was a pursuit of monetary gain: the women sold false prophecies and received food in return (through barter, as was common). But the historical reality of the period, particularly the hunger that represented an existential challenge to all inhabitants of Jerusalem (as we saw in the prophecies in chapters 4–5) may indicate that the women's deceptive activity, although unquestionably a grave misdeed, was a desperate attempt to obtain food in the famine-ravaged city, rather than an attempt to make money through deceptive means. Indeed, what they demand in exchange for their "prophecies" is nothing more than "handfuls of barley and morsels of bread," which will keep them alive.

Regardless, God will not allow them to continue to deceive the people. Their garments will be torn and the people caught up in their words will be freed:

> I will tear them from your arms and free the persons whose lives you hunt down like birds. I will tear off your bonnets and rescue My people from your hands, and they shall no longer be prey in your hands; then you shall know that I am the Lord. (vv. 20–21)

Unlike the male prophets addressed above, who God punishes with annihilation, either in exile or as part of the Destruction, Ezekiel emphasizes only that the women must recognize God, and that they will be prevented from continuing their false prophecies, in order that the people will not be "hunted." There is no mention of any punishment for the women prophets, indicating that the women prophets acted out of despair and desperation.

THE SEEKERS OF PROPHECY (14:1–8)

Thus far Ezekiel has spoken to those who seek out his prophecy – apparently in Babylonia. At this point the series of units dealing with different types of false prophecies is interrupted. But the response that God conveys via Ezekiel to those who come to listen to him indicates that even those who recognized Ezekiel as a true prophet and came to hear the word of God from him would not merit hearing any true prophecy, because of their betrayal of God.[7] This leads us to the conclusion that there are two preconditions to hearing a prophecy from God: first, of course, avoiding false prophets and resisting their temptations; second, as we learn from this chapter, the seekers of prophecy can only approach the prophet if they themselves are innocent. They will receive no message from God if they serve idols at the same time. Ezekiel describes: "Certain elders of Israel came to me and sat down before me" (Ezek. 14:1). The identity of these "elders of Israel" is not made clear,[8] but unlike the description of the divine vision that Ezekiel experiences when the "elders of Judah" are before him in chapter 8, here the elders' request is denied (as in the appeal of the elders in chapter 20:1–4) because of their sins: "And the word of the Lord came to me: O mortal, these men have turned their thoughts upon their fetishes and set their minds upon the sin through which they stumbled: Shall I respond to their inquiry?" (14:2–3). In other words, why should people

---

7. The language of the verses in this chapter resembles the language in Leviticus 17 and 20. Here, as in chapters 6 and 8 above, the similarity of language is meant to indicate the severity of the actions of the people. (In our earlier discussion, we noted that this technique serves to reinforce the prophetic message.)
8. Yehiel Moskowitz describes them thus: "But their approach is hesitant; their voice is inaudible, their request is unclear and in their heart of hearts they also serve idols, as though seeking to assure themselves assistance from every possible source." (Moskowitz, *Sefer Yeḥezkel*, 80).

who worship idols merit hearing the word of God? Nevertheless, they are not simply ignored and rejected; they are rebuked for their actions:

> Now speak to them and tell them: Thus said the Lord God: If anyone of the House of Israel turns his thoughts upon his fetishes and sets his mind upon the sin through which he stumbled, and yet comes to the prophet, I the Lord will respond to him as he comes with his multitude of fetishes. Thus I will hold the House of Israel to account for their thoughts, because they have all been estranged from Me through their fetishes. (vv. 4–5)

Notably, and uniquely in this book, Ezekiel calls upon them to repent – perhaps because these people have, after all, come to hear God's word from the prophet: "Now say to the House of Israel: Thus said the Lord God: Repent, and turn back from your fetishes and turn your minds away from all your abominations" (v. 6).

The punishment for those who come to seek God's word while still serving idols will be harsh: "I will set My face against that man and make him a sign and a byword, and I will cut him off from the midst of My people. Then you shall know that I am the Lord" (v. 8). Like the false prophets, they will be cut off from the people. This is another indication of the severity of the elders' dual loyalty.

"IF A PROPHET IS SEDUCED" (14:9–11)

Finally, we are told of a rather surprising group: prophets who have been tempted by God to mislead the people with their words. In contrast to the false prophets who "prophesied out of their own imagination," this last group has been guided by God Himself: "And if a prophet is seduced and does speak a word [to such a man], it was I the Lord who seduced that prophet" (v. 9).

The existence of this group raises the obvious question: How can Ezekiel blame prophets whom God has caused to speak falsely? And how are the people supposed to know that they are not speaking the truth? The commentators offer different solutions to this question. Rashi explains: "I opened a doorway for him to [do] whatever he wishes. And from here we can learn that if one wishes to defile himself, [a door] is opened for him." Thus, God's tempting of the prophet is, in fact, part of his punishment. A similar interpretation is offered by Rabbi Eliezer of Beaugency:

> "It was I the Lord who seduced…" – in other words, having already made known to him the nature of the wickedness he has come to seek, I test him without offering any further warning or caution. I allow him to be tempted by it, and then I will punish him.

In contrast, Rabbi Joseph Kara explains that it is not God who tempts the prophet to speak falsely:

> He says something that he did not hear from Me, and the people listen to him. "It was I the Lord who seduced that prophet" – for he came to seduce My people, so he finds himself being seduced. How do I seduce him? As the verse says later on: "I will stretch out My hand against him, and will destroy him from the midst of My people Israel."[9]

These prophets, too, will be punished with annihilation: "I will stretch out My hand against him and will destroy him from the midst of My people Israel" (Ezek. 14:9).

Verses 10–11 are a continuation of the unit concerning the prophet who is seduced, but also serve as a conclusion of the series of units dealing with prophets and prophecies: "Thus they shall bear their punishment: The punishment of the inquirer and the punishment of the prophet shall be the same, so that the House of Israel may never again stray from Me and defile itself with all its transgressions." The people, we find, will be punished along with their prophets, if they come and seek God's words while sinning at the same time.

---

9. See also the interpretations of Radak, Rabbi Menachem ben Shimon, Rabbi Isaiah di Trani, and especially Rabbi Joseph ibn Caspi, who concludes his comment here with the words, "And all these matters are tremendous secrets which would not be proper to explain in this book."

"Prophets" and Their Prophecy

Nevertheless, this series of prophetic units concludes with the covenantal formula: "Then they shall be My people and I will be their God – declares the Lord God" (v. 11).

This is the second time since the beginning of the book (the first instance was in Ezekiel 11:20) that the prophet concludes by emphasizing the bond between God and His people. In both instances, following a harsh prophecy, this formula brings some measure of consolation. The difficult words of retribution and even annihilation are thus moderated by God's affirmation that He maintains His bond with the nation.

Chapter 10

Individual Righteousness and Salvation

Ezekiel 14:12–23

After considering the various categories of false prophets and prophecies, Ezekiel returns to the question: Who might nevertheless be saved? This prophecy is uttered four times, each time similarly, but with slight stylistic variations. This technique echoes the prophet's earlier rhetorical devices and his repeated efforts to persuade his audience of the veracity of his message. The prophet begins by describing the famine that will befall the city; then he depicts the wild animals that will pass through the land, followed by the sword, and finally, the pestilence. Describing these imminent miseries raises the question of whether any righteous people will survive the onslaught. And if so, might their families also be saved in their merit, as in similar situations described in the Torah? The prophetic response to this question is that if indeed there are any righteous individuals to be found in the city, they alone will be saved.

Perhaps this prophecy indicates that Ezekiel's audience is concerned with the question of the fate of the righteous. This may show they have

Ezekiel 14:12–23

internalized the fact that the Destruction is on its way, and the speculation now is about its scope.

To understand the content of this prophecy, let us examine it in a format that reveals its structure:

(v. 13) O mortal, if a land were to sin against Me and commit a trespass, and I stretched out My hand against it and broke its staff of bread, and sent **famine** against it and *cut off* man and beast from it,	(v. 15) Or, if I were to send **wild beasts** to roam the land and they depopulated it, and it became a desolation with none passing through it because of the beasts,	(v. 17) Or, if I were to bring the **sword** upon that land and say, "Let a sword sweep through the land so that I may *cut off* from it man and beast,"	(v. 19) Or, if I let loose a **pestilence** against that land, and poured out My fury upon it in blood, *cutting off* from it man and beast,
(v. 14) even if these three men – Noah, Daniel, and Job – should be in it, **they would by their righteousness save only themselves** – declares the Lord God.	(v. 16) as I live – declares the Lord God – those three men in it would save neither sons nor daughters; **they alone would be saved**, but the land would become a desolation.	(v. 18) if those three men should be in it, as I live – declares the Lord God – they would save neither sons nor daughters, but **they alone would be saved**.	(v. 20) should Noah, Daniel, and Job be in it, as I live – declares the Lord God – they would save neither son nor daughter; **they would save themselves alone by their righteousness**.

Individual Righteousness and Salvation

Each section of the prophecy, as we can see, begins by naming an affliction that will befall the people, in most cases using the phrase "cut off" or "cutting off," and ends by noting that the righteous alone will be saved.

THE FAMINE THAT AWAITS THE INHABITANTS OF JERUSALEM (14:13–14)

Prophecies about the famine in Jerusalem are found in chapters 4, 5, 6, 12, and 14; they constitute part of the punishments facing the city. Of all the imminent afflictions, the inhabitants will initially feel the effects of the famine, the first tangible punishment, growing increasingly severe as the siege continues. Perhaps this is why the famine is emphasized in the early chapters that rebuke the city (4–14) rather than in the later ones (15–24). For instance, in chapter 4, the symbolic act that Ezekiel performs is meant to dramatize the approaching famine:

> O mortal, I am going to break the staff of bread in Jerusalem, and they shall eat bread by weight, in anxiety, and drink water by measure, in horror, so that, lacking bread and water, they shall stare at each other, heartsick over their iniquity. (4:16–17)

Then, in chapter 5, the famine is mentioned again:

> When I loose the deadly arrows of famine against those doomed to destruction, when I loose them against you to destroy you, I will heap more famine upon you and break your staff of bread. I will let loose against you famine and wild beasts and they shall bereave you; pestilence and bloodshed shall sweep through you, and I will bring the sword upon you. (5:16–17)

Ezekiel speaks of the famine (among the other punishments) once again in chapter 6:

> ...who shall fall by the sword, by famine, and by pestilence. He who is far away shall die of pestilence, and he who is near shall fall by the sword, and he who survives and is protected shall die of famine. Thus I will spend My fury upon them. (6:11–12)

Ezekiel 14:12–23

And again in chapter 12:

> But I will spare a few of them from the sword, from famine, and from pestilence, that they may recount all their abominable deeds among the nations to which they come; and they shall know that I am the Lord! (12:16)

Finally, we encounter the famine in Ezekiel's symbolic act:

> O mortal, eat your bread in trembling and drink your water in fear and anxiety. And say to the people of the land: Thus said the Lord God concerning the inhabitants of Jerusalem in the Land of Israel: They shall eat their bread in anxiety and drink their water in desolation, because their land will be desolate of its multitudes on account of the lawlessness of all its inhabitants. (12:18–19)

Moreover, as noted earlier, the price demanded by the false women prophets – "handfuls of barley and morsels of bread" (see 13:19) may also be an expression of the famine in the city.

Apart from these similarities, the prophecies describing the famine that the inhabitants of the city will suffer also diverge. First, in chapter 4, through his symbolic act and its interpretation, Ezekiel announces that, among the other punishments that will befall them, the inhabitants of the city will hunger and thirst to death. In chapter 6, he emphasizes that this punishment will be shared by all. After the distant and the nearby die, the remnant, still besieged in the city, will also die of hunger. In the description of the famine in chapter 12, Ezekiel first mentions the possibility of survivors. He emphasizes that they will remain alive in order to recount the abominations perpetrated in the city. Finally, in chapter 14, the prophet addresses the identity of the survivors and makes it clear that if indeed there are righteous people, they will save only themselves.

The description of the punishment awaiting the city (and especially the "evil beasts," 14:15) in these prophecies fits the description of the punishment set forth in the book of Leviticus:

Individual Righteousness and Salvation

I will loose wild beasts against you, and they shall bereave you of your children and wipe out your cattle. They shall decimate you, and your roads shall be deserted.... I in turn will smite you sevenfold for your sins. I will bring a sword against you to wreak vengeance for the covenant; and if you withdraw into your cities, I will send pestilence among you, and you shall be delivered into enemy hands. When I break your staff of bread, ten women shall bake your bread in a single oven; they shall dole out your bread by weight, and though you eat, you shall not be satisfied. (Lev. 26:22–26)

THE IDENTITY OF THE RIGHTEOUS (14:12–20)

Nowhere in the book is there any mention of the possibility that the people might be saved by the merit of their ancestors. But throughout our chapter, the prophet states that the city will not be saved by virtue of the righteous dwelling in it. Twice (and only twice) he even names the three individuals who represent the righteous who might be saved through their own merit: Noah, Daniel, and Job. Jeremiah, like Ezekiel, rejects the possibility that the inhabitants of Jerusalem could be saved by virtue of the righteous present there: "The Lord said to me, 'Even if Moses and Samuel were to intercede with Me, I would not be won over to that people. Dismiss them from My presence, and let them go forth!'" (Jer. 15:1).

This comparison with Jeremiah adds to our surprise at the particular figures named by Ezekiel: Noah, Daniel, and Job. It is difficult to know what particular aspect or manifestation of righteousness is represented by each individual. Perhaps what they share is their universality. Noah lived at the time of the Flood, before the patriarchs of the Jewish nation. Daniel appears to have been known internationally for his wisdom, as we find in Ezekiel's prophecy to Tyre: "Yes, you are wiser than Daniel; In no hidden matter can anyone compare to you" (Ezek. 28:3).[1]

---

1. The biblical book of Daniel appears to be of later origin than the book of Ezekiel. The name Daniel as mentioned by Ezekiel is consistent with the Daniel who is famed among the nations as a sage. The name Daniel (or Danel) was a universal name; this is documented as early as the Ugaritic *Epic of Aqhat*, where Danel is a wise man and righteous judge. See Umberto Cassuto, "Daniel," in *Encyclopedia Mikrait* (Jerusalem: Bialik, 1954), 2:683–85.

Ezekiel 14:12–23

While the commentaries are divided about the identity of the biblical Job, he too represents a universal symbol of a righteous person who suffers.[2]

Ezekiel emphasizes that even the sons and daughters of such exceptional individuals will not be saved; certainly other inhabitants of the city will not be saved. The comparison to Noah makes the anticipated Destruction seem even more devastating than the Flood. Noah saved his entire family; now, even that possibility does not exist. Similarly, Daniel remained alone after he and his friends earned the king's recognition, and Job, too, remained alone. The fulfillment of this prophecy is illustrated very tangibly in Ezekiel 9:6, where the man clothed in linen is commanded to slay even the little children.

Ultimately, there are some survivors of the Destruction of Jerusalem. However, they are left alive not by virtue of the righteous individuals, but because of God's desire that the terrible actions and the resulting punishment of the city's inhabitants be made known. The prophet thus deflects his opponents' claim that the punishment that he foretells for Jerusalem does not match its deeds. He emphasizes that the punishment is indeed proportional: "not without cause did I do all that I did in it" (14:23); "it was not without cause that I the Lord resolved to bring this evil upon them" (6:10). The importance of this prophetic message is reinforced by the fact that another prophecy, in chapter 21, reiterates that God's sword will leave no survivors in the city – neither righteous nor wicked – and this will make God recognized:

> I will draw My sword from its sheath, and I will wipe out from you both the righteous and the wicked. In order to wipe out from you both the righteous and the wicked, My sword shall assuredly be unsheathed against all flesh from south to north; and all flesh

---

2. Commenting on 14:14, Radak cites the midrash: "These three righteous individuals are mentioned because each of them saw three worlds: [a world that was] built, [a world that was] destroyed, and [a world that was re-] built." In Noah's case this refers to the physical world; in Daniel's case, the "world" is the Temple; and for Job, the "world" was his family. Thus, although Ezekiel's prophecy foretells that the inhabitants of Jerusalem will not be saved by virtue of the righteous, the mention of these three men nevertheless carries a covert message of consolation that Jerusalem will eventually be rebuilt.

shall know that I the Lord have drawn My sword from its sheath, not to be sheathed again. (21:8–10)

THREE AND FOUR (14:21–23)

Following the verses that foretell that there will be no survivors from the city, the prophet goes on to enumerate, for the first time, not only the number of righteous individuals, but also the number of punishments that they will suffer: "Assuredly, thus said the Lord God: How much less [should any escape] now that I have let loose against Jerusalem **all four[3] of My terrible punishments – the sword, famine, wild beasts, and pestilence – to cut off man and beast from it!**" (Ezek. 14:21).

Note that the number of hypothetical righteous individuals (three) is smaller than the number of punishments that will befall the city (four) – another indication that ultimately the four punishments will prevail over the three righteous people.[4] The prophet now adds that not only will all the human inhabitants of the city be annihilated, but the animals too, just as was foretold in Leviticus.

The prophecy then ends on a surprising note: despite everything we have heard until this point, there will be survivors after all: "Yet there are survivors left of it, sons and daughters who are being brought out. They are coming out to you" (v. 22).

The purpose of leaving this remnant is for the exiles to know what happened to the city:

> And when you see their ways and their deeds, **you will be consoled** for the disaster that I brought on Jerusalem, for all that I brought on it. **You will be consoled through them**, when you see their ways and their deeds and realize that not without cause did I do all that I did in it – declares the Lord God. (vv. 22–23)

---

3. In Jeremiah 15:2–3 (continuing from v. 1, which mentions the potential righteous individuals in whose merit the city might be saved) we likewise find a "four-fold" punishment. Verse 2 speaks of death, the sword, famine, and captivity, and verse 3 reads, "I will appoint over them four kinds [of punishment]."
4. For a discussion of three and four as a numerical model for a situation of ranking or hierarchy, rather than merely as defined numbers, see Meir Weiss, "Al Shlosha... Ve'al Arba'a," *Tarbiz* 36 (1966): 307–18.

Ezekiel 14:12–23

These verses inform us – much like 12:16 – that despite everything there will be a remnant: sons and daughters of Jerusalem who will survive, their purpose being to testify that the Destruction was deserved. Throughout the book of Ezekiel there is a noticeable lack of expressions of consolation. So it is startling that it is specifically here that the prophet states *twice* that the survivors of the Destruction will bring consolation: "you will be consoled." It may be that the very survival of this remnant is itself a consolation (as Rabbi Eliezer of Beaugency explains). But the language of the text seems to suggest that the surviving sons and daughters, along with their consolation, are the exception; their survival and the consolation are unusual, and remind us of the norm: a picture of utter desolation, with no community that lives on, and none of the longed-for consolation.[5]

APPENDIX: "IF A LAND WERE TO SIN" (14:13) – REALITY OR RHETORICAL DEVICE?

In many of his prophecies, Ezekiel begins by addressing the land – or specific places in the land – rather than the people. He speaks to "the mountains of Israel" (Ezek. 6:1–2; 36:1, 4), the "Land of Israel" (7:2, 21:8), "the brushland of the Negeb" (21:2–3), "Jerusalem" (16:2), "city of blood" (24:6, 9), "the city of bloodshed" (22:2), and "Mount Seir" (35:2). Introducing a prophecy in this manner is uncommon in Tanakh and therefore commands our attention. In some of these prophecies the "land" is addressed not only as an opening statement, but as the target audience throughout the prophetic unit (for instance, the prophecy to the "mountains of Israel" in 6:1–11). What is the significance of the prophet's appeal to the land? While such a call is found in five different chapters of the book, chapter 14 is the central instance, as we will see.

The appeals to the land, in order, are as follows:

1. In chapter 7, Ezekiel speaks of the destruction of the land: "Doom is coming upon the four corners of the land" (7:2). This prophecy

---

5. Radak explains: "Your seeing them in their wickedness will be a consolation for you, for [it will be clear that] I acted justly in bringing all that I brought upon it." However, it is difficult to conceive of the punishment itself – even if it was clearly just and well-deserved – bringing consolation to the exiles.

Individual Righteousness and Salvation

begins with an appeal to the land (ground) of Israel with no explicit mention of its inhabitants.

2. In chapter 14, it is the land itself that sins: "If a land were to sin against Me and commit a trespass (*lime'al maal*)" (14:13).[6] The land's sin here contains no description of human actions; rather, it depicts the trespass of the land itself against God. God's response to the land's actions is formulated with the words, "If a land were to sin … and I stretched out My hand against it and broke its staff of bread, and sent famine against it and cut off man and beast from it" (v. 13). This is an earthly, natural punishment; not a political one relating to human deeds. In its proper state, the land causes food to grow and crops to flourish. Now, owing to its sin, it can no longer offer a staff of bread. As a result, its inhabitants, both human and animal, go hungry; they will no longer be able to live in it. Verses 15–20, too, seem to describe the land's desolation as a punishment to the land rather than to the inhabitants, who are exiled and are gone.

3. In Ezekiel 22:24 we find: "O mortal, say to her: You are an uncleansed land, not to be washed with rain on the day of indignation." The land is "uncleansed" (or "not pure") and the prophet goes on to enumerate the reasons for this, all of which relate to the actions of the office-bearers:

> Her gang of prophets are like roaring lions in her midst, rending prey.… Her priests have violated My teaching.… Her officials are like wolves rending prey in her midst.… Her prophets, too, daub the wall for them with plaster.… And the people of the land have practiced fraud and committed robbery. (22:25–29)

4. In Chapter 36, the prophet addresses himself to the Land (or ground) of Israel: "And say to the mountains and the hills, to the watercourses and to the valleys, Thus said the Lord God: Behold, I declare in My

---

6. This expression is quite common in the book of Ezekiel – it is found in 14:13; 15:8; 17:20; 18:24; 20:27; 39:23, 26.

blazing wrath: Because you have suffered the taunting of the nations" (36:6). Later on, Ezekiel speaks to the mountains of Israel and the ground of Israel in a prophecy of consolation, in which the land flourishes: "But you, O mountains of Israel, shall yield your produce and bear your fruit for My people Israel." (36:8). These verses describe the restoration of the people hand in hand with the flowering of the land. In doing so, the book emphasizes the scope of the restoration, against the backdrop of the present state of the land. Note that even here, God's motivation for causing the land to flourish is the "taunting of the nations" that has been inflicted on it, rather than Israel's actions.[7]

The more common references to the land describe the Destruction, impurity, and exile as the result of the actions of the land's inhabitants. The prophetic units examined here are different: Ezekiel conveys his prophetic message by presenting the land as an independent entity. While this change appears to be merely semantic, used for the sake of rhetoric diversity, the contrast with the biblical perspective that appeals to man and his actions is another way in which the prophet draws the attention of his target audience.[8] Out of a desire to make a real impression and affect his listerners' very core, Ezekiel presents his messages in a way that draws them in, using different devices: the use of harsh and blatant language (for instance, the term "*gilulim*"); the awarding of "independence status," as it were, to the land; and the use of animation (anthropomorphism). Thus, the prophet emphasizes that the land is given to Israel by God, but the connection between the nation and the land is conditional upon the people's actions and God's will.

---

7. To these verses we might also add Ezekiel 25:3, 6, which expresses an animation of the land: "Say to the Ammonites.... Because you cried 'Aha!' over My Sanctuary when it was desecrated, **and over the Land of Israel when it was laid waste**, and over the House of Judah when it went into exile...."
8. In many places throughout Tanakh we see that human actions influence the land to the extent that God's words, or the prophet's words, are addressed to the land rather than its human inhabitants. Thus, for instance, the sin of Adam brings in its wake a punishment to all of mankind whose object is actually the land: "Cursed be the ground because of you.... Thorns and thistles shall it sprout for you" (Gen. 3:17–18). In the description of the punishment meted out to Cain, we read, "If you till the soil, it shall no longer yield its strength to you" (Gen. 4:12), and so on.

Chapter 11

Parables: The Vine and the Adulterous Wife

Ezekiel 15:1–16:63

T he prophecies in chapters 15–24 present a series of parables through which the prophet describes the fate of Jerusalem, its inhabitants, and its leaders.[1] The reader who has followed the chapters of the book of Ezekiel from the start now discovers a new device through which the prophet conveys his message, in addition to the symbolic acts (especially in chapters 4–5[2]) and the image of the building of a house (13:10–16) which preceded our chapter.

Allegories and metaphors are used more often in Ezekiel than in the other Prophets to convey prophetic messages. This again attests to the

---
1. The term *mashal*, often translated as "parable" or "proverb," is taken from the prophecy (16:44; 21:5) and is also used by Ḥazal. However, we refer here also to "allegory," "metaphor," and "personification," which are more commonly used terms in modern scholarship. The parables of chapter 17 have been discussed above in chapter 8.
2. The death of Ezekiel's wife, and is its placement in chapter 24, are also significant, as is the echo of a further symbolic act in 7:23.

Ezekiel 15:1–16:63

literary diversity and rhetorical precision of Ezekiel's messages. In chapters 15, 17, and 19, the parable of the vine appears; chapter 19 contains the parable of the lioness; and in chapters 16 and 23 we read the parable of the harlot. Each prophecy between chapters 15 and 24 is introduced with a parable. Thus, chapter 18 begins with a parable proposed by the children of Israel concerning divine reward and punishment;[3] chapter 21 starts with the parable of the fire; chapter 22 presents the parable of the furnace, and chapter 24 has the parable of the cauldron, concluding this series of prophetic units. It seems that indeed Ezekiel's style succeeded in gaining the people's attention. From the words that the prophet addresses to God we see that the nation's response to this device was not long in coming: "And I said, 'Ah, Lord God! They say of me: He is just a riddlemonger'" (21:5).

A review of Ezekiel's allegories shows that in many cases we cannot match the allegory to any historical reality with precision. Sometimes an entire prophecy appears to end with the conclusion of the parable. Hence, the interpretations of the parables in Ezekiel's prophecies must be sought within the parables themselves. Greenberg describes this phenomenon eloquently.[4] He explains that over the course of the narrative, various major or minor "interventions" of the reality to which the parable refers appear. These may include a series of verses (as in 16:17–22), or nothing more than a single word that deviates from the continuous description of the parable, which alludes to the interpretation.[5] The parable and its interpretation are interwoven to the point where sometimes it is difficult (or even impossible) to define which of the prophet's words are which. For instance, some of the descriptions of the harlot's actions in chapter 16 can be interpreted as the actions of the woman (which are an allegory for

---

3. In this instance, the word *mashal* actually means a fable, by means of which the nation or the prophet makes a statement. The same is the case in 12:22–23. Notes Kasher: "This term is used in the Bible to denote different literary genres, such as idioms, lyrical speeches, allegories, etc. The term itself seems to be derived from the root *M-SH-L*, which means similarity, comparing something with something else. The term is repeated several times in the book of Ezekiel, being used in the sense of an allegorical story (17:2; 24:3) or in the sense of a brief fable (12:22; 18:2–3)" (Kasher, *Yeḥezkel 1–24*, 289).
4. See Greenberg, *Ezekiel 1–20*.
5. One example is 23:29, in which the word *"yegi'ekh"* ("all you have toiled for") describes the reward of the man, rather than the accessories of the woman.

Parables: The Vine and the Adulterous Wife

the idolatry committed by the people). But they can also be interpreted as descriptions of the idolatry committed by the people. Or, perhaps, these actions were a ritual harlotry which would suit both the message of the parable and its interpretation. For this reason, our discussions of parables will, for the most part, not distinguish between each parable and its meaning; rather, we will address the general meaning of the prophecy.

"FIRE SHALL CONSUME THEM" (CHAPTER 15)

Chapter 15, unlike the chapters that follow it, makes a clear distinction between the parable (vv. 1–5) and its meaning (vv. 6–8). The parable describes a vine that is burned and therefore no longer serves any purpose: It cannot be used for work nor to make any vessel. In his explanation, the prophet reveals that the vine is a symbol for the inhabitants of Jerusalem, who will be devoured by fire.[6] The main message, perhaps, is that Ezekiel does not propose – even in the parable – any possibility of the vine producing grapes; the city is fated to be as useless as the burned vine: "I will make the land a desolation, because they committed trespass – declares the Lord God" (v. 8).

This third-person reference to the inhabitants of Jerusalem ("they committed trespass") indicates that Ezekiel is addressing the exiles in Babylonia. He aims to inform them not only that the city's end is very near, but that the entire land will be desolate. The land's desolation appears and reappears over the course of the book. Through it, the prophet tells the exiles that for the first time in its history, the lineage of the Jewish people lies not with the remnant in Jerusalem, but with the exiles themselves.

"NOW, O HARLOT, HEAR THE WORD OF THE LORD!" (CHAPTER 16)[7]

Having used all the means at his disposal to convey God's word about the nation's fate, Ezekiel compares Jerusalem to an abandoned woman, and in the interpretation, to the inhabitants of the city or the Jewish people as a

---

6. A. E. Rivlin discusses the literary structure of this chapter in "Mashal HaGefen VeHaEsh: Mivneh, Miktzav, VeDiktzia BeShirat Yeḥezkel," *Beit Mikra* 20, no. 4 (1975): 562–66.
7. In this section, our aim is to examine the way in which Ezekiel prophesies and not to provide a close, literal interpretation of the verses.

whole. This stark image constitutes a cry through which the prophet conveys his message to the people. Our assumption in explaining this metaphor is that the literary device and its meaning are deliberately indistinct – that is, there is a blurring between the harlot, with her real punishment, and the concrete situation in Jerusalem, with its impending destruction.

The image of the harlot is clearest in chapter 16, but the chapters dating to the years prior to the Destruction (1–24) generally contain words and terms that relate to women. This motif is especially noticeable in chapters 16 and 23, where Jerusalem is metaphorically compared to a woman. The image is fully realized at the end of this series of chapters (24:15–24), with the death of the prophet's wife, symbolizing, inter alia, the final destruction of the city.[8] Chapters 25–48 are almost completely devoid of images and terms belonging to the semantic field of women – to the point where there is no mention, whether explicit or implied, of any "woman" in the description of the future city.

JERUSALEM'S DEEDS (16:1–34)

Verses 1–34 describe the unfaithfulness of Jerusalem. The prophetic message in this chapter is conveyed through the literary adoption of a repetitive vocabulary, among other things: "naked and bare" (vv. 7, 22, 39); "covered/expose your nakedness" (vv. 8, 36, 37); blood (vv. 6, 9, 22, 38), and garments (vv. 10, 16, 39). These depict the city's deeds with great impact.

The prophet begins by describing the origin (v. 3) and birth of the "girl" in the field, with none to care for her (vv. 4–5). God sees her weltering in her blood and gives her life (v. 6). Then the prophet describes her growing and becoming a young woman (v. 7), and God's act of covering her and entering into a covenant with her ("I entered into a covenant with you by oath" v. 8). The city/girl is gathered up by God, who provides for all her needs and extends His patronage (vv. 9–14), but gradually, step by step, she loses everything she has been given. God gave her fine garments and ornaments, but she offers them over to idolatry, builds high places (v. 16), sacrifices to foreign gods (v. 19), and even offers up her own children (vv. 20–21). God cries out, as it were, over her playing the harlot "in every street," receiving

---

8. This idea is presented by Julie Galambush, *Jerusalem in the Book of Ezekiel*, SBLDS 130 (Georgia: Atlanta Scholars Press, 1992).

nothing in return (vv. 33–34): "After all your wickedess (woe, woe to you!) – declares the Lord God" (v. 23). This harlotry symbolizes the bonds maintained between Jerusalem and Egypt (v. 26), Assyria (v. 28), and Chaldea (v. 29). The description of the unfaithfulness of this woman – Jerusalem – emphasizes the chasm between her humble beginnings, with no lineage and no identity, and the abundance God bestowed upon her and His favors done for her. Perhaps the descriptions of her betrayals in this chapter can be mitigated if we consider the background to her need to assert her identity, which she absorbs "from the outside."

GOD'S RESPONSE (16:35–43)

The next verses in the chapter show the city punished measure for measure for her deeds. Now God will reveal her nakedness (vv. 36–38). She is punished with every possible form of death, including stoning, burning, and the sword (vv. 39–42, with parallels in 23:9–10, 22–29, 45–48). Concerning this punishment, Ishay Rosen-Zvi writes:

> This "hyper-punishment" makes sense in light of Ezekiel's tendency in these chapters to present the Destruction as a total annihilation, a punishment unprecedented in its severity. He presents the imminent Destruction as the "punishment to end all punishments," and therefore constructs a punishment that has no precedent; nothing like it exists in reality. At the same time, he also describes the sin in exceedingly severe terms, which provides justification for such a terrible punishment. To this end, these chapters bring together adultery, bloodshed, and idolatry – the three gravest sins. Ezekiel creates his own original punishment, which is prescribed neither for adulteresses nor for killers; he calls it "punishment of women who commit adultery and murder" (16:38) jointly, just as he binds together the sin of the adulteress and that of the harlot. A sin that has no parallel justifies a punishment without precedent.[9]

---

9. Ishay Rosen-Zvi, "'VeAsita Otkha KaAsher Asita:' Mabat Nosaf al Anishat HaNo'afot BeYeḥezkel 16 Ve- 23," *Beit Mikra* 50, no. 2 (2005): 163–93 (the citation is taken from pp. 186–87). See his article for a full picture of the punishment in chapters 16 and 23 and its uniqueness.

Ezekiel 15:1–16:63

JERUSALEM AND HER SISTERS – SAMARIA AND SODOM (16:44–58)

Ezekiel now goes on to compare the deeds of Jerusalem to those of her "elder sister," Samaria (which had a greater number of inhabitants and was exiled earlier than Jerusalem) and her "younger sister," Sodom. The comparisons emphasize that Jerusalem's deeds were worse than those of her sisters. Since Samaria and Sodom were destroyed, Jerusalem's fate can be deduced by simple logic.

It is interesting to note the sins that are attributed here to the city of Sodom: "Only this was the sin of your sister Sodom: arrogance! She and her daughters had plenty of bread and untroubled tranquillity; yet she did not support the poor and the needy" (16:49).

The sin of Sodom, as depicted here, is that despite its inhabitants' economic stability and strength, they did not support the poor and needy. In other words, the sins are socioeconomic ones. This description is rather surprising, in light of the fact that in the book of Genesis, Sodom is destroyed because "the outrage of Sodom and Gomorrah is so great, and their sin so grave!" (Gen. 18:20), and the story there seems to suggest that their sins included rape or homosexuality (19:1–9).[10] The book of Ezekiel attributes "social welfare" sins to Sodom, in contrast to the actions described in the book of Genesis. This fits the prophet's message about the severity of Jerusalem's sins in chapter 16. The surprising disparity between the deeds of Sodom in Genesis and the deeds attributed to it in Ezekiel makes more sense in the context of the prophetic message arising from the comparison between Sodom and Jerusalem: The comparison emphasizes that Jerusalem's sins – sins of a religious and adulterous nature – are even worse than those of Sodom: "You were almost more corrupt than they in all your ways. As I live – declares the Lord God – your sister Sodom and her daughters did not do what you and your daughters did" (16:47–48).

Thus, Ezekiel attributes only social sins to Sodom in order to emphasize the more grievous sins of Jerusalem, which are described as unfaithfulness. The end of this prophetic unit emphasizes that Jerusalem

---

10. See the medieval commentators on Genesis 19:5, "that we may be intimate with them."

will be disgraced through God's rehabilitation of its sisters, Sodom and Samaria. Jerusalem itself will be rebuilt only after these cities have been restored to their former state (16:53–58).

RENEWAL OF THE COVENANT (16:59–63)

The prophecy in chapter 16 ends with the promise that God will not break His covenant with the Jerusalem/Israel of earlier times; He will make an everlasting covenant with them. This renewed covenant will cause Jerusalem to feel shame for her deeds (16:63).

These verses conclude what is one of the harshest prophecies – if not the harshest – in the book of Ezekiel. It is fitting that this concluding prophecy of restoration differs from the other prophecies. First, it lacks elements that are found in all the other prophecies of redemption in this book. Second, it includes elements that are common among the other prophets but unusual for Ezekiel, including the establishment of an "everlasting covenant" (16:60) and divine forgiveness for the people's actions. These verses – their prophetic message, their location at the conclusion of the prophecy, the language and in its context – all emphasize to the people that the cataclysm and the amendment are bound up with one another. Even the sins that the people have committed – including violating the covenant with God – will not lead to the breaking of the bond between God and His people. Despite the people's actions in the present, the covenant that God remembers and maintains even in the future is a covenant of youth; at the time of their sin, this historical covenant will stand. This is also why the nation is rebuked just as it is being forgiven: "Thus you shall remember and feel shame, and you shall be too abashed to open your mouth again, when I have forgiven you for all that you did – declares the Lord God" (Ezek. 16:63).

APPENDIX: THE WOMAN – JERUSALEM

Throughout the first part of the book, Ezekiel addresses Jerusalem by comparing the city to a woman. A fuller understanding of the verses in their context and an examination of the images interwoven throughout these prophecies as a whole points to a trend that becomes clear in chapters 16 and 23, and concludes with the description of the prophet's own wife in chapter 24.

Verses 8–17 of chapter 5, for example, deal with the punishment of the city; in verse 14 we read: "I will make you a ruin and a mockery… in the sight of every passerby." The language with which the prophet describes the scorn of the nations suits the description of the deeds of Jerusalem in chapter 16. Sometimes the deeds of the people are described using vocabulary that corresponds even more explicitly to chapters 16 and 23. For example, "…their faithless hearts…and their eyes which lusted…" (6:9); "their gold shall be treated as something unclean… therefore I will make them an unclean thing to them" (7:19–20). The word used in these verses for "unclean" is *nidda* which is specifically associated with the impurity of a menstrual woman. Likewise, the use of the word *damim* (blood), also connotes menstrual women: "the city of bloodshed…. O city in whose midst blood is shed…. You stand guilty of the blood you have shed…" (22:2–4); "Woe to the city of blood – A caldron whose scum is in it.… For the blood she shed is still in her" (24:6). We propose[11] that this accumulation of examples demonstrates that the comparison of Jerusalem with a harlot is actually maintained, on some level, throughout the chapters of the book that contain prophecies of destruction.[12]

In light of the above it not surprising that no use is made of the image of a woman in the vision of the future. The woman is an image that symbolizes the impurity of the city that has led to the Destruction of the Temple. The death of the prophet's wife may perhaps symbolize metaphorically that the city will not be made unclean again. If this is correct, then Ezekiel differs in this respect from the other prophets, since they also use images of women in a positive sense; for Ezekiel, this metaphor is purely negative.

---

11. Following the example of Galambush, *Jerusalem*.
12. It should be noted that women appear in other contexts, too, in these chapters: there are the women who weep for Tammuz (8:14); the false prophetesses (13:17–23); and the wife of his neighbor (mentioned in 18:6, 11, 15, and 22:10–11).

Chapter 12

Justice and Responsibility
Ezekiel 18:1–32

The concept of divine justice is treated in four separate places in the book of Ezekiel: 3:16–21; 14:12–23; chapter 18; and 33:1–20. We have already discussed three of these. Now, with our study of chapter 18, we will conclude our analysis of this subject.[1]

SOCIAL INJUSTICES (18:1–20)

Unlike the other sections in Ezekiel that address this subject, this chapter is unique by virtue of the nature of the sins that it enumerates. Elsewhere in the book, social and moral injustices seem to be pushed aside, perhaps owing to the paucity of prophecies addressing them. Not so in this chapter.

Our chapter opens with the people questioning the situation: "Parents eat sour grapes and their children's teeth are blunted" (18:2).

---

1. One study of these four chapters and the concepts of divine justice and retribution they raise is Gershon Brin's *Iyunim BeSefer Yeḥezkel* (Tel Aviv: Hakibbutz Hameuchad, 1975), 80–105.

Ezekiel 18:1–32

What follows is the prophet's response: "The person who sins, only he shall die" (v. 4). He then lists the deeds of the righteous man, which include avoidance of idolatry and prohibited sexual relations (vv. 8–9). In this sense, the list here resembles the list of the deeds of his wicked son which follows (vv. 10–13), as well as the deeds of his righteous grandson (vv. 14–17). Following a description of the deeds attributed to each of the three generations, Ezekiel emphasizes that the wicked son will be punished for his actions (v. 18), and concludes with the same idea with which he began: "The person who sins, he alone shall die" (v. 20). The prophetic unit concludes with a reiteration of individual responsibility. Each person, throughout his life, is responsible for his own actions. A person may turn back from the path on which he or she began. A formerly wicked person who repents will live (vv. 21–23), but a righteous person who turns to sin will be punished (18:24). It appears that the people, who claim "the way of the Lord is unfair" (vv. 25, 29), do not at first grasp the distinction that Ezekiel draws between the nation as a whole (whose actions have brought about the imminent Destruction of the Temple and the exile, both of which are now irreversible) and the responsibility of all individuals for their actions and the life-and-death consequences that follow. Therefore, throughout the chapter, the prophet emphasizes this message repeatedly.

Ezekiel concludes by stating that the people's claim – that the son dies because of the sins of the father – is simply incorrect: "A child shall not share the burden of a parent's guilt, nor shall a parent share the burden of a child's guilt" (18:20).

Thus, chapter 18 is unique for its explicit discussion of individual responsibility. Apparently, the people of Ezekiel's generation claimed that, with the Destruction now inevitable, their individual actions no longer had any importance. It made no difference whether they remained loyal to God's commandments or not. The prophet refutes this erroneous view. Without casting the slightest doubt on the imminent Destruction, Ezekiel nevertheless does not exempt anyone from personal responsibility.[2]

---

2. This idea has been discussed at length above, chapter 2.

Justice and Responsibility

THE GATES OF REPENTANCE (18:21–32)

In verses 21–30, the prophet declares that the gates of repentance remain open to the individual, and this is emphasized at the end of the prophecy:

> Be assured, O House of Israel, I will judge each one of you according to his ways – declares the Lord God. Repent and turn back from your transgressions; let them not be a stumbling block of guilt for you. Cast away all the transgressions by which you have offended, and get yourselves a new heart and a new spirit, that you may not die, O House of Israel. For it is not My desire that anyone shall die – declares the Lord God. Repent, therefore, and live! (18:30–32)

Addressed mainly to the inhabitants of Judah and Jerusalem prior to the Destruction, these verses are quite unusual given that nowhere in the book is there any call for the people to mend their ways so that God will not destroy His Temple. Although the prophet here calls upon the people to repent, he offers no promise that this will prevent the Destruction; he only speaks of sinners' deliverance from death when the Destruction comes. It may be that in the context in which this prophecy appears, the righteous individuals will be the remnant that will survive in Jerusalem or among the exiles.

The sins that brought about the imminent destruction of the city can be categorized. The main group consists of different forms of idolatry. Unquestionably the most prominent in the book of Ezekiel, these sins receive attention every time the prophet talks about the nation's transgressions. The second group of sins includes sexual immorality (such as the acts performed as part of pagan ritual mentioned in chapters 16 and 23 as well as adultery). Finally, the prophet notes the sin of bloodshed. This too is sometimes connected to idolatry, as well as being an obvious violation of proper social conduct. In contrast, when Ezekiel mentions "social" sins, there is a distinction between those committed privately (ch. 18, 33) and those of the office-bearers and leaders of the nation. Ezekiel, it emerges, does not seem to attribute the Destruction of the First Temple to the social transgressions of the nation as a whole – neither in the prophecies before the Destruction nor in those after it.

SOCIAL INJUSTICES AFTER THE DESTRUCTION (CHAPTER 33)

Aside from chapter 18, the prophet also addresses individual retribution in chapter 33, verses 1–20.[3] In the latter, the target audience consists of the exiles in Babylonia; accordingly, the prophet must address a different claim: "This is what you have been saying: 'Our transgressions and our sins weigh heavily upon us; we are sick at heart about them. How can we survive?'" (v. 10).

The prophet once again emphasizes that a person is judged for his present actions. In describing the wicked person who mends his ways, he mentions social misdeeds: "If the wicked man restores a pledge, makes good what he has taken by robbery, follows the laws of life, and does not commit iniquity…" (v. 15). As is clear from the context, the prophet is talking about the deeds of the exiles after the Destruction, not the deeds that caused it. The subject of retribution is repeated because even after the Destruction, the inhabitants of the land who had survived did not despair of the possibility that they would inherit the land in the future. In response, Ezekiel enumerates the sins that led to the Destruction and emphasizes that as long as such behavior continues, the land will not be given to them as an inheritance:

> Therefore say to them: Thus said the Lord God: You eat with the blood, you raise your eyes to your fetishes, and you shed blood – yet you expect to possess the land! You have relied on your sword, you have committed abominations, you have all defiled other men's wives – yet you expect to possess the land! (vv. 25–26)

The sins noted here explicitly are the kind that continue to be committed in the absence of the Temple. Among these sins are social injustices; note the explanation given to Ezekiel for the people's failure to change their ways even after the Destruction: "and their hearts pursue nothing but gain" (v. 31).

The role of interpersonal sins in bringing about the Destruction of the First Temple is discussed in the Talmud: "Why was the

---

3. See the discussion in chapter 2, above.

Justice and Responsibility

first Sanctuary destroyed? Because of three [evil] things which prevailed there: idolatry, sexual immorality, and bloodshed" (Yoma 9b). Accordingly, it was not interpersonal sins alone that brought about the Destruction of the Temple. Indeed, we have noted that it is idolatry, in its various forms, that Ezekiel points to as the main factor that defiled the Temple: the *shikkutzim* (detestable things), the *gilulim* (fetishes), the *to'evot* (abominations), the passing of children through fire (which constitutes bloodshed as well). In addition, Ezekiel also mentions sexual immorality (including, for example, adultery).

THE SINS OF THE OFFICE-BEARERS

In contrast to the idolatry and sexual immorality, the social sins committed by the people's office-bearers affect their status. Indeed, the Talmud questions explicitly whether causeless hatred did not exist at the time of the First Temple, citing in support a verse from Ezekiel:

> But [during the time of] the first Sanctuary did not groundless hatred prevail? Surely it is written: "They shall be cast before the sword together with My people; oh, strike the thigh [in grief]" (Ezek. 21:17)? And R. Eleazar said: This refers to people who eat and drink together and then stab each other with the daggers of their tongue! That [passage] speaks of the *nesi'im* in Israel, for it is written, "Cry and wail, O mortal, for this shall befall My people" (ibid.), etc. [The text reads] "Cry and wail, O mortal." One might have assumed [it is upon] all [Israel], therefore it goes on, "This shall befall all the chieftains of Israel." (Yoma 9b)

While R. Eleazer's interpretation of the verse seems far removed from its plain meaning, a closer look at the text reveals that along with the prophet's warning about the fate of the people, he also features interpersonal sins in his description of the leaders' sins.

Chapter 22 includes a unique list of sins, out of character with the rest of the book. As the Destruction of Jerusalem draws nearer ("that your hour is approaching"; 22:3; "You have brought on your day; you have reached your year"; v. 4) the prophet appears to place more of an emphasis on the personal responsibility borne by the leaders of

Ezekiel 18:1–32

the people for their actions, along with the dire consequences of their corrupt leadership for the nation as a whole. This chapter attributes sins, both social and religious in nature, to the office-bearers in leadership positions. The fate of the city is sealed because of idolatry, sexual immorality, bloodshed, and – finally – the deeds of the leadership. In practical terms, not all of these sins were committed during the generation of the Destruction; rather, the city's fate and decree are the result of the accumulated wrongdoing (similar to the description of the sins of idolatry in chapter 8). However, every individual, and every leader, is able to determine his or her own personal fate (as we saw in chapters 18 and 33). To this end the prophet lists the sins and punishments of the various officials: the *nesi'im* (princes) (22:6–13)[4], the prophets (vv. 25, 28), the priests (vv. 22, 26), the officials (v. 27) and finally – the common people (v. 29).

In his post-Destruction guidance to the office-bearers of the future near the end of the book, Ezekiel notes social sins. Thus, for example, the priests are meant to fill a judicial function: "In lawsuits, too, it is they who shall act as judges; they shall decide them in accordance with My rules. They shall preserve My teachings and My laws regarding all My fixed occasions; and they shall maintain the sanctity of My sabbaths" (44:24).

The prophet exhorts the *nesi'im*, reminding them of their past social sins:

> Thus said the Lord God: Enough, *nesi'im* of Israel! Make an end of lawlessness and rapine, and do what is right and just! Put a stop to your evictions of My people – declares the Lord God. Have honest balances, an honest ephah, and an honest bath.[5] The ephah and the bath shall comprise the same volume, the bath a tenth of a homer and the ephah a tenth of a homer; their capacity shall be gauged by the homer. (45:9–11)

---

4. In the list of sins attributed to the *nesi'im*, the number of socio-moral transgressions is equal to the number of transgressions in the religio-ritual realm (eight of each, though the division is not entirely clear-cut).
5. Ephah and bath are biblical measures of volume.

Justice and Responsibility

Along with their personal responsibility for what is happening on the national level the prophet once again emphasizes the personal sphere in which their fate is determined. Thus, the excoriation of the people and the demand that they take individual responsibility also includes an appeal directly to the nation's leaders that they, too, exhibit more worthy behavior.

APPENDIX: THE TERM ḤAMAS AS A DESCRIPTION OF THE PEOPLE'S SINS

In chapter 5, we discussed the word *ḥamas* and noted that at times it was understood to relate to social infractions but might also refer to religious sins. Indeed, the term *ḥamas* appears several times in Ezekiel's descriptions of the people's sins. The common meaning of the word as used elsewhere in Tanakh is robbery, extortion, or exploitation of the poor by the rich. This has led many scholars to likewise interpret all such instances in the book of Ezekiel as referring to social sins, and to conclude that it is to these types of sins that the prophet attributes the Destruction. However, closer study of Ezekiels' usage of the term reveals that this interpretation is not entirely correct; in some instances, it is even inappropriate.

The word first appears in chapter 7, where Ezekiel prophesies the imminent Destruction. In mentioning the sins that have brought about this catastrophe, he refers to "abominations" (7:3, 4, 8, 9, 20), "detestable abominations" (v. 20), and "bloody crimes" (v. 23). Verses 11 and 23 also mention *ḥamas* as a cause of the Destruction. In verse 11 the prophet declares that "lawlessness (*ḥamas*) has grown into a rod of wickedness." The meaning of the word here is rather ambiguous. It may be interpreted as a general description of the actions of the people: "The *ḥamas* that you have committed" (Radak and Rabbi Joseph Kara), or alternatively, as Kasher suggests:

> The ambiguity of the previous verse continues here. Perhaps the image refers to what is happening in Judah, such that *ḥamas* would be the rod with which the wicked strike. Or the verse may be describing the enemy: The *ḥamas* that is embodied in

Ezekiel 18:1–32

the enemy develops and rises up into a rod of wickedness that strikes cruelly at the inhabitants of Judah.[6]

Either way, the word *ḥamas* here does not specifically describe social sins. It may be a general description of the behavior of the people, or of the rod, or of the enemy.

In contrast, the reason for the Destruction in verse 23 seems to be set down more explicitly: "for the land is full of bloody crimes, and the city is full of lawlessness (*ḥamas*)." The term "bloody crimes" (*mishpat damim*) appears nowhere else in Tanakh, and it may refer to social laws (*mishpatim*) whose violation entails the death penalty (hence "bloody"); therefore, the prophet adds that the city is "full of *ḥamas*." From the context, we can deduce that this sin – along with idolatry (7:20) and bloodshed – has brought about the desecration of the Temple. The next appearance of *ḥamas* in the book of Ezekiel is in chapter 8, where it describes violations of a religious nature. Thereafter the term *ḥamas* is noted in the context of the people's sins, in chapter 12: "because their land will be desolate of its multitudes on account of the lawlessness (*ḥamas*) of all its inhabitants" (12:19). Like the examples above, the word *ḥamas* here is used in a general sense. The land will be desolate and bereft of its inhabitants because of the *ḥamas* perpetrated in it. An alternative (but similar) explanation is that the land will be desolate and emptied of the *ḥamas* that now fills it.

The word *ḥamas* also occurs later on in relation to the sins of the office-bearers in 22:26, where the prophet talks about the sins of the priests: "Her priests have violated (*ḥamsu*) My teaching,"[7] and likewise in 45:9, in describing the sin of the *nesi'im*: "Enough, *nesi'im* of Israel! Make an end of lawlessness (*ḥamas*) and rapine …"[8]

It is thus clear that the word *ḥamas* in the book of Ezekiel does not necessarily indicate social sins. It may be a more general term

---

6. Kasher, *Yeḥezkel 1–24*, 231.
7. For use of the word in the same sense, namely violation of Torah commands, see Zeph. 3:4.
8. For a similar occurrence, see the description of the sin of Tyre in 28:16: "By your far-flung commerce You were filled with lawlessness (*ḥamas*) And you sinned"; here, *ḥamas* means unfair or dishonest trade.

referring to all the sins of the people against God – especially the most serious transgressions, including idolatry and bloodshed. The verses that contain the word *ḥamas* do not represent proof that Ezekiel refers to interpersonal sins. The prophet refers to these sins in the chapters in which he speaks about individual reward and punishment. But when he speaks about the causes of the Destruction, he mentions bloodshed and sexual immorality along with religious sins, making no specific mention of social injustice. For this reason, the general picture arising from the book of Ezekiel seems to be that the Destruction of the Temple was caused not by the moral transgressions of the people in a general sense, but only as a result of the religious violations that cause the Temple to be desecrated – including idolatry and bloodshed. The prophet addresses moral transgressions and the need for repentance and amendment only when he speaks about the fate of the individual, as opposed to the fate of the people as a whole and the fate of the Temple, both of which have already been sealed.

Chapter 13

The Beginning of the End

Ezekiel 20:1–21:37

Ezekiel's prophecy in chapters 20 and 21[1] turns to the nearing Destruction and God's increasingly severe responses. Listing the deeds that led the nation to its dire fate and describing the sword wielded by the king of Babylonia, Ezekiel's narrative leads up to the horrors of the massacre at the hands of Nebuchadnezzar.

"THE ABHORRENT DEEDS OF THEIR FATHERS" (CHAPTER 20)

Our prophecy opens with a date: "In the seventh year, on the tenth day of the fifth month" (20:1). This is two years before the siege of Jerusalem began, a year after the last date mentioned (at the beginning of chapter 8), and two years after the date noted at the beginning of the book. In other words, the Destruction is drawing nearer.[2]

---

1. For discussion on Ezekiel chapter 19, see chapter 8 above.
2. If Ezekiel's prophecies in chapters 1–24 are indeed arranged in chronological order, then chapters 1–7 belong to the fifth year of Jehoiachin's exile; chapters 8–19 to the sixth year; chapters 20–23 to the seventh year; and chapter 24 to the ninth year.

Now, the prophet notes, "Certain elders of Israel came to inquire of the Lord, and sat down before me" (20:1). It seems reasonable to connect these elders of Israel with those mentioned in chapter 14. It is also possible they have come before Ezekiel not as an official body of representative elders, but rather as individuals concerned for their own fate. In either case, their request is quickly rejected, and Ezekiel rebukes them as representatives of the nation:[3] "Speak to the elders of Israel and say to them: Thus said the Lord God: Have you come to inquire of Me? As I live, I will not respond to your inquiry – declares the Lord God" (v. 3). Instead, the prophet is commanded, "Arraign, arraign them, O mortal! Declare to them the abhorrent deeds of their fathers" (v. 4).

Ezekiel then reviews the Israelites' history, beginning with nationhood in Egypt. A pattern of behavior is repeated – first the nation acts, then God responds. This pattern includes establishing statutes for the nation of Israel (or giving a reminder or rebuke concerning statutes that have been given), followed by violation of the statutes by the nation, then divine anger and a desire to annihilate the nation, and ultimately God's forgoing the full punishment for the sake of His name. His review of this pattern covers three distinct periods:

Period	The Israelites in Egypt (20:5–10)	The generation that left Egypt, in the wilderness (20:11–17)	The wilderness generation (20:18–26)
Giving of statutes and reminder	On the day that I chose Israel, I gave My oath to the stock of the House of Jacob; when I made Myself known to them **in the land of Egypt,**	I gave them My laws and taught them My rules, by the pursuit of which a man shall live. *Moreover, I gave them My sabbaths to serve as a sign between Me*	I warned **their children in the wilderness:** Do not follow the practices of your fathers, do not keep their ways, and do not defile

---

3. See Yair Hoffman, "LiShe'elat HaMivneh VeHaMashma'ut shel Yeḥezkel Perek 20," *Beit Mikra* 20, no. 4 (1975): 473–89.

The Beginning of the End

Period	The Israelites in Egypt (20:5–10)	The generation that left Egypt, in the wilderness (20:11–17)	The wilderness generation (20:18–26)
	I gave my oath to them. When I said, "I the Lord am your God," that same day I swore to them to take them out of the land of Egypt into a land flowing with milk and honey, a land which I had sought out for them, the fairest of all lands. I also said to them: Cast away, every one of you, the detestable things that you are drawn to, and do not defile yourselves with the fetishes of Egypt – I the Lord am your God.	*and them, that they might know that it is I the Lord who sanctify them.*	yourselves with their fetishes. I the Lord am your God: Follow My laws and be careful to observe My rules. *And hallow My sabbaths, that they may be a sign between Me and you, that you may know that I the Lord am your God.*
Rebellion against God	But they defied Me and refused to listen to Me. They did not cast away the detestable things they were drawn to, nor did they give up the fetishes of Egypt.	But the House of Israel rebelled *against Me* **in the wilderness**; they did not follow My laws and they rejected My rules – by the pursuit of which a man shall live – *and they grossly desecrated My sabbaths.*	But the children rebelled against Me: they did not follow My laws and did not faithfully observe My rules, by the pursuit of which man shall live; *they profaned My sabbaths.*

Ezekiel 20:1–21:37

Period	The Israelites in Egypt (20:5–10)	The generation that left Egypt, in the wilderness (20:11–17)	The wilderness generation (20:18–26)
God's intention to punish with annihilation	Then I resolved to pour out My fury upon them, to vent all My anger upon them there, in the land of Egypt.	Then I thought to pour out My fury upon them in the wilderness and to make an end of them;	Then I resolved to pour out My fury upon them, to vent all My anger upon them, in the wilderness.
God acts for His name's sake	But I acted for the sake of My name, that it might not be profaned in the sight of the nations among whom they were. For it was before their eyes that I had made Myself known to Israel to bring them out of the land of Egypt.	but I acted for the sake of My name, that it might not be profaned in the sight of the nations before whose eyes I had led them out.	But I held back My hand and acted for the sake of My name, that it might not be profaned in the sight of the nations before whose eyes I had led them out.
God's action	I brought them out of the land of Egypt and I led them into the wilderness.	However, I swore to them in the wilderness that I would not bring them into the land flowing with milk and honey, the fairest of all lands, which I had assigned [to them], for they had rejected My rules, disobeyed My laws, and	However, I swore to them in the wilderness that I would scatter them among the nations and disperse them through the lands, because they did not obey My rules, but rejected My laws, *profaned*

Period	The Israelites in Egypt (20:5–10)	The generation that left Egypt, in the wilderness (20:11–17)	The wilderness generation (20:18–26)
		desecrated My sabbaths; their hearts followed after their fetishes. But I had pity on them and did not destroy them; **I did not make an end of them in the wilderness.**	My sabbaths, and looked with longing to the fetishes of their fathers. Moreover, I gave them laws that were not good and rules by which they could not live: When they set aside every first issue of the womb, I defiled them by their very gifts – that I might render them desolate, that they might know that I am the Lord.

According to this prophecy, Israel's history since becoming a nation has consisted of a series of appeals by God which the nation rejects, followed by divine responses that become increasingly severe. The nation rebels by adhering to the idols of the nations and the corrupt ways of their fathers. Despite the nation's passivity, God brings it out of Egypt and leads the people to the land which He had sought out for them.[4]

---

4. See Moshe Greenberg, "Yeḥezkel 20 VeHaGalut HaRuḥanit," in *Oz LeDavid: Kovetz Meḥkarim BeTanakh, Mugash LeDavid Ben-Gurion BeMele'at Lo Shivim VeSheva Shanim*, ed. Yeḥezkel Kaufmann et al. (Jerusalem: HaḤevra LeḤeker HaMikra BeYisrael, 1964), 433–42.

This is the only place in the book in which there is any direct mention of the Egyptian Exodus. Ezekiel makes no reference to that historical event in his prophecies to Egypt (ch. 29–32), nor even in the context of his words about Passover (Ezek. 45:21).

Following this litany, the prophet rebukes his generation for its behavior. But the relevance of Egypt involves more than a description of the nation's recurrent backsliding; their future redemption is also based on the model made familiar by the story of the departure from Egypt in the book of Exodus. The stages of this future restoration are: an ingathering of the exiles ("With a strong hand and an outstretched arm and overflowing fury I will bring you out from the peoples and gather you from the lands where you are scattered"v. 34); a wilderness ("and I will bring you into the wilderness of the peoples; and there I will enter into judgment with you face to face"v. 35); a covenant ("I will make you pass under the shepherd's staff, and I will bring you into the bond of the covenant"v. 37); a winnowing of sinners, and an arrival in the Land of Israel. The amendment for the desecration of God's name, which is a recurring motif throughout the chapter, is sanctification: "When I bring you out from the peoples and gather you from the lands in which you are scattered, I will accept you as a pleasing odor; and **I will be sanctified through you in the sight of the nations**" (v. 41).

This chapter illustrates clearly the cyclical process of history: Israel violates God's laws and as a result is deemed unworthy of redemption – even survival. But nonetheless the nation is restored to its land to prevent God's name from being desecrated in the eyes of the nations. The desecration of God's name lies not only in the actual transgression of His laws, but also in how God's abandonment of His people would be perceived by the nations. Thus the remedy of this desecration – the sanctification of God's name – must likewise also be "in the sight of the nations," through the ingathering of the nation of Israel from the places to which they have been scattered.[5]

---

5. It is for this reason that this chapter includes an additional theme: the praise of the Land of Israel (vv. 6, 15, 28, 40).

The Beginning of the End

"THEY PROFANED MY SABBATHS" (20:21)

The commandment of Shabbat enjoys a place of honor in the book of Ezekiel. This chapter has repeated mentions of Shabbat along with the "laws and rules" "by the pursuit of which a man shall live" (vv. 12–13, 16, 20–21, 24). Furthermore, Shabbat is mentioned among the sins of the priests and the people in chapters 22 and 23, and is also awarded a special place in the vision of the future Temple (ch. 44–46).

The special status of Shabbat in the book of Ezekiel is addressed by the medieval commentators. Rashi and Rabbi Joseph Kara explain (apparently in light of Exodus 31:16–17) that the sanctity that God bestows on the nation is apparent from God giving them His own day of rest after the creation. Rabbi Joseph Kara comments, "When the children of Israel observe the Shabbat, they testify thereby that I created the world in six days, and rested on the seventh." However, since Ezekiel does not mention Creation as the reason for the nation's observance of Shabbat, Rabbi Eliezer of Beaugency provides a more precise reading: He notes that the Creation of the world does not, in itself, draw any distinction between the people of Israel and the other nations; God's sanctification of the nation is the reason for them to observe Shabbat. Other reasons for the special prominence of Shabbat in the book of Ezekiel are offered (for example, by Radak and Rabbi Joseph ibn Caspi), explaining that the special characteristics of Shabbat transform it into a symbol for the commandments as a whole.

What makes Ezekiel's attitude towards Shabbat special is not that he mentions it more often than do other prophets, but that he views Shabbat as a sign and symbol – not of the Creation of the world, but of the special sanctity of Israel "that you may know that I the Lord am your God" (20:20). He gives two different meanings for this "sign": "Moreover, I gave them My sabbaths to serve as a sign between Me and them, **that they might know that it is I the Lord who sanctify them**" (v. 12); "And hallow My sabbaths, that they may be a sign between Me and you, **that you may know that I the Lord am your God**" (v. 20).

The first meaning of the sign is familiar to us from the book of Exodus: "You must keep My sabbaths, for this is a sign between Me and you throughout the ages, **that you may know that I the Lord have consecrated you**" (Ex. 31:13). But the second meaning – Shabbat's testimony that "I the Lord am your God" – is a concept unique to Ezekiel; there is no parallel to it elsewhere in the Torah. This accentuates the importance of Shabbat: Through its observance, the nation not only expresses its sanctity, but also testifies to and calls to consciousness the fact that the Lord is their God. Conversely, desecration of the Shabbat violates this testimony.

As Ezekiel points out, immediately after the commandment of Shabbat was given to the generation of the wilderness, it was violated (see Num. 15:32–36). The nation thereby testified publicly that it was not faithful to God and preferred to worship other gods. This is why Shabbat occupies such a special place in the prophecy of Ezekiel, uttered in the generation of the Destruction. The breach of Shabbat attests to the distance between the nation and its God. This ultimately led to the defiling of the Temple and its destruction. This is also why, apart from our chapter, Shabbat is mentioned elsewhere (Ezek. 22:8; 23:38) among the reasons for the Destruction.

Shabbat only appears again in the book of Ezekiel in the chapters dealing with the vision of the future rebuilt Temple, but is omitted from the chapters preceding that vision (34–39). This suggests that Shabbat as testimony to the God of Israel is only relevant when the nation recognizes Him and no longer sins. This will come about only when the Temple is rebuilt. It will not come about through the Destruction, nor while the nation dwells in exile.

"I GAVE THEM LAWS THAT WERE NOT GOOD" (20:25)

Verses 25–26 of chapter 20 are especially problematic:

> Moreover, I gave them laws that were not good and rules by which they could not live: When they set aside every first issue of the womb, I defiled them by their very gifts – that I might render them desolate, that they might know that I am the Lord.

How are we to understand the words of the prophet? The commentators offer different approaches.[6] *Targum Yonatan* offers the following interpretation:

---

6. For further discussion see Kasher, *Yeḥezkel 1–24*, 404–406, appendix IV.

> So I too – after they rebelled against My words and did not listen to My prophets – I distanced them, and gave them over into the hands of their foolish inclination; they went and made [for themselves] unbefitting statutes and practices whereby they would not live.

Thus, the creation of the bad laws is attributed to the nation; God's role is simply to allow the people to follow their own inclination, which causes them to follow the statutes in an improper way. In other words, God allows the people to sin (which is what they want to do). In the wake of the *Targum*, Rashi comments:

> I delivered them into the hands of their temptation to stumble over their iniquity…. Those gifts that I legislated for them to hallow for Me every firstborn delivered them into the hands of their temptation: to pass those firstborn to the Molech. Hence the statutes that are not good.

Rabbi Eliezer of Beaugency, who understands the nation's sin as mixing divine service with idolatry, explains that the statutes are described as "not good" in the sense that the nation will not receive a reward for them, because of the severity of their sins.

Either way, these interpretations offer an understanding not found in the plain text alone. A different approach is presented with great clarity by Moshe Greenberg:

> Since exile has already been decreed for Israel, it is necessary to ensure that they will persist in their wickedness to the end, until their measure is full and they have completed their sin. If God seeks to put someone to death, He puts a stumbling block before him that causes him to die (20:3). As in many other places where he describes divine punishment, the prophet describes the stumbling block here in terms of "measure for measure:" twice they despised God's good statutes "by the pursuit of which a man shall live" choosing [instead] the statutes and judgments of their fathers (which were not good, and by which people do

not live). What was God's retribution? He upheld their choice, giving them, instead of good statutes, "laws that were not good and rules by which they could not live." Therefore he is able to fulfill the promise, "I will treat them in accordance with their own ways and judge them according to their deserts" (7:27).... Thus we conclude that the prophet viewed the entire First Temple period as a time of filling the measure of sin, so as to justify the annihilation that had already been decreed.[7]

It seems that the "laws that were not good" are those related to the people's offering of gifts that defiled them: "When they set aside every first issue of the womb." Perhaps the prophet is attributing to the people the false notion that sacrifice of the firstborn is permitted. This act – offering children to Molech and passing them through fire – was common among pagans and is echoed in the story of the binding of Isaac. It led to a perception that seems to have been prevalent amongst the nation that such practices had divine legitimacy. Ezekiel's words come into sharper focus against the background of Jeremiah's descriptions of the nation's actions during this period:

> And they have built the shrines of Topheth in the Valley of Ben-hinnom to burn their sons and daughters in fire – which I never commanded, which never came to My mind. (Jer. 7:31)

> They have built shrines to Baal, to put their children to the fire as burnt offerings to Baal – which I never commanded, never decreed, and which never came to My mind. (Jer. 19:5)

> And they built the shrines of Baal which are in the Valley of Ben-hinnom, where they offered up their sons and daughters to Molech – when I had never commanded, or even thought

---

7. Greenberg, "Yeḥezkel 20," 436. In his article he also points out the similarity between the history of Israel as presented in this chapter, climaxing in the giving of "laws that were not good," and the history of the Egyptians in Exodus 7–15, climaxing in the hardening of Pharaoh's heart.

> [of commanding], that they should do such an abominable thing, and so bring guilt on Judah. (Jer. 32:35)[8]

Jeremiah emphasizes, in each of the three verses in which the burning of children by fire is mentioned, that the act violates God's command; that such an idea never "came to [God's] mind," and that God would never mislead His people this way. Such emphasis is unusual in descriptions of the people's sins; usually, the prophets do not take the trouble to spell out that the actions of the people were not commanded by God. Moreover, it is possible that the people adopted a literal interpretation of the verse in Exodus 22:28: "You shall give Me the firstborn among your sons."

If indeed – as it appears from Ezekiel – the prevalent view was that this act was legitimate in God's eyes, then it is clear why Jeremiah repeatedly states that there is no basis for it. This message is also emphasized in Ezekiel's own words:

> And if to this very day you defile yourselves in the presentation of your gifts by making your children pass through the fire to all your fetishes, shall I respond to your inquiry, O House of Israel? As I live – declares the Lord God – I will not respond to you. (Ezek. 20:31)

"I WILL BE SANCTIFIED THROUGH YOU IN THE SIGHT OF THE NATIONS" (20:30–38)

The periods in Jewish history recalled in chapter 20 of Ezekiel are not randomly chosen, and a review of them offers important insights into the process of restoration as expressed in the book. The restoration of the nation in the future is described in verses 32–38 as follows:

> And what you have in mind shall never come to pass – when you say, "We will be like the nations, like the families of the lands, worshipping wood and stone." As I live – declares the Lord God – I will reign over you with a strong hand, and with an outstretched

---

8. See also Micah 6:7: "Shall I give my firstborn for my transgression, the fruit of my body for my sins?"

arm, and with overflowing fury. With a strong hand and an outstretched arm and overflowing fury I will bring you out from the peoples and gather you from the lands where you are scattered, and I will bring you into the wilderness of the peoples; and there I will enter into judgment with you face to face. As I entered into judgment with your fathers in the wilderness of the land of Egypt, so will I enter into judgment with you – declares the Lord God. I will make you pass under the shepherd's staff, and I will bring you into the bond of the covenant. I will remove from you those who rebel and transgress against Me; I will take them out of the countries where they sojourn, but they shall not enter the Land of Israel. Then you shall know that I am the Lord.

Yehuda Elitzur makes an interesting observation on these verses:

> Here, too…there is an allusion to exile.… We can say this is the other side of the coin of Israel's existence…. The text maintains…that the nation of Israel is destined to have two spheres of existence: one of light and grandeur – the sphere of the Land of Israel – and the other of punishment and darkness – the sphere of exile. Both are legitimate spheres of existence that were destined for Israel in advance, with one anticipated and the other a constant threat.[9]

In view of this, Elitzur explains "the wilderness of the peoples" as a symbolic expression for the cruel mechanism of exilic existence. The expression "the bond of the covenant," *masoret habrit* (adopting the interpretation of the Septuagint) refers to "counting." The prophet says, "I will make you pass under the shepherd's staff" (v. 37); like a shepherd counting his flock, He keeps the ones that need to be kept and sends to slaughter those that must be slaughtered. Elitzur concludes:

---

9. Yehuda Elitzur, "Yisrael BeMidbar HaAmim (Yeḥezkel 20:32–38)," in *Iyunim BeSefer Yeḥezkel*, ed. Yitzhak Avishur (Jerusalem: Kiryat Sefer, 1982), 46–47. For an explanation of this prophetic unit (and a comparison to Amos 9:8–9), the article should be read in its entirety (pp. 43–66).

In summary...these verses in Ezekiel 20 seem to me to convey a vision of exile, of the great concept that passes through and accompanies all the generations – the statutes that apply in exile. He states that any Israelite gathering in exile that dreams of becoming "like the nations" – i.e., that is proceeding towards assimilation – is told by Ezekiel that it will not succeed in assimilating. It will be annihilated before becoming assimilated... This is hinted at for the first time in Leviticus 26: "the land of your enemies shall consume you" (v. 38) where no explanation is given. We propose that the "consuming" that takes place in the exile is not arbitrary, but rather selective.... Ezekiel comes along and reveals the secret. This selection is based on a principle: Those Israelites who dwell in exile but wish to remain children of Israel will live; those who do not wish to remain children of Israel will not live.... This prophecy pertains to the fundamental concept of exile that is interwoven through all generations, but here it is a warning given to the exiles in Babylonia....[10]

"ON MY HOLY MOUNTAIN" (20:39–44)

The concluding verses of the chapter are explained beautifully by Moshe Greenberg:

> In verse 39 the prophet introduces a new subject: he turns to his listeners angrily and tells them: Better that you serve the idols for the time being; only do not defile God's service any more with your abominable gifts! The time and place that are appropriate for divine service are only when the entire nation is able to participate, after the redemption and in the Land of Israel. "On My holy mountain...*there*, in the land, the entire House of Israel, all of it, must worship Me. *There* I will accept them, and *there* I will take note of your contributions and the choicest offerings of all your sacred things..." (v. 40). The three-fold repetition of the word "there" indicates the proper place for God's service, contrasting with the four-fold mention of "there" and its portrayal in verse 28.[11]

---

10. Ibid., 52.
11. Greenberg, "Yeḥezkel 20," 438.

Ezekiel 20:1–21:37

Only then does the process of restoration reach its conclusion:

> I will accept you as a pleasing odor; and I will be sanctified through you in the sight of the nations. Then, when I have brought you to the Land of Israel, to the country that I swore to give to your fathers, you shall know that I am the Lord. (vv. 41–42)

But the prophet emphasizes once again that even after the nation is gathered and returned to the land, the people will persist in sinning because their return did not follow a process of repentance or a change in their behavior:

> There you will recall your ways and all the acts by which you defiled yourselves; and you will loathe yourselves for all the evils that you committed. Then, O House of Israel, you shall know that I am the Lord, when I deal with you for My name's sake – not in accordance with your evil ways and corrupt acts – declares the Lord God. (vv. 43–44)

The unit 20:30–44 is the third and final prophecy of restoration preceding the Destruction (preceded by 11:14–21 and 16:59–63). It seems that the aim of this prophecy, which concludes Ezekiel's review of the history, is to emphasize through unique devices the severity of the nation's sins. The expression "corrupt acts" (*alilot nishḥatot*; v. 44) – with which the unit concludes – is reminiscent of the two previous prophecies of restoration that precede the Destruction. All of them emphasize the deeds of the nation, such that the vision of the future restoration that is offered prior to the Destruction is overshadowed by their sins.[12]

According to Ezekiel's prophecy (as we have seen), the nation's future restoration will not result from the covenant of the

---

12. The other prophecies of restoration similarly conclude on a note that emphasizes the nation's sins. See 11:21, concerning their hearts following despicable things and abominations, and 16:63, concerning the remembrance and shame over the nation's disgrace.

forefathers – which is not mentioned here at all – nor from repentance. It will be a "forced" restoration, motivated by the desecration of God's name inherent in the very fact of the nation's exile: "These are the people of the Lord, yet they had to leave His land" (36:20). This is emphasized and repeated throughout chapter 20 (vv. 9, 14, 22, 41). The nation should therefore be ashamed of its deeds because of the divine motivation to restore them to their land. This restoration is forced upon the people, as it were; they will have no opportunity to exercise free choice – perhaps it will even be against their will. It is for this reason that the Return will not include the entire nation. God will choose some members of the nation of Israel while they are in the "wilderness of the nations." It is no coincidence that this description of the future restoration differs from the descriptions of consolation familiar to us from Jeremiah and of redemption familiar to us from Isaiah – a difference that extends also to the chapters of restoration in Ezekiel 34–39.

GOD'S SWORD IN THE HAND OF THE KING OF BABYLON (CHAPTER 21)

The series of prophecies in chapter 21 which describe the end of the Kingdom of Judah seem to have been uttered in close proximity to the siege on Jerusalem laid on the tenth of Tevet. Chapter 19, dealing with the fate of the kings of Judah, did not mention God's name at all; our chapter – in stark contrast – mentions God's name fifteen times in different forms ("the word of the Lord," "thus said the Lord," etc.). This emphasis is meant to counter the popular perception – prevalent in pagan thought – that God would not destroy His own land, and to emphasize that events would come about by God's will.

The Drawn Sword (21:1–10)

Ezekiel begins the chapter by addressing himself to the south. He does so as a parable, but the people apparently do not understand the parable; or perhaps they understand it but refuse to accept and internalize its message. So Ezekiel repeats his prophecy, this time explicitly addressing Jerusalem:

21:2–4	21:7–10
O mortal, set your face toward Teman, and proclaim to Darom, and prophesy against the brushland of the Negeb.	O mortal, set your face toward Jerusalem and proclaim against her sanctuaries and prophesy against the Land of Israel.[13]
Say to the brushland of the Negeb: Hear the word of the Lord. Thus said the Lord God: I am going to kindle a fire in you, which shall devour every tree of yours, both green and withered. Its leaping flame shall not go out, and every face from south to north shall be scorched by it.	Say to the Land of Israel: Thus said the Lord: I am going to deal with you! I will draw My sword from its sheath, and I will wipe out from you both the righteous and the wicked. In order to wipe out from you both the righteous and the wicked, My sword shall assuredly be unsheathed against all flesh from south to north;
Then all flesh shall recognize that I the Lord have kindled it; it shall not go out.	And all flesh shall know that I the Lord have drawn My sword from its sheath, not to be sheathed again.

The nation's response to the first part of the prophecy is disbelieving: "And I said, 'Ah, Lord God! They say of me: He is just a riddlemonger'" (v. 5). Following the more explicit prophecy addressed to Jerusalem, the prophet adds his own response, by God's command:

> And you, O mortal, sigh; with tottering limbs and bitter grief, sigh before their eyes. And when they ask you, "Why do you sigh?" answer, "Because of the tidings that have come." Every heart shall sink and all hands hang nerveless; every spirit shall

---

13. The text creates a parallel among three descriptions of place: "Jerusalem," "the holy places," (*mikdashim*), and "the Land of Israel." Since it appears more appropriate that a comparison be drawn between different geographical places, rather than between an area and a structure, the expression *mikdashim* should be understood as the sanctified area in general, rather than specifically referring to the Temple.

grow faint and all knees turn to water because of the tidings that have come. It is approaching, it shall come to pass – declares the Lord God. (vv. 11–12)

The prophet's reaction to the events underlines the immediacy with which they are about to occur.

"A Sword, A Sword" (21:13–22)

The next prophetic unit deals with the sword of the king of Babylon, and describes the campaign of conquest approaching Jerusalem. The verses are difficult to translate and explain literally, as Rabbi Samuel David Luzzatto[14] writes in his commentary on verses 15 and 18:

> Ultimately, we understand nothing of all of this allegory (v. 15). This verse and the later one (v. 18) are examples of verses concerning which Ben-Zeev[15] describes (in his introduction) as incomprehensible and unintelligible…. And the commentators and scholars despair of seeking their meaning. Despite all their forced and roundabout attempts at elucidation, it (the verse) remains as unreachable as before, enveloped in mist and cloud and surrounded by a darkness so thick that it is almost tangible.

As an example of the difficulty in explaining this chapter, we find the following statement by Rashi, commenting on verse 18: "I heard many explanations for it, and I saw [others] in books of interpretations, but they did not appear correct to me." For this reason, we shall not attempt a continuous literal elucidation of the verses, but rather focus on the prophetic message on the eve of the Destruction, which Ezekiel repeats here once again: Jerusalem will not be saved; not only that, but the city is about to suffer a large-scale massacre, and the sword that slaughters will do so as commissioned by God. This sword, which has been mentioned previously (6:11–12; 12:16; 14:17) now returns with even greater

---

14. Also known by the acronym "Shadal;" 1800–1865, Italy.
15. Yehuda Lieb Ben-Zeev, *Mavo el Mikra'ei Kodesh* (Vienna, 1810). Ben-Zeev was one of the first to accept some of the conclusions of modern biblical criticism.

emphasis (eight appearances in these verses), with the prophet stating in each instance that the sword is ready to slaughter (the inhabitants of Jerusalem):

> A sword! A sword has been whetted and polished. It has been whetted to wreak slaughter; [therefore] it has been ground to a brilliant polish.... It has been given to be polished and then grasped in the hand; for this has the sword been whetted, for this polished – to be put into the hand of a slayer. (vv. 14–16)

Along with the sword there are the cries of lamentation ("Cry and wail, O mortal," v. 17), and expressions of sorrow ("Oh, strike the thigh [in grief]" [v. 17]; "striking hand against hand" [v. 19]) on the part of Ezekiel, as well as the fear on the part of the nation in view of the approaching sword ("They shall be cast before the sword together with My people" [v. 17]; "Thus hearts shall lose courage" [v. 20]). This sword is "the mother of all swords" ("it is a sword for massacre, a sword for great carnage" v. 19), and it does not pass over anyone, neither to the right nor to the left ("Be united, go to the right, turn left; whither are you bound?" v. 21). Ultimately, God's wrath will subside, with an echo of His sorrow ("I, too, will strike hand against hand and will satisfy My fury upon you"; v. 22).

The King of Babylon (21:23–32)

Now the prophet addresses the sword of the king of Babylon. The proximity of these two units seems to highlight the idea that the sword of the king of Babylon is none other than the sword of God, on whose mission the king is acting.

> And you, O mortal, choose two roads on which the sword of the king of Babylon may advance, both issuing from the same country; and select a spot, select it where roads branch off to [two] cities. Choose a way for the sword to advance on Rabbah of the Ammonites or on fortified Jerusalem in Judah. For the king of Babylon has stood at the fork of the road, where two roads branch off, to perform divination: He has shaken arrows, consulted teraphim,

The Beginning of the End

and inspected the liver. In his right hand came up the omen against Jerusalem – to set battering rams, to proclaim murder, to raise battle shouts, to set battering rams against the gates, to cast up mounds, to erect towers. In their eyes, the oaths they had sworn to them were like empty divination; but this shall serve to recall their guilt, for which they shall be taken to task. (vv. 24–28)

In verses 23–32, the prophet describes the military campaign of Nebuchadnezzar, king of Babylon, at the conclusion of which Jerusalem is conquered. In previous chapters we discussed Zedekiah in light of chapters 12 and 17, and noted that the potential for renewal of the monarchy in Israel lay with those exiled to Babylonia. We have also discussed the fate of the kings of Judah according to chapter 19, and there we addressed the verses in our chapter that speak of Zedekiah's fate. We will now examine the political context in the Land of Israel and in Babylonia at the time these prophecies were uttered, as well as discussing Nebuchadnezzar's identity.

"To Perform Divination: He Has Shaken Arrows, Consulted Teraphim, and Inspected the Liver" (21:26)

The king of Babylonia used the magical practices of the time to decide whether to advance his army towards Jerusalem or Ammon (Rabbath Ammon). The "shaking of arrows," Rimon Kasher explains, consisted of "filling a quiver with arrows, with different answers written on them. The diviner would shake the arrows, and the first to fall from the quiver was considered to represent the answer of the gods."[16] In addition, the king "consulted teraphim," divining the future using idols (see Gen. 31:34; II Kings 23:24; Zech. 10:2).

---

16. Kasher, *Yeḥezkel 1–24*, 426. It is interesting to note Luzzatto's commentary on verse 26: "*'kilkel baḥitzim'* – this means 'shaking' them, in Arabic… This is one of the ways of casting lots, and this was the custom of the Arabs when in doubt as to whether or not to follow a certain course of action: they would take three arrows. On one they would write, 'My master has commanded me,' on the second – 'My master forbids me,' and the third was left unmarked. They would then shake them in a container. If the first came up, they would do whatever the action was. If the second came up, they would refrain. If the third came up, they would return the arrow to the container, until one of the other two appeared."

Ezekiel 20:1–21:37

What is particularly interesting is that he "inspected the liver." This corresponds to archaeological and textual evidence about people "looking in the liver" – namely, they would divine the future and their fate in accordance with the state of a liver taken from an animal that was offered as a sacrifice. (This custom is mentioned in Ecclesiastes Rabba 12:7.) Ettie Koryat-Aharon writes about a finding from Megiddo:

> It seems that the custom of "looking in the liver" is based on the idea that the liver, as the seat of the psyche, reflects the psyche of the god who receives the sacrifice, and divining through the liver of the sacrifice may reveal the god's hidden desire. The discovery of the form of a liver, found in Megiddo, shed light on the process of this "looking," which was performed by a priest, starting with an examination of the innards of the animal (usually the liver), following which the liver was separated from the other organs and placed upon the palm of the priest's left hand or upon the altar. The priest would then look closely at the liver and, depending on its shape and the lines that had formed in it, would divine or resolve a certain question. In order to teach priests this technique, the various appearance of the liver were copied on tin molds, and sometimes explanations were even engraved in handwriting on these molds. [Such] tin molds have been found in many archaeological sites throughout the Ancient East.[17]

AMMON – TEMPORARY SALVATION (21:34–37)

The chapter concludes with a prophecy addressed to the children of Ammon, foretelling its imminent demise as well. The prophet begins with Jerusalem and then moves to Ammon; while Jerusalem preceded Ammon, it did not replace it. The language of this prophecy recalls that used towards Jerusalem both in this chapter and also elsewhere:

> O sword! O sword unsheathed for slaughter, polished to the utmost, to a flashing brilliance! Because they have prophesied falsely about you and have divined deceitfully concerning you,

---

17. Ettie Koryat-Aharon, "Mamlekhet HaIr Megiddo," *Moreshet Derekh*, November 2001, 95.

The Beginning of the End

> you shall be wielded over the necks of the dishonored wicked ones, for their day has come, the time set for their punishment. Return it to its sheath! In the place where you were created, in the land of your origin, I will judge you. I will pour out My indignation upon you, I will blow upon you with the fire of My wrath; and I will deliver you into the hands of barbarians, craftsmen of destruction. You shall be fuel for the fire, your blood shall sink into the earth, you shall not be remembered. (vv. 33–37)

The "sword," the "slaughter," and "divining" are all reminiscent of the prophecy earlier in the chapter; the "end," the "sheath," the "fire," and the "blood" appear in other chapters in which Ezekiel prophesies the city's impending destruction. The linguistic similarity between his prophecy to Jerusalem and his prophecies to other nations does not appear to be coincidental. We will discuss this further in the chapters addressed to the nations.

The prophecies contained in chapters 20 and 21 lend to the sense of a spiraling situation; Ezekiel prepares the nation for the impending Destruction by both recounting the deeds that led to it and depicting the sword of Nebuchadnezzar as it draws nearer. It is on this ominous note that we enter chapter 22 and its descriptions of the Destruction.

APPENDIX: NEBUCHADNEZZAR'S EXILE IN EZEKIEL'S PROPHECIES AND EXTRABIBLICAL SOURCES

Ezekiel's perception of Nebuchadnezzar's role is different from the conventional view, found primarily in Jeremiah's prophecies. Jeremiah sees Nebuchadnezzar as God's emissary, charged with implementing His universal decrees among the nations, including Judah. In contrast, Ezekiel views Nebuchadnezzar as a tool in God's hand, but in a more limited role. Nebuchadnezzar is sent by God to punish the Israelites for their sins and for their violation of their covenant with God, which have led to a desecration of God's name (17:11–14) – but Babylonia also conquered the nations that rejoiced over Israel's destruction. In our chapter, Nebuchadnezzar first chooses Jerusalem, but then turns to the children of Ammon, who had cursed Israel and celebrated their downfall. These justifications for punishment are different from those set down by Jeremiah, whose prophecy to Nebuchadnezzar (whom he calls "God's servant") broadens his role as God's emissary (Jer. 27:6–7). Jeremiah also predicts that after the conquest of Jerusalem, Babylonia's sins will bring about its own downfall (Jer. 50–51), while Ezekiel does not prophesy about the end of Nebuchadnezzar or the end of the Babylonians.

Ezekiel's silence is even more noteworthy when we compare his attitude towards Babylonia to that of Jeremiah. Jeremiah calls upon the nation of Israel to place the reins of power in the hands of the Babylonians for seventy years (ch. 25) and prophesies that instead of banding together with a view to rebelling, the people should submit to Babylonian rule (ch. 27) and even deepen their ties with Babylonia. These prophecies are uttered as part of his struggle against representatives of the Jewish leadership (ch. 36) and the false prophets in his own environs (ch. 28), who believe that the exiles in Babylonia will be back in their land within two years (ch. 29). The prophecies of Ezekiel, who now dwells in Babylonia, say nothing on this subject.

Life in the Babylonian Exile, according to Extrabiblical Sources[18]

We know of a considerable number of extrabiblical sources from the time of Nebuchadnezzar that can shed light on the Destruction and exile: a Babylonian chronicle that records the surrender of the Kingdom of Judah to Babylonia in the seventh year of the king;[19] a tablet listing the members of his court, with Nebuzaradan (Akkadian: Nabû-šarrūssu-ukīn) appearing in second place;[20] and administrative lists that were discovered

---

18. See Kathleen Abraham, "The Reconstruction of Jewish Communities in the Persian Empire: The Al-Yahudu Clay Tablets," in *Light and Shadows – The Catalog – The Story of Iran and the Jews*, ed. H. Segev and A. Schor (Tel Aviv: Beit Hatfutsot, 2001), 264–68. My thanks to Prof. Abraham for all her help in writing this appendix.
19. See Jean-Jacques Glassner, *Mesopotamian Chronicles* (Atlanta: Society of Biblical Literature, 2004) 226–35 (no. 24; r. 11'–13').
20. Nevuzaradan, the chief eunuch (in Akkadian: rab ša rēši) is listed as having sent a quantity of gold with a eunuch to the temple of the god Marduk in Babylon. Confirmation of receipt in the presence of two witnesses is recorded on the eighteenth of Shevat in the tenth year of Nebuchadnezzar (595 BCE). The tablet was publicized by Michael Jursa, "Nabû-Sarrussu-Ukin, Rab Sa-Resi, and 'Nebusarkesim' (Jer. 39:3)," *Nouvelles Assyriologiques Brèves et Utilitaires* 5 (2008), 9–10.

The Beginning of the End

in the palace of Nebuchadnezzar in Babylonia, in which Jehoiachin is recorded (with his title "King of Judah"), along with his sons and eight of his men, as receiving allowances of oil from the king's treasury.[21] In recent years, additional sources have come to light.

Until recently, the primary source for research on the day-to-day life of the Judeans in Babylonia in ancient times has been the hundreds of private legal documents from Babylonia that are still extant, mostly in the Murashu Archive. This archive belonged to a Babylonian family, and Jewish names appear in the documents, occupying different statuses (as parties to contracts and/or as witnesses to them), and thus we may conclude that they were free men. Some 163 Jewish names have been identified in the Murashu documents so far.[22] Another important source, known to scholars since the late 1990s, is the Al-Yahudu Archive, whose texts shed new light on the daily life of the exiles.[23] The archive contains almost 250 legal documents, including promissory notes, tenancies, sales of agricultural merchandise, and receipts for various payments such as rental and taxes. Of these, about fifty-five were written in Al-Yahudu ("the village of Judah"). These texts are uniquely valuable owing to the fact that they date back further than those of the Murashu Archive. The earliest document in the Al-Yahudu Archive is from 572 BCE, about twenty-five years after the first exile, predating the Murashu

---

21. This is dated in the texts to Nebuchadnezzar's second decade. See Mark William Chavalas, ed., *The Ancient Near East: Historical Sources in Translation* (Malden, MA: Blackwell, 2006), 387–88.
22. An individual appearing in a Babylonian document is considered Judean when his first name, or that of a blood relative, includes the name of God. The son of Neria, for example, is considered Judean even if his name is Zerubbabel. Most Babylonian documents are dated, and thus we are able to trace the Judeans of Babylonia from 582 BCE until 350 BCE. Since each document also notes the place where it was written, we are also able to trace their geographic distribution throughout Babylonia. See Ran Zadok, "The Jews in Babylonia During the Chaldean and Achaemenian Periods According to the Babylonian Sources," *Studies in the History of the Jewish People and the Land of Israel* 3 (Haifa: University of Haifa, 1979); idem, *The Earliest Diaspora: Israelites and Judeans in Pre-Hellenistic Mesopotamia* (Tel Aviv: Tel Aviv University, 2002). In Hebrew, see Bustenay, *Galut Yisrael VeYehuda*.
23. Laurie E. Pearce and Cornelia Wunsch, *Documents of Judean Exiles and West Semites in Babylonia in the Collection of David Sofer*, CUSAS 28 (Bethesda: CDL: Press, 2014).

Archive by roughly one hundred years. Of the names appearing in the archive, 15 percent – over one hundred names on roughly two hundred tablets – are Judean.[24]

The evidence leads us to conclude that the Judeans adapted well to the local customs and internalized Babylonian legal procedures. Their Jewish origins appear not to have influenced either the formulation or the content of the legal documents written in their name. Despite all of this, the members of this exiled community maintained their Jewish names, even though nearly a hundred years had passed since the first exile from Judah. They were absorbed into the local economy and engaged, for the most part, in agriculture, but did not become especially wealthy. The picture that arises from the sources indicates that while they integrated in the community, the exiles did not fully assimilate.

---

24. Kathleen Abraham, "An Inheritance Division among Judeans in Babylonia from the Early Persian Period," in *New Seals and Inscriptions, Hebrew, Idumean and Cuneiform*, (*Hebrew Bible Monographs* 8) ed. Meir Lubetski, (Sheffield: Sheffield Phoenix Press, 2007), 206–21. See also Ran Zadok, "Judeans in Babylonia – Updating the Dossier," in *Encounters by the Rivers of Babylon: Scholarly Conversations between Jews, Iranians and Babylonians in Antiquity*, ed. Uri Gabbay and Shai Secunda, TSAJ 160 (Tübingen: Mohr Siebeck, 2014), 109–29. As Zadok puts it, "the new material from Yahūdu almost doubles the prospographical pool from Babylonia to circa 316–320 Judeans."

Chapter 14

The Destruction of Judah and Jerusalem
Ezekiel 22:1–24:14

God's sword has been described approaching Jerusalem, held by the king of Babylonia, and the subsequent chapters prophesy what happens in the city during the siege and the Destruction: Chapter 22 addresses the sins of Jerusalem and its punishments; chapter 23 describes the treachery of the sisters Oholah (Samaria) and Oholiba (Jerusalem) against their husband (God).[1] Then, at the start of chapter 24 (vv. 1–14) Ezekiel returns to the parable of the pot.

Chapter 24 opens with a date: the tenth of Tevet, in the ninth year of the reign of Zedekiah. This was the day the siege was laid on

---

1. In chapter 23, as in chapter 16, the parable about the adulterous sisters and its interpretation intermingle. The severity of their actions is made all the more deplorable in that they betray not only their husband but also their lovers. This leads to the conclusion that disloyalty is embedded in the nation's character from even before it became a nation in Egypt. We have briefly discussed chapter 23 in chapter 11 above and will not expand further here.

Jerusalem (II Kings 25:1; Jer. 39:1; 52:4). Highlighting the date at the start of the chapter indicates that these prophecies about events taking place in Jerusalem are uttered by Ezekiel in Babylon. Once the news of the Destruction spreads, his listeners (who still doubt the veracity of his words) will know that he spoke prophetically about events in Jerusalem as they occurred. The doubters will thus conclude that "a prophet has been among them" (Ezek. 2:5; 33:33).

These chapters bring different circles to completion and sharpen the prophetic messages that have been conveyed thus far. For instance, the emphasis on the time having come (22:3) is a further development of the prophecy in chapter 7. While on one hand these chapters share common features with earlier ones (especially in the imagery of the fate of the city in chapters 4–5 and the description of the sins of its inhabitants in chapters 16 and 20), the prophecy here is conveyed with unusually powerful expressions, both in context and in substance. The prophet emphasizes the primary motifs of his prophecies in order to describe what is now occurring in the defiled city.

THE SINS OF JERUSALEM AND ITS PUNISHMENTS (CHAPTER 22)

Chapter 22 is divided into three units: verses 1–16, verses 17–22, and verses 23–31. The first and third units deal with the sins of the people, while the second focuses on the punishment. What is common to all three units is the status of Jerusalem. The prophecy concerning the imminent fate of the city resembles the destruction that Ezekiel prophesied in the past (ch. 8–11), but he no longer reacts with cries of surprise or distress, as he did earlier (9:8–9); now he is apathetic. From this point on, his pre-Destruction prophetic mission is limited to describing the situation in the city.

The description begins by presenting a city that is full of bloodshed: "O city in whose midst blood is shed" (22:3); "You stand guilty of the blood you have shed" (v. 4); "for the shedding of blood" (v. 6); "were intent on shedding blood" (v. 9); "to shed blood" (v. 13); and above all – the expression "city of bloodshed" (v. 2), an appellation that appears again only in chapter 24 (vv. 6, 9).[2]

---

2. This appellation recurs in only one other place in Tanakh: Nahum 3:1.

The Destruction of Judah and Jerusalem

Ezekiel's accusation is against all of Jerusalem's inhabitants – all classes and positions (vv. 25–30). This seems to be why the prophet repeats again and again that the actions were perpetrated within Jerusalem.[3]

Apart from bloodshed, Ezekiel mentions a broad spectrum of sins (vv. 6–12) including idolatry, sexual immorality, ritual transgressions, and moral and social corruption. The prophetic message is further amplified by the biblical warnings that echo in the background: Verse 9 should be read against the backdrop of Leviticus 19:16, and may be an instance of intra-biblical exegesis, alluding to the connection between gossip mongering and standing by the blood of the innocent. That is, it may imply that one who goes about spreading gossip will end up spilling blood.[4]

Comparing Ezekiel's images with those of other prophets also amplifies the severity of his rebuke. For instance, in verse 18, the entire nation is compared to dross,[5] and the prophetic message is that the inhabitants of Jerusalem will be killed in their own city, and will not be saved. Using the same imagery, Isaiah (1:22) expresses the opposite message: removing the dross will leave the righteous and the pursuers of justice alive in Jerusalem. Similarly, the gathering of the inhabitants of Jerusalem in the city in order to kill them (Ezek. 22:19–21) is an image that recalls Jehu, who gathered the prophets of Baal in order to annihilate them (II Kings 10). The chapter thus serves as a summary of Jerusalem's disgrace in the eyes of the nations (Ezek. 22:4, 16) and also summarizes the ramifications that the destruction will have on God's status in the eyes of the nations.

JERUSALEM

To examine the status of Jerusalem in the book of Ezekiel, let us briefly review the various appellations the prophet uses to refer to the city, along with the occasions when he mentions it by name.[6] Admittedly, God's

---

3. The word "*bah*" (in it) occurs eight times in the chapter, along with two variations (*betokha, betokhekh*).
4. See also Rashi's interpretation of verse 7: "All the abominations in the section of 'You shall be holy' (Lev. 19–20) about which they were warned, are enumerated here."
5. Dross is removed from precious metals in a melting pot (i.e., through fire).
6. The name "Jerusalem" appears in many other contexts in these chapters. In this connection, there is a significant difference between the prophecies preceding the

anger was already apparent earlier, both in the prophet's cry, "pouring out Your fury upon Jerusalem" (9:8), and in his declaration that its fate will be the opposite of that foretold by the false prophets "who prophesy about Jerusalem and see a vision of well-being for her when there is no well-being" (13:16).

Nevertheless, God's anger seems to reach a climax in chapter 22 (vv. 2–5), where Ezekiel speaks of "city of bloodshed…city in whose midst blood is shed." Likewise, he describes the worship of abominations as defiling the name of the city, such that Jerusalem is called "besmirched of name," and by the same token, in verse 24, "an uncleansed land." And because the name of Jerusalem has been defiled, the city will no longer be referred to by name, but rather by negative appellations. For instance, in chapter 24, Jerusalem is referred to again as a city of blood: "Woe to the city of blood…. For the blood she shed is still in her… Woe to the city of blood…" (24:6–9).

In the chapters of rebuilding, Ezekiel mentions Jerusalem by name only once: "As Jerusalem is filled with sacrificial sheep during her festivals, so shall the ruined cities be filled with flocks of people. And they shall know that I am the Lord" (36:38). However, the reader should note that although Ezekiel mentions the name "Jerusalem," he is not referring to the city of the future, but rather using the name as a way of describing the "holy flock" that filled the city *in the past*. In all of his other prophecies in the chapters of restoration (34–39) and in the vision of the future Temple (40–48),[7] Ezekiel refers to the city by other names.

Avoiding the name "Jerusalem" in their prophecies for the future is one example of the differences between Ezekiel, Jeremiah, and Isaiah. The name "Jerusalem" is ubiquitous in Isaiah's prophecies of redemption (Is. 41:27; 51:22; 52:1–2, 9; 62:1). But it appears only rarely in Jeremiah's prophecies of consolation (appearing mainly in Jer. 3:14–17 and chapters 30–33). In contrast, as we have noted, Ezekiel avoids using the name altogether. Perhaps this is because the actions of the nation have

---

Destruction, in which Jerusalem is mentioned by name some twenty times, and those following the Destruction, where it is not mentioned again (with one exception, discussed below).

7. See Ezekiel 40:1–4; 43:12; 48:35.

not only led to the defiling of the name, but have also caused a rupture in God's attitude towards the eternity of the city.[8]

"This City Is the Pot, and We Are the Meat" (11:2–10; 24:3–14)

Radak offers an eloquent explanation of the prophetic message behind Ezekiel's parable of the pot:

> This is what a person does with a pot: first he places it upon the stove, then fills it with water, and then places meat in it and lights a fire under it, until the meat is cooked. The placing of the pot upon the stove symbolizes the proximity of the king of Babylonia to Jerusalem, for this is the first thing he did there. The pouring of the water into it foretells that the fire will not burn it quickly, for water prevents the meat from cooking quickly: when it is without water, the fire causes it quickly to be roasted, but if there is water in it, the meat will cook slowly. Likewise, the siege lasted from the ninth year of Zedekiah until his twelfth year, with the inhabitants of the city slowly dying off from hunger, the plague, and the sword.

In addition, in his description of the pot in chapter 24 the prophet emphasizes that "no lot has fallen upon it" (24:6) – meaning that there was no lot separating the fate of those killed from those to be saved. Apparently, no one will survive.

Jerusalem is described with the words "the blood she shed is still in her" (24:7). The blood has been poured upon the rock and has not been covered – recalling that covering the blood after slaughter is a basic requirement for the blood of animals and fowl. This blood, symbolizing the bloodshed committed by the people openly and shamelessly, represents, in this chapter, the expression of the fate of this "city of blood" upon which God will pour His fury.

---

8. Some scholars maintain that the city that Ezekiel refers to (and even mentions explicitly in 45:6; 48:15, 30–35) is not Jerusalem, and that the Temple will not be located in it. For a review see Ben-Yashar, "HaMerkava BeSefer Yeḥezkel," 22f.

DEPARTURE (24:15–27)

Chapter 24 contains two accounts of loss: the loss of Ezekiel's wife[9] and the loss of the Temple. To these the prophet adds another loss – "the sons and daughters" (further to their mention in chapter 14). The connection between Ezekiel's private loss and the nation's loss of the Temple echoes in the words of the Talmud:

> R. Yoḥanan also said: He whose first wife has died [is grieved much] as if the Destruction of the Temple had taken place in his days, as it is written: "O mortal, I am about to take away the delight of your eyes from you through pestilence; but you shall not lament or weep or let your tears flow" (Ezek. 24:16). Again it is written, "In the evening my wife died… and when I spoke to the people that morning…" (v. 18). And further it is written, "I am going to desecrate My Sanctuary, your pride and glory, the delight of your eyes and the desire of your heart" (v. 21). (Sanhedrin 22a)

However, the verses also indicate clearly the difference between the two partings: while the prophet's wife is *taken* ("I am about to take away [*loke'aḥ*]…" [v. 16], using the same expression that is employed to describe the deaths of Enoch and of Elijah[10]), the Temple is *profaned* ("I am going to desecrate My Sanctuary…" v. 21). This comparison indicates that the profaning of the Temple is irreversible: in other words, the Temples that will be built after the Destruction of the First Temple represent a new creation, not a recreation of the Temple that existed.

Ezekiel is commanded not to mourn for his wife, just as Aaron is commanded not to mourn after the death of his sons (Lev. 10:6–7; similarly, Lev. 21:10–12). In both instances, the verses speak not of the impurity of the dead, but rather of mourning. In both instances the close relative of the deceased is forbidden to mourn by virtue of his public position. In the book

---

9. Rabbi Menachem ben Shimon addresses the question of how God could put the prophet's wife to death for the sake of conveying a prophetic message. His conclusion is that "God did not shorten her life; rather, it was her time to die, so she died."
10. In Tanakh, the verb L-K-Ḥ is used in the sense of "being taken (by death)" only in relation to righteous individuals: Enoch (Gen. 5:24), Elijah (II Kings 2:3), and the children of Job – "The Lord gave and the Lord has taken away" (Job 1:21).

of Leviticus, mourning violates the sanctity of the priests; if they mourn, they are not able to serve in the Sanctuary. In Ezekiel's case, mourning is forbidden because his role is to "be a portent for them" (Ezek. 24:27).[11]

Why, then, is the nation of Israel commanded not to mourn over the Temple? Perhaps it is difficult to bear the thought that the party directly responsible for the catastrophe will mourn over it when it happens. But the withholding of mourning may also represent a sort of divine punishment – or, alternatively, an act of acceptance of God's will. Rashi offers two other interpretations, and these are instructive as to the essence of mourning. In the first explanation Rashi says the people must not mourn "because you have no consolers ... and there is no mourning except where there are consolers" (Rashi, v. 22). The message here is that giving comfort is itself the essence of mourning. The mourning customs exist to highlight that state as one that is different and exceptional, which thereby draws comforters. In a large-scale catastrophe, (according to this view) there is no room for mourning, since there is no one who can offer comfort.

Rashi's second explanation is, "For you will be afraid to weep before the Chaldeans in whose midst you are." According to this view, the essence of mourning is weeping and the outward display of emotion – which can sometimes express a lack of acceptance of the situation as it is. Such a display might be interpreted by the Babylonians as a revolt against their supremacy.

This prophecy concludes Ezekiel's prophecies of rebuke uttered before the Destruction, bringing the book's first section to an end. At the same time, with the period of muteness ending, a gateway is opened to his prophecies after the Destruction:

---

11. The impression arising from a review of the mourners described in Tanakh is that there is no clear obligation to mourn. Jacob tears his garments when he believes that his son has been torn apart by wild beasts (Gen. 37:34); the Israelites weep over the death of Aaron (Num. 20:29) and over the death of Moses (Deut. 34:8). In II Samuel (3:31) David instructs the people to mourn for Abner, telling them to "rend their clothes, gird on sackcloth, and make lament [eulogize] before Abner." These descriptions suggest that mourning is a spontaneous act that also represents local custom. Nevertheless, Ḥazal (Moed Katan 15a–b) derive many of the laws of mourning from the verses of our chapter using negative induction. In other words, the actions that Ezekiel is commanded to refrain from performing become, for Ḥazal, laws that are incumbent upon the mourner.

> You, O mortal, take note: On the day that I take their stronghold from them, their pride and joy, the delight of their eyes and the longing of their hearts – their sons and daughters – on that day a fugitive will come to you, to let you hear it with your own ears. On that day your mouth shall be opened to the fugitive, and you shall speak and no longer be dumb. So you shall be a portent for them, and they shall know that I am the Lord. (vv. 25–27)

These verses are a fitting summary of this series of prophecies. Through them, the prophet now binds the past with the future; and his role as "a portent for them" with the death of his wife is bound up with the Destruction of Jerusalem, but also, in his words, with the prophecies of restoration.

APPENDIX: EZEKIEL'S PERSONAL WORLD (DOV KIMCHE)[12]

Ezekiel son of Buzi, the priest-prophet, tells us nothing about himself. This stems from a profound awareness that his own individual concerns are infinitesimally small in relation to the mission of eternity that he has taken upon himself, or which has been placed upon him by God. Throughout the narrative, we glean only small hints of who Ezekiel is.[13] Ezekiel himself shies away from autobiography. What was his life like in exile? What were his sources of joy and pain? There is not a word. He focuses only on the matter at hand, which is the great political question of the time, the young Babylonian Empire, and the most critical question of all: the future of his people within the tide of current events. That is all we know.

And yet here, all of a sudden, the prophet has a wife, and she is dear to him. She is "the delight of [his] eyes" (24:16), a beloved, precious soul of whom the prophet has made not the slightest mention up until this last moment. Now a plague breaks out in his city, in Babylonia, and she, too, dies. And since she was dear to him, he notes the date, "On the

---

12. The following is adapted from Kimche's book, *Bein HaShittin shel HaTanakh* (Jerusalem: Ahiasaf, 1941), 51–53.
13. See, for example, chapter 7, footnote 4 above.

tenth day of the tenth month" (24:1), the tenth of Tevet, a fateful day of national punishment. His short phrase is an aside, almost swallowed up in the narrative: "In the evening my wife died" (v. 18). It is as though not connected. But no, his personal tragedy is but a symbol of the national cataclysm, and the two poignant expressions, "the delight of your eyes" and a "desire of your heart" (v. 21), which could well express his intimate relationship with his wife, refer to what is to follow: Jerusalem, about to perish in a plague. Nevertheless, we are touched by this hint of human emotion behind the prophetic mask.

Section II

Prophecies Concerning the Nations

Ezekiel's second section, comprised of chapters 25–32, contains prophecies about the nations. Concentrated in a single continuum, the prophecies are located between the prophecies of rebuke and destruction and those of restoration. This placement is no minor matter. A similar collection of prophecies for the nations is found in other prophetic books (Is. 13–23; Jer. 46–51; Amos 1–2). Their purpose: to lay the foundation for Israel's restoration. Israel's restoration will cause the all the nations to recognize the unique transcendence and absolute control of of the God of Israel; it will counter the desecration of His name among the nations which reached its nadir in the Destruction and exile. The prevailing idea in the Ancient East that kings were emissaries of the gods (or even gods themselves) and that gods ensured military victory is countered here with the compilation of the prophecies about the nations; it emphasizes that God, Lord of the entire world, decides the fate of each and every nation.

Unlike the prophecies addressed to other nations by other prophets, these chapters make scant mention of Israel's restoration, with the exception of two brief prophetic units (in the prophecies to Tyre and Egypt).

Section II

The prophecies in these chapters are devoted to seven nations: Ammon, Moab (and Seir), Edom, Philistines, Tyre, Sidon, and Egypt (the number seven may express the wholeness of God's supremacy over the world; it is also repeated in Ezekiel's prophecy to Egypt). The order of the prophecies to the nations is not chronological. The first, to Egypt (29:1–15) was conveyed prior to the prophecy to Tyre (26:1–6), and the prophecy with the latest date (29:17–21) is not the last one in the collection. Perhaps they are ordered by geographical location, starting from the east, and then moving along the coastline to the west: the prophecies in chapter 25 speak of Ammon, Moab, Seir, Edom, and the Philistines; chapters 26–28 address Tyre and Sidon; and chapters 29–32 focus on Egypt. Alternatively, the order of prophecies may be related to their content: the prophet begins with the nations' reactions to the Destruction (Ammon, Moab, Seir, Edom, Philistines); then he speaks at greater length to Tyre and Egypt, whose status at the time of the Destruction represented a real challenge of faith for the nation of Israel. Rather conspicuous is the absence of any prophecy for Babylonia, which actually destroyed the Temple (as discussed previously; this recalls Isaiah's addresses to the nations, which contains no words for Assyria, which exiled Israel at the time).

Chapter 15
Brief Prophecies Concerning the Nations
Ezekiel 25:1–17

In chapter 25, Ezekiel conveys brief prophecies concerning Ammon, Moab, Edom, and the Philistines, each of which has a lengthy historical relationship with Israel.[1] These prophecies share a uniform structure: The sin is detailed using the word "*ya'an*" ("because" or "since"); the punishment is described beginning with the word "*lakhen*" ("therefore" or "assuredly"); and this is followed by a concluding message, "they shall know that I am the Lord" – which is clearly the purpose of the prophecy as a whole (see the chart below for a detailed comparison).

---

1. In this respect, too, Babylonia is different from the other nations addressed by Ezekiel in these chapters, since Babylonia has no long common history with Israel. From this perspective, as from many others, including the substance of the sins of the nations that are mentioned, this chapter is similar to Amos 1–2.

AMMON (25:1–7)

The word of God that comes to Ezekiel begins as follows: "O mortal, set your face toward the Ammonites and prophesy against them. Say to the Ammonites: Hear the word of the Lord God" (25:2–3). This preamble is unique to the prophecy to Ammon. The multiple introductory expressions ("set your face," "say," "hear") seem to serve as a transition between the first part of the book and the second, an indication that the content of the prophecy changes at this point.

Whether the order of the prophecies here is geographical or related to content, Ammon may be the nation that appears first because the two prophecies to Ammon in our chapter (vv. 1–5 and 6–7) complement the previous prophecy to Ammon, in chapter 21 (vv. 33–37). Alternatively, Ammon may be first because of the severity of the prophet's accusation – their rejoicing over the fall of Israel, which is depicted twice in these verses: once through their cries of joy, and again through their clapping of hands and stamping of feet.[2] Perhaps another technique that Ezekiel adopts in his efforts to depict the disdain of Ammon is his use of the word "*she'at*," a term unique to the book of Ezekiel, denoting scorn.[3]

A similar depiction of Ammon's attitude towards Israel is found in Zephaniah's prophecy:

> I have heard...the jeers of the Ammonites, who have insulted My people and gloated over their country. Assuredly...and the Ammonites like Gomorrah: Clumps of weeds and patches of salt, and desolation evermore. The remnant of My people shall plunder them, the remainder of My nation shall possess them. That

---

2. *He'ah*, "Aha!" here expresses schadenfreude (likewise in vv. 3 and 6 of our chapter, and again in the prophecy to Tyre –26:2 – and in the description of Israel's enemies in general [36:2]). This is a contrast to *ah*, expressing the prophet's own sorrow of the sins of the people (6:11). Similarly, we must distinguish between the clapping of hands in our chapter, expressing pleasure over the downfall of Israel, and the clapping by means of which the prophet conveys God's sorrow over the Destruction of Jerusalem (6:11; 21:19, 22; 22:13).
3. The word appears six times throughout the book. Two appearances are in our chapter, in verses 6 and 15; it also appears in 16:57; 28:24, 26; and 36:5. The word is also part of the Akkadian language: šâṭu (meaning scorn). See Menachem Zvi Kaddari, *Milon HaIvrit HaMikrait* (Ramat Gan: Bar-Ilan University Press, 5766), 1066.

is what they'll get for their haughtiness, for insulting and jeering at the people of the Lord of Hosts. (Zeph. 2:8–10)[4]

The many years of Ammon's scorn towards Israel may be the reason that Ezekiel introduces his prophecies to the nations by foretelling the destruction and downfall of Ammon. The transition between the first and second parts of the book is indirectly shown here through the content of the prophecy to Ammon, too: their joy over the desecration of the Temple and the desolation of the land and the exile of the inhabitants of Judah serve to define the book's transition to the post-Destruction prophecies.

In response to Ammon's glee, Ezekiel prophesies their annihilation. Further indications of the context are found in Jeremiah's attitude towards the relationship between Israel and Ammon. His prophecy indicates some degree of fear that Ammon would conquer the land: "Concerning the Ammonites. Thus said the Lord: Has Israel no sons, Has he no heir? Then why has Milcom dispossessed Gad, and why have his people settled in Gad's towns?" (Jer. 49:1).

Against the backdrop of this fear, we gain a better understanding of the importance of Ezekiel's prophetic message to Ammon, including its destruction.[5]

MOAB AND SEIR (25:8–11)

For Moab, the Destruction represents proof that Israel is a nation like any other. Moab has an ongoing conflict with the children of Israel, extending back to the period of the wilderness, when Balaam was enlisted to curse them. The inclusion of Seir along with Moab in this brief prophetic unit is rather surprising, since elsewhere in Tanakh (as well as in Ezekiel 35:3 and 15), Seir is usually mentioned along with Edom. Opinions are divided as to the geographic location of Seir; it would seem to be in the southern Negeb region.

---

4. This description accords with the humiliation of Israel at the hands of Ammon described in I Samuel 11:2.
5. The prophet mentions Ammon again in verse 10, at the end of the next prophecy about Moab, and emphasizes that Ammon will not be remembered among the nations. It is possible that verses 10–11 represent a concluding unit for verses 1–11, which explains why Ammon is once again mentioned.

The Moab prophecy follows immediately after Ammon; the reason for this may relate to the idolatrous influence that both nations had on Israel. This had already begun filtering into Israel during the time of Solomon and had thus become implanted deeply in the Temple from its very inception: "At that time, Solomon built a shrine for Chemosh the abomination of Moab on the hill near Jerusalem, and one for Molech the abomination of the Ammonites" (I Kings 11:7).

The Temple's destruction in the days of Ezekiel's prophecy therefore, to a great extent, brings an end to the direct and indirect influence that nations had exerted over Jerusalem for many years.[6]

EDOM (25:12–14)

The prophecy to Edom is concise and proportionate: God repays the vengeance of Edom on Israel. Although the relationship between the two nations had its ups and downs over the years, Edom has systematically harmed Israel throughout its existence. Another prophecy is devoted to Edom in chapter 35, within the prophecies of restoration, and there the prophet deals with the long-term ramifications of the hostility between Edom and Israel (with its roots in the relationship between Jacob and Esau, as we will see).

THE PHILISTINES (25:15–17)

Like the other nations addressed in this chapter, the Philistines, too, have an age-old relationship with the Israelites. In fact, the Philistines determined the location of the country's southwestern border for many years. It would seem that it is for this reason that the prophet emphasizes that the Philistines will disappear, and the coastline that they controlled will no longer be under their rule. The prophet thus indirectly ties the fate of the Philistines to the expansion of Israel's southern border. The long

---

6. In contrast to Ezekiel, Isaiah (ch. 15–16) and Jeremiah (ch. 48) record lengthy prophecies about Moab. The discrepancy between the respective lengths of the prophetic units devoted to Moab by the different prophets may perhaps symbolize the fact that the prophecies in Isaiah and Jeremiah (which overlap partially) are profoundly bound up with the geographical areas in which they were uttered (a phenomenon made even more prominent by the proliferation of names of places and areas). The conciseness of Ezekiel's message, in contrast, reflects the distance from which Ezekiel addresses Moab.

and convoluted relationship between these nations, and perhaps the sharp words of revenge that Ezekiel hurls at the Philistines, are related to Israel's wars with them, which began in the days of Samson at the end of the book of Judges.

A UNIFORM STRUCTURE AND MESSAGE

The prophecies, as noted earlier, follow a uniform structure in this chapter, each with the same four elements and similar language:

Ammon 1	*Ammon 2*	*Moab and Seir*	*Edom*	*Philistines*
Thus said the Lord God	For thus said the Lord God	Thus said the Lord God	Thus said the Lord God	Thus said the Lord God
Because you cried "Aha!" over My Sanctuary when it was desecrated, and over the Land of Israel when it was laid waste, and over the House of Judah when it went into exile –	Because you clapped your hands and stamped your feet and rejoiced over the Land of Israel with such utter scorn –	Because Moab and Seir said, "See, the House of Judah is like all other nations"	Because Edom acted vengefully against the House of Judah and incurred guilt by wreaking revenge upon it	Because the Philistines, in their ancient hatred, acted vengefully, and with utter scorn sought revenge and destruction

Ezekiel 25:1–17

Ammon 1	Ammon 2	Moab and Seir	Edom	Philistines
assuredly, I will deliver you to the Kedemites as a possession. They shall set up their encampments among you and pitch their dwellings in your midst; they shall eat your produce and they shall drink your milk. I will make Rabbah a pasture for camels and Ammon a place for sheep to lie down.	assuredly, I will stretch out My hand against you and give you as booty to the nations; I will cut you off from among the peoples and wipe you out from among the countries and destroy you.	assuredly, I will lay bare the flank of Moab, all its towns to the last one –Beth-jeshimoth, Baal-meon, and Kiriathaim, the glory of the country. I will deliver it, together with Ammon, to the Kedemites as their possession. Thus Ammon shall not be remembered among the nations, and I will mete out punishments to Moab.	assuredly, thus said the Lord God: I will stretch out My hand against Edom and cut off from it man and beast, and I will lay it in ruins; from Tema to Dedan they shall fall by the sword. I will wreak My vengeance on Edom through My people Israel, and they shall take action against Edom in accordance with My blazing anger;	assuredly, thus said the Lord God: I will stretch out My hand against the Philistines and cut off the Cherethites and wipe out the last survivors of the seacoast. I will wreak frightful vengeance upon them by furious punishment;

Ammon 1	Ammon 2	Moab and Seir	Edom	Philistines
And you shall know that I am the Lord.	And you shall know that I am the Lord.	And they shall know that I am the Lord.	And they shall know My vengeance, declares the Lord God.	and when I inflict My vengeance upon them, they shall know that I am the Lord.

The uniform structure brings home the same message time and again – God's words to the different nations is meant to ensure that ultimately they will all recognize His supremacy.

Chapter 16
Prophecies to Tyre
Ezekiel 26:1–28:26

The nations of Tyre and Egypt (treated in the next chapter) differed from the other nations to whom Ezekiel prophesied: They were not always in conflict with Israel. On the contrary, they were occasionally allies. Perhaps this is why the prophet treats them at greater length than he does the other nations. In this way he addresses the uniqueness of Israel while also, indirectly, addresses the complicated relationship between Israel and these nations. A longer prophecy may also be devoted here specifically to the nations whose existence represents an indirect challenge to the eternity of Israel.

TYRE AND SIDON

Ezekiel devotes no less than three chapters to his prophecy concerning Tyre (26–28:19), concluding with a brief prophecy addressed to Sidon (28:20–24). The scope of this prophecy suggests that Ezekiel takes a special interest in Tyre: His message is longer than parallel prophecies made by other prophets. Perhaps Tyre's extraordinary economic success

Ezekiel 26:1–28:26

during this period and its withstanding the prolonged Babylonian siege represented a challenge to Ezekiel's prophecies.

The prophecy to Tyre starts with a reference to the date – the eleventh year of Jehoiachin's exile, the first of the month (which month is not noted). Many of Ezekiel's prophecies to the nations note their date (about half of all the dates mentioned in the book are linked to prophecies to the nations), and most indicate that they are close to the time of the Destruction. Perhaps these prophecies have a proliferation of dates because they are ordered thematically, in contrast to all the other prophecies in the book which appear in chronological order.

Tyre: Historical Background[1]

Until the era of Alexander the Great, Tyre lay between Acre and Sidon on an island located at a distance of a few hundred meters from the coast; during the biblical period, it was accessible solely by boat. It was only during the time of Alexander the Great that a connecting embankment was created and gradually built up over the years.

The people of Tyre seem to be a very ancient nation (Is. 23:7), mentioned in Egyptian execration texts. If Philo of Byblos (a Greek Phoenician writer of the first and second centuries CE) is correct, it was the people of Tyre who invented boats, and their advanced commerce was widely admired in ancient times.

Tyre was an economic and cultural power throughout the duration of the Israelite kingdom. This was the source of various problems: starting from the time of Solomon, who went after the gods of Sidon (I Kings 11:5), via Ahab, who married Jezebel, who was responsible for the introduction of idolatry throughout the Israelite kingdom (I Kings 16), up until the time of Nehemiah, after the return from Babylonia, when commercial cooperation between Israel and Tyre presented a challenge to Shabbat observance (Neh. 13:16–22). All of this may explain

---

1. The background presented here is taken partially from H. Jacob Katzenstein, *The History of Tyre: From the Beginning of the Second Millennium B.C.E. until the Fall of the Neo-Babylonian Empire in 538 C.E.* (Beer Sheva: Ben-Gurion University of the Negev Press, 1997).

Prophecies to Tyre

why Ezekiel devotes such a long prophecy to Tyre. Other prophets who address Tyre include Isaiah (ch. 23), Joel (4:4–8), and Amos (1:9).

Despite these problems, there were periods when positive ties prevailed between Israel and Tyre. Examples include the building of David's house by emissaries from Tyre (II Sam. 11–12) and Huram's assistance in building the Temple (II Chr. 2–7).[2] It seems that the Israel-Tyre connection was bound up over the years with the royal house and, especially, with the Temple. The topics of Ezekiel's prophecy to Tyre are not limited to events that took place during his own lifetime, but rather reflect the substantial and long-term relationship described above.

During the period of Ezekiel's prophecies, Tyre was a kingdom ruled by Ithobaal III (591–573 BCE), and shared an anti-Babylonian policy with the neighboring nations of the region. Jeremiah (27:3) provides a hint of its involvement in this policy, suggesting that Tyre, together with Zedekiah, king of Judah, and other nations, formed an alliance against Babylonia. In view of this threat, Nebuchadnezzar journeyed to the region and laid siege to Tyre for thirteen years (585–572 BCE). While Jerusalem was conquered by the Babylonians, Tyre withstood the siege throughout the period of the Babylonian Empire. The steadfastness of Tyre in contrast with the Destruction of the Temple served to compound the psychological difficulty facing the inhabitants of Jerusalem: now, God's status in the eyes of the nations had sunk to even greater depths. Not only had the god of the Babylonians seemingly prevailed over the God of Israel, but there seemed to be a different god, one that watched over Tyre and was even stronger than the Babylonians. In effect, Nebuchadnezzar's conquest of Jerusalem proved to the nations what they had wanted to demonstrate – the weakness of the God of Israel. This challenge of faith, and the desecration of God's name among the nations, are apparently the reason for the length and vehemence of the prophecy to Tyre.

The Sin and Its Punishment (Chapter 26)

The prophecy to Tyre begins with a description of the kingdom's joy over the Destruction of the Temple, in a manner reminiscent of the prophecy

---

2. This assistance continued despite the fact that Huram was dissatisfied with the compensation for his efforts; I Kings 9:10–14.

to Ammon (ch. 25): "Because Tyre gloated over Jerusalem, 'Aha! The gateway of the peoples is broken, it has become mine; I shall be filled, now that it is laid in ruins'" (26:2). In this prophecy, as in earlier ones, the prophet interweaves the allegory and its meaning. The substance of his prophetic message concerning the downfall of Tyre is connected to the form, with images that are characteristic of and unique to Ezekiel. Ezekiel's style, as we have previously noted, entails explanations (or interpretations) of analogies and images that must be sought within the analogy itself, since the actual reality emerges within the allegoric description. Thus the prophecy of the punishment awaiting Tyre comes in the form of a sea analogy, fitting for a nation that lives by the sea:

> I will hurl many nations against you, as the sea hurls its waves. They shall destroy the walls of Tyre and demolish her towers; and I will scrape her soil off her and leave her a naked rock. She shall be in the heart of the sea a place for drying nets; for I have spoken it – declares the Lord God. She shall become spoil for the nations, and her daughter-towns in the country shall be put to the sword. And they shall know that I am the Lord. (26:3–6)

The Babylonian Conquest of Tyre: An Unrealized Prediction

Ezekiel attributes the downfall of Tyre to the king of Babylonia: "I will bring from the north, against Tyre, King Nebuchadrezzar of Babylon, a king of kings" (v. 7). Nebuchadnezzar conquers Tyre using horsemen and chariots that surround the city and an earthen rampart that is built against its walls. When the walls begin to collapse, the horsemen complete the work of destruction: The walls and houses are shattered, the city is plundered and covered with water. Ultimately, the city becomes a heap of ruins. The result is described in real terms – "I will put an end to the murmur of your songs, and the sound of your lyres shall be heard no more" (v. 13) – but it is also seen from the divine perspective: "I will make you a naked rock, You shall be a place for drying nets; You shall never be rebuilt. For I have spoken – declares the Lord God" (v. 14). To this description the prophet adds the lamentation of the leaders of the local islands over the destruction of Tyre (vv. 15–18). From these lamentations we deduce the status of Tyre prior to its conquest: "O renowned city!

Prophecies to Tyre

Mighty on the sea were she and her inhabitants, who cast their terror on all its inhabitants" (v. 17). The final end of Tyre, which likewise integrates allegory and reality, describes its descent to the depths of the sea forever:

> Then I will bring you down, with those who go down to the Pit, to the people of old. I will install you in the netherworld, with those that go down to the Pit, like the ruins of old, so that you shall not be inhabited and shall not radiate splendor in the land of the living. I will make you a horror, and you shall cease to be; you shall be sought, but shall never be found again – declares the Lord God. (vv. 20–21)

This evocative description, however, is one that never materialized; as noted, Tyre withstood its siege.

The Boat and Its Demise (Chapter 27)

In chapter 27, Ezekiel provides a detailed description of Tyre as a ship at sea, with sophisticated equipment (27:3–9) as well as military strength (vv. 10–11), which allows it to trade with many countries and ensures its key position in international commerce through involvement in many different manufacturing and commercial spheres (vv. 12–25).[3] But the description of Tyre's greatness is abruptly cut short. In a sharp reversal, which is also part of the prophetic message, Ezekiel describes the sinking of the ship of Tyre (vv. 26–27) and the lamentation of the people of Tyre who dwell on this ship and on the islands around it (vv. 29–36). The detail with which the prophet describes the power of Tyre creates a false impression. Despite the long elaboration of the prophecy, there is in fact a lack of clarity in Ezekiel as to the state of Tyre during the years of the Destruction. This may stem from a desire to separate the written prophecy from its concrete historical or political context, thereby conveying a timeless message.

---

3. An overall view of Tyre's extensive commercial ties is presented on a map that appears in the *Daat Mikra* edition of Ezekiel (Moskowitz, *Sefer Yeḥezkel*, 207). The map shows the countries with which Tyre maintained commercial ties, as well as the merchandise that each of these countries produced.

King and Temple, Tyre and Jerusalem (28:1–19)

Chapter 28 includes two prophecies to the king of Tyre. At the center of the first prophecy stands the godly pride of Tyre's prince and God's response to it (28:1–10), while at the center of the second prophecy is the pride of the king who is compared to a cherub banished from Eden. The images that Ezekiel uses in this prophecy are surprising ("I created you as a cherub with outstretched shielding wings; and you resided on God's holy mountain" v.14). Tyre – which, from the earliest history of the Israelite monarchy maintained commercial ties with it – has grown arrogant to the point where it has presumed itself above the Lord God of Israel.[4]

First we learn of the presumptuousness of the king of Tyre: "Because you have been so haughty and have said, 'I am a god; I sit enthroned like a god in the heart of the seas,' whereas you are not a god but a man, though you deemed your mind equal to a god's" (v. 2). This description vividly illustrates the ongoing battle waged by the Jewish prophets against the pagan worldview. The pagan view, with the king as a god – or, at the very least, the god's exclusive representative – is easily discerned in the description of his great wealth. The divine view, in contrast, regards the king as a messenger or agent of God and therefore subject to His laws and commandments, like everyone else – which is reflected, inter alia, in the prohibition on accumulating excessive wealth or too many wives or horses.

The final part of the lamentation over the fall of the king of Tyre in chapter 28 describes the fall of he who dwells in "Eden the garden of God" (v. 13). In this section Ezekiel mentions the temples of Tyre:

> By the greatness of your guilt, through the dishonesty of your trading, you desecrated your sanctuaries. So I made a fire issue from you, and it has devoured you; I have reduced you to ashes on the ground, in the sight of all who behold you. (v. 18)

---

4. The translations and midrashim grapple with this world of imagery and its relationship with that of the Torah. See Rimon Kasher, *Yeḥezkel 25–48*, *Mikra LeYisrael* (Tel Aviv: Am Oved/Magnes, 2004), 558–61, appendix VII; see also Ilana Goldberg, "HaItzuv HaOmanuti shel HaKina al Melekh Tzor," *Tarbiz* 58, no. 2 (1989): 277–81, who suggests that the lamentation should be understood through its structural completeness.

Prophecies to Tyre

This is a unique occurrence; nowhere else in the book of Ezekiel is any mention made of foreign sanctuaries.[5] Even this source offers little information about Tyre's sanctuaries. The literal meaning of the term "your sanctuaries" itself is not clear. The term appears here in the plural, and perhaps Ezekiel is indeed speaking of a number of sanctuaries that existed in Tyre, not just one. Alternatively, there may, in fact, be only one such sanctuary, and the plural is used to refer collectively to all of its contents.[6]

Either way, the explicit reference to desecration of Tyre's sanctuary is unusual, and finds no parallel in Ezekiel's prophecies to the other nations. Since it is difficult to imagine that Ezekiel views the sanctuary of Tyre – a place of idolatry – as a holy site that has been defiled, perhaps his description is meant to convey something of the way in which this sanctuary is perceived by the nations. Indeed, Ezekiel emphasizes the personal dimension of the people of Tyre: "By the greatness of your guilt, through the dishonesty of your trading, you desecrated your sanctuaries" – it is the king of Tyre's iniquities that have caused the defilement of his sanctuary. Therefore, no comparison should be drawn between the sanctity and defilement attributed to the Temple in Jerusalem and the parallel expressions referring to the sanctuary of Tyre. The reason for which the sanctuary in Tyre is defiled (commerce) is likewise different from the causes of the Destruction in Jerusalem (primarily idolatry). This may also explain why the punishment for defilement of Tyre's sanctuary is included within the description of the fate awaiting Tyre as a whole: "All

---

5. In the whole of Tanakh there is only one other mention of a sanctuary that is not the Temple (or *Mishkan*) – and this sanctuary is not even desecrated. It belongs to Moab: "And when it has become apparent that Moab has gained nothing in the outdoor shrine, he shall come to pray in his temple – but to no avail" (Is. 16:12). The glory of this sanctuary is reminiscent of that of Solomon's Temple.
6. Support for the possibility that the prophet is speaking of a single sanctuary is found in 21:7 – "O mortal, set your face toward Jerusalem and proclaim against her sanctuaries and prophesy against the Land of Israel." Here the prophet is speaking of the Temple in Jerusalem, yet he uses the plural (see likewise in Leviticus 21:23). In contrast, Moskowitz, *Sefer Yeḥezkel*, 222 interprets Ezekiel's expression "defiled your sanctuaries" in a non-literal way, such that "your sanctuaries" means "your sanctity." Thus, the verse is not referring to a specific temple or to actual sanctuaries, but rather to sanctity in the general sense.

who knew you among the peoples are appalled at your doom. You have become a horror and have ceased to be, forever" (v. 19).

SIDON (28:20–24)

Sidon was an ancient Canaanite port city on the coast to the north of Tyre. It is a major city in Tanakh, both because it is one of the earliest cities in Canaan and because of the history that it shares with Israel. As early as the days of Joshua, Sidon already marked the northern border of the territory conquered by Israel upon entering the land (Josh. 11:8; 19:28), and in fact it was never inhabited by Israelites. It is therefore possible that this prophecy contains an echo of the historical accounting that concludes with God's destruction of Sidon. If this is the case, it comes as no surprise that in Ezekiel's brief prophecy to Sidon he emphasizes that the purpose of God's word is to cause the people of Sidon to recognize Him:

> I am going to deal with you, O Sidon. I will gain glory in your midst; and they shall know that I am the Lord, when I wreak punishment upon her and show Myself holy through her. I will let pestilence loose against her and bloodshed into her streets. And the slain shall fall in her midst when the sword comes upon her from all sides. And they shall know that I am the Lord. Then shall the House of Israel no longer be afflicted with prickling briers and lacerating thorns from all the neighbors who despise them; and they shall know that I am the Lord God. (28:22–24)

In addition to the purpose of the prophecy, Ezekiel also notes the anticipated result: a sanctification of God's name in the eyes of the nations, after God punishes Sidon.

THE NATIONS' JUDGMENT PRIOR TO THE INGATHERING OF ISRAEL (28:25–26)

Ezekiel's prophecy to Tyre and to Sidon ends with the ingathering of Israel in its land. This does not appear to be an afterthought; it is, rather, an essential component, a conclusion that completes the prophecies of destruction to the nations. The sanctification of God's name in the eyes of the nations begins with their downfall, but it will not be visible and clear until God gathers His nation together. Although the end of the prophecy refers to Israel, it should not be viewed as a prophecy of consolation addressed to Israel; rather, it is the finale of the prophecies of destruction addressed to the nations:

> When I have gathered the House of Israel from the peoples among which they have been dispersed, and have shown Myself holy through them in the sight of the nations, they shall settle on their own soil, which I gave to My servant Jacob, and they shall dwell on it in security. They shall build houses and plant vineyards, and shall dwell on it in security, when I have meted out punishment to all those about them who despise them. And they shall know that I the Lord am their God. (vv. 25–26)

The prophecy does not include elements of consolation and redemption other than the image of God's people dwelling safely and prosperously in their land.

Chapter 17
Prophecies to Egypt
Ezekiel 29:1–32:32

Egypt's long-term stability in the region, its geographic proximity, and its historic connection with Israel form the foundation of these prophecies. The prophet points an accusing finger at Egypt in three arenas.

The first and most central accusation, common to Tyre and Egypt, is the sin of arrogance towards God. The kings of Tyre and of Egypt pride themselves on their successes, boasting about them and scorning the God of Israel (Tyre in 27:3; 28:2; Egypt in 29:9; 31:2). Ezekiel therefore emphasizes God's rule: Even when the Temple is in ruins and God's nation is exiled, it is God who determines the fate of all nations, including Egypt, and its king.

The second accusation concerns the king of Egypt's pride in his political successes. The essence of this prophecy is directed towards the king of Egypt (Pharaoh Apries) who, during this period, exerted great efforts to banish Babylonian influence from the area. He wished for Jerusalem to join him in his rebellion against Babylon.[1] We thus find,

---

1. See Danel Kahn, "Yehuda bein Bavel LeMitzrayim (594–586 BCE)," *Shnaton LeḤeker HaMikra VeHaMizraḥ HaKadum* 17 (2007): 147–59.

Ezekiel 29:1–32:32

at the beginning of the prophecy (29:6–9), that the backing Pharaoh gave to the rebellion against the king of Babylon is what prompted the prophecy of punishment. In fact, this was a period when Egypt hoped to become a superpower with influence beyond the region, following the fall of Assyria and prior to Babylon reaching its zenith. Ezekiel's prophecies put an end to this, not only in the worldly realm, but also from the divine perspective. From now on, as in the past, Egypt would be a "lowly kingdom," and not an empire.

Finally, Egypt is accused of the religious harlotry that infiltrated Israel.

All three issues are part of Egypt and Israel's joint history, going back to the period of Israelite slavery. In describing the faithlessness of Jerusalem, Ezekiel describes it as having played the harlot with Egypt, as part of its betrayal of God (16:26; 23:3, 8, 19, 21, 27), and the deeds of the people are described as "the fetishes of Egypt" (*gilulei Mitzrayim*) (20:7, 18). On the other hand, their common history also includes positive elements: Egypt is the furnace in which the nation of Israel was forged, the place of God's revelation to His people (20:5–6), the place from which He brought them out for His name's sake (20:9–10, 36).

DATES OF THE PROPHECIES

Ezekiel notes many different dates in his prophecy to Egypt. The inclusion of these days may serve to attest to Ezekiel's status even before the Destruction: They emphasize that Ezekiel prophesied, in advance, that Egypt would fall into the hands of Nebuchadnezzar, at a time when such a scenario seemed impossible to the exiles.

Ezekiel 29:1–16

According to the date at the beginning of the prophecy, it was uttered during the tenth year of Jehoiachin's exile, on the twelfth of Tevet. This means that it came at the beginning of the year 587 BCE, a year after the beginning of the siege on Jerusalem, and about a year prior to the Destruction. Some scholars connect the date of this prophecy to Jeremiah 37:5: "The army of Pharaoh had set out from Egypt; and when the Chaldeans who were besieging Jerusalem heard the report, they raised the siege of Jerusalem." If so, then Ezekiel, like Jeremiah, was speaking out against relying on Egyptian power,[2] even though the Egyptian intervention did lead to the removal of the Babylonian siege on the city, at least briefly. Nevertheless, Ezekiel does not explicitly mention Nebuchadnezzar, king of Babylon, as the figure who will punish Egypt (29:19; 30:10, 24–25; 32:11) for its intervention in Judah during the years of the siege on Jerusalem. And indeed – Egypt was not ultimately conquered by the Babylonians.

Ezekiel 29:17–21

As we have noted, this is the latest date mentioned in the book of Ezekiel. The content of this prophecy is rather unusual: Egypt will be given into the hand of the king of Babylon as recompense for Tyre not having fallen into his hands. While the might of Tyre is described at length, we have seen that the prophecy concerning Egypt annuls, to some extent, Ezekiel's previous prophecy of punishment to Tyre, where he foretold that it would fall to the Babylonians. Indeed, according to historical records, the Babylonian siege on Tyre continued for thirteen years (585–572 BCE) and concluded without a conquest by Nebuchadnezzar, such that in effect there was no clear outcome. However, even this "alternative" prophecy presents a problem: According to the historical records, Ezekiel's prophecy was not realized. Babylon never actually conquered Egypt; Egypt was conquered for the first time only in the year 525, by Cambyses king of Persia.

Ezekiel 30:20–26

The date of this prophecy is approximately four months prior to the Destruction. Indeed, its content accords with its date. It is possible that this prophecy is meant to complement Jeremiah's description (Jer. 34:21) of Pharaoh emerging to help Jerusalem, but suffering defeat at the hands of the Babylonians. Against the backdrop of this defeat, Ezekiel foretells an even greater downfall for Egypt in the future (vv. 22–25), and, consequently, Egypt is unable to save Jerusalem from the Babylonians.

---

2. See Kasher, *Yeḥezkel 25–48*, 570.

Ezekiel 31

This prophecy is uttered about two months after the previous one, with another two months left until the Destruction. It includes God's message both to the children of Israel and to the nations in anticipation of the Destruction: even though what is happening to God's people and His land now causes the kings and their gods to be arrogant, their pride will be short-lived, and they will eventually go down to Sheol.

THE GREAT CROCODILE AND ITS DOWNFALL (29:3–9; 32:1–16)[3]

The king of Egypt is compared to a crocodile that is captured by God, and his Nile dried up (29:10; 32:2–3). This description engages in a covert polemic against the ancient Egyptian belief in the crocodile as one of the major gods in the Egyptian pantheon. Extrabiblical sources speak of crocodile worship in Egypt, including sanctifying it during its life and embalming and burying it in special cemeteries after death. These sources also paint a picture of the king of Egypt as a crocodile ruling over the rivers of Egypt, as the god who created the rivers, and even as having created himself. Thus, Ezekiel combines the crocodile who was part of the Egyptian natural environment with the crocodile as a mythological creature. The prophecy concludes with a graphic description of the quiet and barrenness after the Nile subsides (32:13–14).

THE DAY OF THE LORD AND THE DOWNFALL OF EGYPT (CHAPTERS 30–32)

In these chapters, Egypt's downfall is described as part of a broader group of events. The imminent "day of the Lord" (30:2–3) is the definitive moment, and it comes about through Nebuchadnezzar, king of Babylonia (v. 10).[4] The fact that the prophecy about the day of the Lord is the only prophetic unit in this series that is not introduced by any date perhaps conveys the message that the it transcends time. Thereafter, the

---

3. See Joseph Braslavy, "Sofo shel Paro: HaTanim HaGadol LeOr Pulḥan HaTanim BeMitzrayim (Yeḥezkel 29:32)," *Beit Mikra* 18, no. 2 (1973): 143–49.
4. For more on the day of the Lord in the book of Ezekiel, see Kasher, *Yeḥezkel 25–48*, 589–90, appendix VIII.

prophecy describes the inhabitants dying by the sword, the Nile drying up, and Egypt with all its cities being left desolate.

The description of the destruction of Egypt (vv. 13–19) is emphasized through the group of twelve verbs comprising the message in these six verses: "destroy," "put an end to," "be no more," "desolate," "set fire to," "work judgments," "pour out fury," "cut off," "be convulsed," "readily breached," "fall by the sword," and "break."[5] Different elements are emphasized in the repeated descriptions, in various prophecies, of the fall of Egypt: First there is military defeat (30:2–26), depicted as the "breaking of the arm" of its king (vv. 21, 22, 24, 25) as opposed to the "strengthening of the arm" of the king of Babylon (vv. 24, 25); afterwards there is the loss of its status, the end of its pride, and its descent to Sheol (ch. 31). These aspects arise from within the interweaving of analogy and interpretation in depicting the trees of the "garden of God" (31:8), "all the trees of Eden envied it in the garden of God" (v. 9), "the trees of Eden" (vv. 16, 18), and contrasting them with the pagan "Sheol" that awaits Egypt. There is also lamentation over the death of the crocodile (32:1–16), symbolizing the fall of Pharaoh, king of Egypt, which is now placed in even sharper focus through the contrast between God's power and Pharaoh's nothingness. Finally, we read a description of Pharaoh's own descent to Sheol (vv. 17–32).

Here end the prophecies to the nations; their future downfall predicted, their recognition of the God of Israel secured, Ezekiel now turns to a new subject: the future restoration of the people.

---

5. See Moshe Greenberg, *Ezekiel 21–37*, The Anchor Bible (Garden City, NY: Doubleday, 1983), 628.

Section III

Post-Destruction Prophecies

The third section of Ezekiel consists of the prophecies concerning Israel's restoration. It is composed of two distinct parts: the first (ch. 33–39) relates to the events leading up to the prophecy regarding the future Temple; the second (ch. 40–48) express a vision of the future Temple.

The first of these chapters begins with the role of the prophet and the change in his status brought about by the Destruction (ch. 33). In the prophecies that follow, Ezekiel speaks to different audiences: the Jewish leaders in the Diaspora, whom he accuses of exploiting and abandoning the people (ch. 34); the mountains of Edom, to which he directs prophecies of fury and destruction (ch. 35); the mountains of Israel, which the prophet promises will once again bloom (ch. 36); and finally the exiles themselves, who are promised a return to the land (ch. 37). Appended to this unit are two chapters describing the war of Gog from the land of Magog (ch. 38–39).

The final nine chapters of the book of Ezekiel set forth a vision of the future Temple. These chapters are rich in detail. They relate to the glory within it (ch. 40–43), the new leadership and rites (ch. 44–46), and a new type of relationship between God and the nation (ch. 47–48).

Chapter 18

The People, the Prophet, and God Respond to the Destruction

Ezekiel 33:1–33

The first chapter in the book's third section, in which Ezekiel is informed of the Destruction of the Temple in Jerusalem, revisits subjects that were mentioned in the book's first section. Verses 1–20 deal with Ezekiel's role as observer (seen earlier in 3:9–21), which we discussed in chapter 2 above; verses 21–23 return to the topic of the prophet's silence (3:25–27) which we examined in chapter 3; and verses 23–30 compare the status of the exiles of Jehoiachin to the fate of those remaining in the land after the Destruction – a matter addressed in the introduction. In addition, relations between the prophet and his environment can be deduced from verses 30–32, representing a sort of repair of the hostile relations that had been maintained with the prophet when he set out on his prophetic mission (2:6). The concluding verse of the chapter, dealing with the purpose of Ezekiel's prophecy, complements the prophecy

Ezekiel 33:1–33

from 2:5. In light of all of this, we may assert that our chapter serves as a continuation of and complement to previous chapters.

BABYLONIA, THE BABYLONIAN EXILES, AND THE REMNANT IN JERUSALEM (33:21–29)

According to the date given at the beginning of the prophecy, it was uttered "in the twelfth year [of the exile of Jehoiachin]...on the fifth day of the tenth month" (33:21). In other words, more than a year and a half passed from the time of the Destruction until the escapee came to report it to Ezekiel. Some scholars have proposed that the exiles counted Jehoiachin's reign from Nisan, while the reign of Zedekiah was counted from Tishrei, such that the Destruction of Jerusalem in the month of Av during the year 586 BCE fell in the twelfth year of the exile of Jehoiachin – the eleventh year of the reign of Zedekiah. According to this calculation, only about five months separated the Destruction from the arrival of the report – a reasonable amount of time for a survivor to travel from Judah to Babylonia. Either way, this unit belongs to the period after the Destruction (which is described in II Kings 25:12 and in Jeremiah 52:16), in which Ezekiel must contend with the claim of the remnant left in the land that they are the ones who will eventually inherit it. Ezekiel refers to this group as "those who live in these ruins" (Ezek. 33:24). The claim they are quoted directing to the exiles is that there must be some divine significance to the fact that there is still an active Jewish center in the land; their status should not be dismissed just because they are few in number (v. 24). This claim is tied to Abraham: while he was a lone individual, they are many. And indeed, size or number is not the decisive factor; Isaiah proceeds from a similar comparison with the forefathers in his words of encouragement and consolation:

> Look back to Abraham your father and to Sarah who brought you forth. For he was only one when I called him, but I blessed him and made him many. Truly the Lord has comforted Zion, comforted all her ruins; He has made her wilderness like Eden, her desert like the Garden of the Lord. Gladness and joy shall abide there, thanksgiving and the sound of music. (Is. 51:2–3)

The People, the Prophet, and God Respond to the Destruction

However, the argument of "those who live in these ruins" is erroneous: their bitter fate is the result not of their small number, but rather of their multitude of sins. The sins enumerated by the prophet are not related to violation of the sanctity of the Temple, but rather to idolatry and sins between man and his fellow, which are just as relevant now as they were prior to the Destruction. This being the case, it is clear that the remnant in the land is not worthy of inheriting it, and therefore there is no substance to their claim. Moreover, they are destined to die by the sword and by pestilence. By the end of the process, the land will be desolate – but this desolation will lead to knowledge of God.

AN ECHO OF THE EVENTS PRECEDING THE MURDER OF GEDALIA

The claim, "We are many; surely, the land has been given as a possession to us" (Ezek. 33:24), which the prophet places in the mouth of those remaining in the land after the Destruction, seems to belong to the period preceding the murder of Gedalia. The fact that Gedalia was appointed over the remnant population (II Kings 25; Jer. 40:7) indicates that those remaining in the land had a defined status, a delineated area of habitation, and clearly formulated rights and obligations vis-à-vis the administration. Indirect evidence of this is found in the bulla engraved with the title "Gedaliahu appointed over the house," found in Lakhish and dating back to the late seventh/early sixth century BCE. The generally accepted academic view[1] is that this was Gedalia son of Ahikam, who was appointed by the Babylonians as head of the administration of Judah following the fall of the Kingdom of Judah – or, at the very least, as official representative of the Jewish remnant to the Babylonian rulers.

The remnant's claim indicates that they assumed that exile was a matter pertaining only to those now in Babylonia; they themselves were continuing Israel's national existence, and were therefore deserving of possessing the land. Ezekiel rejects this view, and informs them that they are destined to join their exiled brethren in Babylonia (see also 11:16; 12:21–25). In light of this, although this is

---

1. For more on this bulla, see Shmuel Ahituv, *Assufat Ketuvot Ivriyot MiYemei Bayit Rishon VeReshit Yemei Bayit Sheni* (Jerusalem: Bialik, 1992), 172.

a prophecy of rebuke and punishment to the inhabitants of the land, it is in fact a prophecy of restoration and continuation for the exiles. For this reason, this prophetic unit is included here among the chapters of restoration.

Gedalia's murder brought this period to an end. Although we lack documentation of numbers and status concerning the remnant after the Destruction, it would seem that as long as Gedalia was in charge, the Judeans under his authority maintained a separate identity; this was lost after he was assassinated and the administration of the Jewish population passed to the Babylonian rulers. Thus, there was a dual turning point: The Judeans in the land lost all hope of autonomy, and in addition, they ceased to view themselves as a distinct group, separate from their brethren in Babylonia.

Viewing the prophecy within its historical context raises two exegetical possibilities. Since the prophecy came in the fifth month (Tevet), the prevailing assumption is that the assassination of Gedalia, which took place in Tishrei, preceded it. However, the words that Ezekiel places in the mouth of the remnant in the land – "We are many; surely, the land has been given as a possession to us" (v. 24) – suggest that they see themselves as an alternative to the exiles in Babylonia, and this, ostensibly, would be less likely after the murder. Likewise, the prophetic response to their claim (33:25–28) seems better suited to the situation prior to the murder, not following it.

According to the first possibility, the murder occurred seven weeks after the Destruction. Since it is likely that it would take the survivor a few months to reach Babylonia, he would probably have left Jerusalem, heading off to inform Ezekiel and the exiles of Jehoiachin of the destruction of the city, before the murder took place. The prophecy describes the situation in the land during the brief period between the Destruction and the assassination. Although we cannot reject this possibility out of hand, it seems difficult to accept: First, the prophet's words are clearly polemical in nature, and this would have been unlikely at a time when all energies would more logically be directed to regrouping and recovery. Second, the divine response should reflect the reality in the land in real time, regardless of when the escapee left and how he perceived the situation.

The other, seemingly more likely, possibility is that this prophecy describes the situation in the land at a slightly later stage – not during the weeks immediately following the Destruction. At this time there were still a good number of Jewish inhabitants in the land, and they still viewed their group as an alternative to the Babylonian exiles. This perspective rests upon the assumption that Gedalia was assassinated not in the month of Tishrei immediately after the Destruction, but rather a year or more later. If we accept this interpretation, then Ezekiel's prophecy assumes special significance: The purpose of the prophecy is to clarify to those remaining in the land that although they had survived the Destruction of the Temple, they were not the future inheritors of the land; rather, the exiles in Babylonia would constitute the nation's continuation.

This also illuminates the connection between the exiles in Babylonia and the inhabitants of Jerusalem. We think of the Babylonian exile as the center of world Jewry, where the nation's religious and cultural life would flourish – but this status was not conferred on it right away. During the period immediately following the Destruction, the survivors in Jerusalem considered themselves the proper inheritors of the land, and viewed their exiled brethren as fated to disappear, like the ten tribes that had now assimilated among the nations. The change in consciousness was triggered by the murder of Gedalia, when the Jewish community in the land lost its power and the remaining Judeans there began to accept that the continued national and spiritual survival of the nation would be based in Babylonia, and that they themselves would remain an insignificant remnant. Their identity as a remnant extended until the beginning of the Return, as evidenced in the references to the "remnant of the people" in Haggai (1:12; 2:3) and Zechariah (8:6, 11, 12).

EZEKIEL'S STATUS FOLLOWING THE DESTRUCTION (33:30–32)

Our chapter concludes with the exiles' attitude towards Ezekiel. The news of the city's desolation, in fact, includes no mention of the Destruction. This is perhaps the basis for understanding the difference between Ezekiel's prophecy and that of Jeremiah during the same years. Ezekiel's prophecy declares:

Ezekiel 33:1–33

> Note well, O mortal: your fellow countrymen who converse about you by the walls and in the doorways of their houses and say to each other and propose to one another, "Come and hear what word has issued from the Lord." They will come to you in crowds and sit before you in throngs and will hear your words, but they will not obey them. For they produce nothing but lust with their mouths; and their hearts pursue nothing but gain. To them you are just a singer of bawdy songs, who has a sweet voice and plays skillfully; they hear your words, but will not obey them. But when it comes – and come it will – they shall know that a prophet has been among them. (33:30–33)

The audience in Babylonia listening to Ezekiel – whose prophecies concerning the Destruction of the Temple have indeed come to pass – has ascertained that Ezekiel is a true prophet. Now there are more people interested in listening to him, in contrast to the period prior to the Destruction, when he would speak to the elders of Judah and Israel alone. The esteem in which he is now held leads to a greater closeness to and bond with the people, leading him to refer to them as "your fellow countrymen" (v. 30). Word has gotten around that Ezekiel is worth listening to. However, the people are not going to follow his instructions; they listen to his words like a "song." Therefore, the prophecy concludes with the words, "They shall know that a prophet has been among them" – just as Ezekiel was told by God at the outset of his mission (2:5). His prophecy will have no effect in real time; it will only become meaningful after his words and his warnings are realized.

The prophet does not focus on the Destruction itself; he looks to the past and to the future. For their part, the exiles have not experienced the direct crisis, but they have already begun to internalize the new reality. The prophet will soon remind them (ch. 34) that he has already spoken in the past of the inhabitants of the land as dwelling in ruins; from here he launches into a series of prophecies describing the nation's restoration in the future. In the following chapters, he revisits his prophecies concerning the ingathering in extended fashion (36:22–35), as well as bringing the message to the leader of the House of David, the vision of the dry bones, Gog and Magog, and the vision of the future

The People, the Prophet, and God Respond to the Destruction

Temple. These prophecies contain nothing in the way of consolation, sorrow, reconciliation, or compassion over what has happened in Jerusalem. This is especially conspicuous if we compare these chapters with Jeremiah, who laments at length over the Destruction. According to the Talmud (Bava Batra 15a), Jeremiah authored Lamentations, which contains his lamentations over the Destruction and its accompanying trauma and suffering. Jeremiah shares the sorrow of the people, and his lamentations resound with the pain and profound shock experienced by the inhabitants of Jerusalem at the time of the Destruction. Ezekiel, in contrast, looks to the future.

Chapter 19

The Past and Future Shepherds of Israel

Ezekiel 34:1–31

In chapter 34, Ezekiel records a harsh prophecy directed against the kings of Israel, the nation's leaders, whom he compares to shepherds who do not tend to their flocks. His words to them leave no room for doubt:

> Thus said the Lord God: I am going to deal with the shepherds! I will demand a reckoning of them for My flock, and I will dismiss them from tending the flock. The shepherds shall not tend themselves any more; for I will rescue My flock from their mouths, and it shall not be their prey. (34:10)

In the future, the leadership will be taken from these shepherds who failed in the past to properly lead the nation. God Himself will gather up the flock, rehabilitate it, and hand it over to a different shepherd who will fulfill his role faithfully: "Then I will appoint a single shepherd over them to tend them – My servant David. He shall tend them, he shall

Ezekiel 34:1–31

be a shepherd to them" (v. 23). The new shepherd is named as David, possibly referring to a descendant of his. The prophecy that the present model of leadership will come to an end will be fulfilled completely. It will not be a mere "technical" replacement of personnel, but rather a fundamental change in the essence of the role: "I the Lord will be their God, and My servant David shall be a ruler among them – I the Lord have spoken" (v. 24).

In chapter 37, too, the prophecy speaks of the future leader: "I will make them a single nation in the land, on the hills of Israel, and one king shall be king of them all. Never again shall they be two nations, and never again shall they be divided into two kingdoms" (37:22).

In addressing the form of leadership that existed in the past, Ezekiel notes that while Israel and Judah had previously existed as two separate kingdoms, from now onwards "one king shall be king of them all." This leadership will be in the hands of David, known to the nation as the king who unified the kingdom in the past, and he will fill the same role in the future, too: "My servant David shall be king over them; there shall be one shepherd for all of them. They shall follow My rules and faithfully obey My laws" (37:24).

Ezekiel connects the prophecy concerning the future leadership with the message of chapter 34: King David will rule over the nation in the future. However, the leadership role has changed, and therefore in speaking of David's future status he is not referred to as "king":

> Thus they shall remain in the land which I gave to My servant Jacob and in which your fathers dwelt; they and their children and their children's children shall dwell there forever, with My servant David as their *nasi* for all time. (37:25)

In the future, David will be a *nasi* (prince) rather than "king" over Israel. During this period, when the leadership will be in the hands of the *nasi*, it will be possible to build the future Temple: "I will place My Sanctuary among them forever.... And when My Sanctuary abides among them forever, the nations shall know that I the Lord do sanctify Israel" (37:26–28).

David's new title appears to be a necessary change. In Ezekiel's prophecies, the term "king" represents the leader during a period in which many sins are attributed to the nation, suggesting that the leadership of the king is a failure. The king, as he appears in the book of Ezekiel, is always portrayed in a negative light. Only in chapters 34 (v. 24) and 37 (v. 25) is any positive mention made of the king, and here the prophet is speaking of the historical kingship of David in which the kingdom was unified, and of his future reign. Nevertheless, although the prophet speaks here of David, he takes care to refer to him as *nasi*. Since the institution of kingship has failed, an alternative form of leadership must replace it. One of the roles of the king of Israel is to facilitate the Divine Presence's resting within the nation. The kings of Israel, as depicted in the book of Ezekiel, brought about the opposite situation: defilement and the distancing of the Divine Presence. Now it is too late; there is no repair for the corrupt kingship. Ezekiel, then, heralds the replacement of the station with a *nasi*, a worthier leader.[1]

---

1. For more on the Ezekiel's use of the term *nasi*, see chapter 8 above.

Chapter 20
God's Eternal Preference for Israel over Edom
Ezekiel 35:1–36:15

MOUNT SEIR AND THE MOUNTAINS OF ISRAEL

The appeal to mountains is a feature that we encounter throughout the book of Ezekiel.[1] Sometimes the mountains are referred to in a general way, without reference to any specific area; other passages refer to a particular place. "Mountains of Israel" is a phrase unique to Ezekiel, appearing sixteen times in the book.

We might hazard a guess about why the prophet chooses to address the nation in this way. In chapter 6 (vv. 2–3) he speaks to the mountains of Israel, describing how the coming destruction will include the mountains, the hills, the riverbeds, and the valleys. The appeal to the mountains seems to arise from the fact that these were the main sites of the altars and the practice of idolatry – and idolatry is the sin these verses focus on.

---

1. Ezekiel utters his prophecies in Babylonia, which geographically is a flat country. It may be that his frequent invocation of mountains is an expression of his longing for the landscapes of the Land of Israel. For elaboration see Yehuda Feliks, *Nature and Man in the Bible* (London: Soncino, 1981), 144–47.

Ezekiel 35:1–36:15

In contrast, in chapter 36 (vv. 1–4) the prophet addresses himself to the mountains of Israel, and also speaks to the desolate ruins and empty cities. This difference arises from the chronological gap: The prophecy in chapter 6 preceded the Destruction; the prophecy in chapter 36 comes afterwards and therefore includes a description of the state of the land in its wake. The prophecy mentions the nations' reaction to the Destruction, with specific mention of the sites of idolatrous worship: "Aha! Those ancient heights have become our possession" (36:2), and the punishment that they deserve as a result (vv. 5–7). This suggests that the nations will suffer a special punishment because of their arrogance and their scorn for events in the high places on the mountains of Israel. The mountains continue to be a central focus even after the Destruction.

THE PLACEMENT OF THE PROPHECY TO MOUNT SEIR WITHIN THE BOOK OF EZEKIEL

The prophecy in chapter 35 is addressed to Mount Seir – home to Edom. The placement of this prophecy among the restoration chapters in the book of Ezekiel deviates from the general structure of the book, in which the prophecies to the other nations appear in chapters 25–32.

Furthermore, the unit of prophecies to the nations already has a message directed specifically to Edom (25:12–14, discussed in chapter 15). This seeming deviation and repetition is not coincidental. The aim of the prophecy in our chapter is different from Ezekiel's prophecies to the other nations. Surprisingly enough, this prophecy is actually addressed to Israel. The shared historical background of Israel and Edom, on one hand, and the habitation of the Edomites to the south of Judah, on the other, presented a challenge of faith that overshadowed Ezekiel's prophecies of restoration, as we will see below.

The crisis of faith receives a prophetic response in chapters 35 and 36:1–15, which together comprise a single prophetic unit. It seems that the chapter division (executed by a Christian theologian in the Middle Ages) in this instance is an impediment to an accurate understanding of the message. The two chapters should not be viewed as two distinct prophecies, one to Mount Seir and the other to the mountains of Israel. Rather, they are part of the same prophecy, whose main message is that the mountains of Israel will be rebuilt on the ruins of Mount Seir. The first part opens with a call to Mount Seir:

> O mortal, set your face against Mount Seir and prophesy against it.... I am going to deal with you, Mount Seir: I will stretch out My hand against you and make you an utter waste. I will turn your towns into ruins, and you shall be a desolation; then you shall know that I am the Lord. (35:2–4)

The second passage starts with a call to the mountains of Israel: Prophesy to the mountains of Israel and say: O mountains of Israel, hear the word of the Lord (36:1).

PERPETUAL HATRED

Ezekiel notes two reasons for the necessity of this attitude and this message to Edom within the prophecies of restoration in the following chapters. The first relates to the long history that the two nations share; the second concerns the Edomites' territorial demands. After addressing each of these reasons separately, Ezekiel connects them and sums up the struggle between the two nations. The structure of the chapter also attests to this prophetic message (see appendix below).

The origins of the relationship between Edom and Israel are found in *Parashat Toledot*, in the story of the birth of Jacob and Esau (Gen. 25:19–34; 27–28:9). The story of Isaac awarding the blessings, in these chapters, in no way points to any wrongdoing on Esau's part. In fact, the reader cannot help but identify with Esau's cry: "And Esau said to his father, 'Have you but one blessing, Father? Bless me too, Father!' And Esau wept aloud" (Gen. 27:38).

Hence, to fill in the picture, Ḥazal chose as the *haftara* for this *parasha* a prophecy from the book of Malachi. The selected passage represents the "final word" of the Tanakh concerning the relations between Jacob and Esau, following their long history, placing these relations in their historical perspective:

> I have shown you love, said the Lord. But you ask, "How have You shown us love?" After all – declares the Lord – Esau is Jacob's brother; yet I have accepted Jacob and have rejected Esau. I have

made his hills a desolation, his territory a home for beasts of the desert. If Edom thinks, "Though crushed, we can build the ruins again," thus said the Lord of Hosts: "They may build, but I will tear down. And so they shall be known as the region of wickedness, the people damned forever of the Lord. Your eyes shall behold it, and you shall declare, 'Great is the Lord beyond the borders of Israel!'" (Mal. 1:2–5)

From these verses it appears that the nation's fear that God preferred Esau prevailed until the beginning of the Return to Zion with Ezra. Even after the Second Temple was built by the returnees, the status of the Edomites – the descendants of Esau – caused the people of Israel to doubt their own standing in God's eyes. This seems to be an echo of the fear that the divine choice of Jacob over Esau was not an eternal one; God might change His mind. Indeed, Ezekiel's need to mention God's eternal hatred is an expression of the nation's fear that God preferred Edom.[2] The impression arising from Ezekiel's response is that the nation feels that perhaps now, following the Destruction of the Temple, after it has been made clear that the people of Israel did not uphold the covenant with God, God will continue His covenant with Abraham via the sons of Esau, rather than through the descendants of Jacob.[3]

The hostility between Israel and Edom throughout the generations grew even stronger during the years of Ezekiel's prophecies, owing

---

2. See Elie Assis, "Why Edom? On the Hostility Towards Jacob's Brother in Prophetic Sources," *Vetus Testamentum* 55 (2005): 1–20; Elie Assis, *Identity in Conflict: The Struggle between Esau and Jacob, Edom and Israel* (Winona Lake, IN: Eisenbrauns, 2016).
3. This tension between Esau and Jacob can be discerned throughout the First Temple period, starting from the time of David's kingdom. At times, the kings of Judah managed to push the Edomites southward, while at other times the Edomites pushed the Kingdom of Judah northward. See II Samuel 8:13–14 (David subjugates Edom); I Kings 11; 15:14–22 (revenge on Edom following the death of David); II Kings 8:20–21 (the rule of Jehoram son of Jehoshaphat); II Kings 14:7 and II Chronicles 25:11–13 (the days of Amaziah); II Kings 14:22 and II Chronicles 26:7, 10 (the days of Azariah); II Kings 16:6 (the exile of the Kingdom of Israel).

to the active participation of some Edomites in shedding Israelite blood during the Destruction: "Because you harbored an ancient hatred and handed the people of Israel over to the sword in their time of calamity" (35:5). The Edomites put themselves at the service of the conquerors, taking part in hunting down the survivors of Judah and handing them over to the Babylonians for slavery or exile. By virtue of this service the Babylonians permitted them to settle in Judah, in place of the Judeans who had been killed or taken captive and exiled. The Edomites established their own autonomy in the area of the northern Negeb and the Judean hills.[4] An echo of this development arises from the prophecies of Joel (4:19) and Obadiah (1:10). Edom's increasing power continued for many years; the evidence suggests that by the time Judah fell in 586 BCE, a substantial Edomite population in southern Judah had been established. It is therefore not surprising that the nation to whom Malachi addresses himself doubts God's love.

An important archaeological finding offers its own evidence of Edom's harsh treatment of Judah, and suggests that at a certain stage the city of Arad was in danger of being conquered by Edom. The finding is an ostracon from Tel Arad, with an inscription that reads:

> …from Arad 5 and from Qinah [5?] and send them to Ramat-Negev under Malkiyahu son of Qerobur. He is to hand them over to Elisha son of Yirmeyahu at Ramat-Negev lest anything happen to the city. This is an order from the king – a life-and-death matter for you. Behold I send [this message] to warn you now the men with Elisha lest Edom come there.[5]

The instruction is that fifty soldiers must be dispatched urgently from the base in Arad, as well as soldiers from Kinah, to Ramat Negeb, lest

---

4. Mordechai Cogan, *Ovadiah, Mikra LeYisrael* (Tel Aviv/Jerusalem: Am Oved, 1993), 8–10.
5. Shmuel Ahituv, *Echoes from the Past: Hebrew and Cognate Inscriptions from the Biblical Period* (Jerusalem: Carta, 2008), 128.

something happen to the city, because Arad is in danger of being conquered by Edom.[6]

In the book of Ezekiel, as in other biblical sources, the reason for the destruction and desolation of Edom is its abuse of the remnant of Judah (35:5). Ezekiel's prophecy states that Edom is punished measure for measure for its actions: Just as in the past its destiny was tied to that of Israel, so it will be in the future – but this time, Israel will have the upper hand.

Indeed, the prophecies in chapters 35 and 36 are inversely connected: As the mountains of Edom are desolate, so will the mountains of Israel flourish. But for now, with the destruction of Edom, the prophetic message is emphasized through the expression, "and you shall know that I am the Lord," a phrase repeated five times throughout the Edom prophecy.

The continuation of this prophecy, in chapter 36, is likewise the inverse of the prophecy concerning Mount Seir, as well as of the prophecy concerning the mountains of Israel in chapter 6 (vv. 1–4). Thus, the contrast between the content of Ezekiel's prophecies prior to the Destruction (ch. 6) and the content of his prophecies in its wake (ch. 36) is clearly manifest.

Finally, this prophetic unit concludes with the restoration of the land in the future (36:7–15). This prophecy aligns well with the preceding message. It begins with the insult of the nations surrounding Israel: "I hereby swear that the nations which surround you shall, in their turn, suffer disgrace" (v. 7), and continues with a description of the mountains of Israel in their abundance: "But you, O mountains of Israel, shall yield your produce and bear your fruit for My people Israel, for their return is near" (v. 8). God's Divine Presence inspires this reality: "For I will care for you: I will turn to you, and you shall be tilled and sown" (v. 9). This finds expression in the fact that the mountains of Judah will once again be teeming with inhabitants:

> I will settle a large population on you, the whole House of Israel; the towns shall be resettled, and the ruined sites rebuilt.

---

6. Ibid., 92, 126–33.

> I will multiply men and beasts upon you, and they shall increase and be fertile, and I will resettle you as you were formerly, and will make you more prosperous than you were at first. And you shall know that I am the Lord. I will lead men – My people Israel – to you, and they shall possess you. You shall be their heritage, and you shall not again cause them to be bereaved. (vv. 10–12)

These elements combine to provide a precise divine response to the nation's fears. This prophecy says nothing about the ingathering from among the nations, nor about the ramifications of the desecration of God's name represented by the Jewish presence in exile, and not a word about the unification of Israel and Judah. The prophecy makes no mention of any future leader, no mention of a future Temple. Each of these issues will be addressed in the prophecies that follow, starting with Ezekiel 36:16, which is a distinct prophetic unit.[7] Why all of these omissions? Because the purpose of this prophecy is to prepare the people's hearts to accept messages about the future restoration. So long as they are fearful, uncertain as to their status as God's nation, the prophecies concerning the future will be met with skepticism. First Ezekiel must deal with the crisis of faith, concluding with the promise that only the mountains of Israel will yield fruit and be inhabited by the people of Israel. Only then does he launch a series of prophecies regarding the nation's future. These prophecies, from 36:16 until chapter 39, are a concise formulation of Ezekiel's message to the nation. The following chapters will be devoted to these units.

APPENDIX: EDOM VERSUS ISRAEL – THE PROPHECY'S STRUCTURE

The structure of the two distinct units within this prophecy bring its messages to the fore, emphasizing the contrast between the nations and the push and pull of their relationship.

---

7. This proposed division is based on the fact that the *haftara* for *Parashat Para* begins at Ezekiel 36:16 (we will return to this in the next chapter).

Ezekiel 35:1–36:15

The Future of Edom (Chapter 35)		The Future of Israel (Chapter 36)	
Edom's actions towards Israel from time immemorial	The Edomites' desire to succeed and inherit Israel's place and their God	Edom's glee at Israel's downfall and desire to inherit Israel	Edom's actions towards Israel from time immemorial
Reasons behind God's response			
Because you harbored an ancient hatred and handed the people of Israel over to the sword in their time of calamity (35:5)	Because you thought "The two nations and the two lands shall be mine and we shall possess them" – although the Lord was there (35:10)	Because the enemy gloated over you, "Aha! Those ancient heights have become our possession!" (36:2)	Because they say to you, "You are [a land] that devours men, you have been a bereaver of your nations" (36:13)
God's response			
Assuredly, as I live, declares the Lord God, I will doom you with blood; blood shall pursue you; I swear that, for your bloodthirsty hatred, blood shall pursue you. I will make Mount Seir an utter waste, and	Assuredly, as I live, declares the Lord God, I will act with the same anger and passion that you acted with in your hatred of them. And I will make Myself known through them when I judge	Therefore… because they eagerly lusted to see you become a possession of the other nations round about, so that you have become the butt of gossip in every language and of the jibes from every people….	Assuredly, you shall devour men no more, you shall never again bereave your nations – declares the Lord God. No more will I allow the jibes of the nations to be heard against you, no longer shall

228

The Future of Edom (Chapter 35)		The Future of Israel (Chapter 36)	
I will keep all passersby away from it. I will cover its mountains with the slain; men slain by the sword shall lie on your hills, in your valleys, and in all your watercourses. I will make you a desolation for all time; your towns shall never be inhabited. And you shall know that I am the Lord. (35:6–9)	you. You shall know that I the Lord have heard all the taunts you uttered against the hills of Israel: "They have been laid waste; they have been given to us as prey." And you spoke arrogantly against Me and multiplied your words against Me: I have heard it. Thus said the Lord God: When the whole earth rejoices, I will make you a desolation. As you rejoiced when the heritage of the House of	Thus said the Lord God to the mountains and the hills, to the watercourses and the valleys, and to the desolate wastes and deserted cities which have become a prey and a laughingstock to the other nations round about. Assuredly…I have indeed spoken in My blazing wrath against the other nations and against all of Edom which, with wholehearted glee and with contempt, have made My land a possession for themselves for pasture and for prey. Yes,	you suffer the taunting of the peoples; and never again shall you cause your nations to stumble – declares the Lord God. (36:14–15)[8]

---

8. Concerning the language of this prophecy see Yonatan Grossman, "'Kefel Keri'a Mivni' BeYeḥezkel 33 – 48," *Beit Mikra* 49, no. 2 (2004): 194 – 224.

The Future of Edom (Chapter 35)	The Future of Israel (Chapter 36)
Israel was laid waste, so will I treat you: the hill country of Seir and the whole of Edom, all of it, shall be laid waste. And they shall know that I am the Lord. (35:11–15)	prophesy about the Land of Israel, and say to the mountains and the hills, to the watercourses and to the valleys, Thus said the Lord God: Behold, I declare in My blazing wrath: Because you have suffered the taunting of the nations… (36:3–6)

Chapter 21

The Nation's Purification and Restoration
Ezekiel 36:16–38

SPRINKLING OF CLEAN WATER (36:16–31)

The climax of Israel's restoration process in the book of Ezekiel is God's purification of the nation. This process, with all its constituent elements, appears in its most comprehensive form in chapter 36, climaxing in the verse, "I will sprinkle clean water upon you, and you shall be clean: I will cleanse you from all your uncleanness and from all your fetishes" (36:25).

The various descriptions of this restoration (in chapters 11, 20, 28, 34, 35, 37, and 39) suggest that the restoration is not dependent on the nation's deeds;[1] the process is carried out in its entirety by God. The fact that it is not contingent on the nation's behavior is especially conspicuous against the background of the detailed description of its sins. The prophet states the reason for this: The ingathering of the exiled takes place solely because of God's desire that His name be sanctified in the nations' eyes (see Ezek. 20:9, 14, 22, 41; 36:20–23). The Destruction and

---

1. There is one exception, discussed above: "And they shall return there, and do away with all its detestable things and all its abominations" (11:18).

the exile do not cause any fundamental change in the nation's attitude towards God, and therefore the desired processes – purification (36:25; 37:23) and atonement (16:63) – will take place without any preconditions (11:19; 36:26; 39:29). Since the people are not active partners in their own purification, Ezekiel devotes relatively little space to this process: It is discussed only in two specific chapters, contrasting with the dozens of times throughout the book that he repeatedly emphasizes their defilement.

The aim of chapter 36 is to prepare the nation to protect the future Temple, which is described in the prophetic vision in chapters 40–48. While many chapters are occupied with restoration, including the nation's return to its land, the nation's purification is mentioned only three times in the entire book. Two of these are in chapter 36, a chapter that offers a detailed description of the restoration, climaxing in the renewal of the covenant between God and the House of Israel. At the center of this prophecy is the stage at which God sprinkles purifying water over the nation, thereby cleansing the people of their defilement and theirs sins:

> I will take you from among the nations and gather you from all the countries, and I will bring you back to your own land. I will sprinkle clean water upon you, and you shall be clean: I will cleanse you from all your uncleanness and from all your fetishes. (vv. 24–25)

> When I have cleansed you of all your iniquities, I will people your settlements, and the ruined places shall be rebuilt. (v. 33)

This purification "ceremony" for the nation as a whole is exceptional in Tanakh. The expression "clean (or 'pure') water" (*mayim tehorim*) likewise occurs only here; nowhere else in Tanakh is there any description, even metaphoric, of God purifying the entire nation, either through sprinkling water over them or by means of any other method.

The other appearance of purifying the nation is found in chapter 37, which offers no description of the process. The prophet declares only "Nor shall they ever again defile themselves by their fetishes… I will cleanse them. Then they shall be My people, and I will be their God" (37:23).

Rabbi Eliezer of Beaugency interprets the verse thus:

> The waters of purification and the sprinkling are a metaphor for the removal of iniquity and the cleaning, clarifying, and cleansing that they will undergo for a long time throughout the captivity to atone for sin and remove wrongdoing, as in the verse, "Purge me with hyssop till I am pure" (Ps. 51:9), and "If I washed myself with soap, cleansed my hands with lye" (Job 9:30). And after you have been purified of all your defilements, then "I will give you a new heart" (Ezek. 36:26) so that you will not commit such great sins that you will be punished as you are now.

We shall adopt this interpretation and attempt to add another layer to it.

"I Will Sprinkle" (*VeZarakti*; 36:25)

The prophet speaks of "sprinkling" clean water. In Tanakh, verbs based on the root Z-R-K and N-Z-H (another word used for sprinkling) usually appear in the context of religious ritual. In some instances in which the blood of a sacrifice must be sprinkled on the altar, the verb Z-R-K is used; in other instances, the Torah uses the verb N-Z-H. There seems to be a general distinction between the two: *zerika* relates to all of the blood, which must be poured on the altar; *hazaah* is a symbolic gesture that uses only a small portion of the blood, effecting a cleansing and sanctification.[2]

Sprinkling (*hazaah*) of the blood is usually performed with the finger (Lev. 4:6, 17; 14:15, 27 and elsewhere), and sometimes by means of some object – for example, the hyssop (Lev. 14; Num. 19). Both the liquid itself and that which is sprinkled change in accordance with the

---

2. This fundamental distinction can be traced through the details of the actions: "Take some of the blood that is on the altar and some of the anointing oil and sprinkle (*vehizeta*) upon Aaron and his vestments…. Thus shall he and his vestments be holy" (Ex. 29:21); "He shall sprinkle (*vehizah*) some of the blood of the sin offering" (Lev. 5:9); "He shall take some of the blood of the bull and sprinkle (*vehizah*) it with his finger over the cover on the east side; and in front of the cover he shall sprinkle (*yazeh*) some of the blood with his finger seven times" (Lev. 16:14).

situation. The liquid that is sprinkled may be blood, anointing oil, or water mixed with the ashes of the red heifer. The objects of sprinkling include the priests, the Levites, the curtain before the Holy of Holies, the covering over the ark and/or the altar as well as impure houses, vessels, or people. In each instance, the sprinkling is part of a ceremony that symbolically expresses transcendence, progress, and perhaps a transition to a higher status or plane.

In contrast to this sprinkling, the purpose of *zerika* is to transfer the blood upon the altar (Lev. 1:3, 8, 9, 17),[3] and this is achieved, one way or another, using all the blood. For this reason, the Torah's instruction is to sprinkle "the blood," rather than "of the blood."[4] This sprinkling is part of the normative process of offering sacrifices, which comprises several stages (leaning on the animal, slaughter, sprinkling of blood, and offering on the altar). In contrast to *hazaah*, where the symbolism of the act is related to the conceptual world of purification or sanctity, *zerika* is part of the sacrificial ceremony only. The reason for the pouring of the blood on the altar may be induced, inter alia, from the verse, "For the life of the flesh is in the blood, and I have assigned it to you for making expiation for your lives upon the altar; it is the blood, as life, that effects expiation" (Lev. 17:11). This pouring of the blood upon the altar is an important part of the sacrificial service; it is the act that brings atonement.[5]

---

3. There are two exceptions to this rule, which appear in Exodus 24 (the sprinkling of the blood of the covenant) and Numbers 18 (the waters of the red heifer); they will be discussed below.
4. See, for example, "and dash the rest of the blood" (Ex. 29:20); "and Aaron's sons, the priests, shall dash its blood" (Lev. 1:11).
5. We have focused on the fundamental distinction as arising from a plain reading of the biblical text. Further clarification of the distinction between the two types of sprinkling in light of the details of the laws involved lies beyond the scope of the present discussion.
   We do encounter an interesting problem with the mixture of both roots, Z-R-K and N-Z-H, in Numbers 19, in the discussion of the red heifer. The main verb in this context appears to be *hazaah* rather than *zerika*. The central verses of this unit – the actual command – use the verb N-Z-H (Num. 19:18–19) and the individual who performs the action is referred to as *mazeh* (19:21). The verb Z-R-K appears in passive form (19:13, 20), in the description of the punishment of one who enters the

"Clean Water" (36:25)

The cleansing of the nation in Ezekiel, achieved by the sprinkling of purifying water upon it, parallels the process required for someone who has become ritually impure through contact with a corpse (Num. 19), using "waters of lustration" (*mei nidda*). Some scholars have also pointed out the similarity between the sprinkling of water in the book of Ezekiel and the purification of the Levites in preparation for their service in the Sanctuary (Num. 8:7), using "waters of purification" (*mei ḥatat*). Nevertheless, it should be noted that in contrast to the waters of lustration and the waters of purification that are used for purification in the book of Numbers, Ezekiel adopts a new and unique definition – "clean water" (*mayim tehorim*) – for the water that will cleanse the nation. Since this expression appears nowhere else in Tanakh, we must try to understand how to interpret it.

The description of the water as *tehorim* – pure or clean – may be to emphasize the idea that this water does not contract impurity, in the same way that we find, "However, a spring or cistern in which water is collected shall be clean" (Lev. 11:36). If so, it is reasonable to assume that the expression *mayim tehorim* is based on the expression *mei nidda*, but expands on it. On the other hand, it may be that the water is referred to here as "clean" because it plays a role in a ceremony of cleansing. The language used here by Ezekiel sits well with the general theme of the chapter, which describes a unique process of purification. From this perspective, the expression *mayim tehorim* appears to be a deliberate departure from the more familiar *mei nidda* and *mei ḥatat*.[6]

Sanctuary in a state of ritual impurity. The reason for the use of z-r-k, in its various forms, would seem to be that along with the connection that exists between *zerika* and the sacrifices, as discussed above, this verb can also serve in a more general sense, without specific reference (as opposed to *hazaah*, which has a clear and precise meaning). Therefore, when the text speaks of sprinkling the waters within a different legal context, such as the punishment of someone who is ritually impure and enters the Sanctuary, it uses the more general and neutral term z-r-k, in passive form, without invoking the more specific *hazaah*.

6. Support for the distinction between the expressions *mayim tehorim* and *mei nidda* is found in the Community Rule scroll (1QS), among the Dead Sea Scrolls; see Jacob Licht, *Megillat HaSerakhim MiMegillot Midbar Yehuda* (Jerusalem: Bialik,

Purification in Numbers 19

The nation's purification of its defilement in the book of Ezekiel may be better understood when placed in the context of the purification ceremony set forth in Numbers 19. The sins of the nation that are described in Ezekiel, such as the *gilulim* (fetishes), are compared to the impurity contracted through contact with a dead body, and God's sprinkling of water is likened to the purifying sprinkling that is performed by the priest. The importance of this metaphor lies in its highlighting the fact that the nation's impurity is so grave that it is compared to one of the central, major types of impurity treated in the Torah, requiring a lengthy and thorough process of purification. Both of these purifications are notable in that the subject (whether the individual or the nation) cannot undertake the purification process independently; someone else is needed for it to happen.

Despite the similarity, however, there is an important difference between the two cases: the causes of impurity. Whereas in Ezekiel the sins that have led to the nation's impurity involve idolatry – including worship of the abominations and passing children through fire – the individual's state of impurity is the result of contact with death. The description of the nation's impurity resulting from idolatry is unique to the book of Ezekiel. In addition, a distinction should be drawn in the way in which the purification is described. Both in Numbers (ch. 8, 19) and in Ezekiel, the purification ceremony involves water – but, as we noted above, in Numbers, the sprinkling of water is described using the word *hazaah*, while in Ezekiel the verb *zerika* is employed.

The Blood of the Covenant (Exodus 24)

The fact that Ezekiel chooses to use the root z-r-k points in the direction of another biblical parallel which offers a fascinating perspective on Ezekiel's prophecy. Two places in Tanakh use the verb z-r-k but do not involve the altar. One is our chapter in Ezekiel, and the other is chapter 24 of Exodus, where the blood of the covenant is sprinkled over the nation. Both instances

---

1996), 78–79, column 3, lines 4–5, and 80, line 9. The text indicates that its author assumes that the purification process includes both the sprinkling of *mei nidda* and sanctification using *mayim tehorim*.

The Nation's Purification and Restoration

involve the sprinkling of a liquid over the Israelites in order to purify them. In the book of Exodus, the ceremony marks the forging of a covenant between the nation and God, and the substance that is sprinkled is blood:

> Moses took one part of the blood and put it in basins, and the other part of the blood he dashed [*zarak*] against the altar. Then he took the record of the covenant and read it aloud to the people. And they said, "All that the Lord has spoken we will faithfully do!" Moses took the blood and dashed it [*vayizrok*] on the people and said, "This is the blood of the covenant that the Lord now makes with you concerning all these commands." (Ex. 24:6–8)

The verb Z-R-K is used here, it appears, in relation to the second half of the blood (the portion sprinkled over the nation) because of its use in relation to the first half (the portion sprinkled upon the altar), and the use of the same verb emphasizes the connection between the two. A comparison of this scene to Ezekiel's prophecy illuminates the reason for the choice of this verb in our context. In the book of Exodus, the focus of the ceremony was the moment when Moses divided the blood of the peace offering in half: One half was sprinkled upon the altar, representing God's side of the covenant (see Sforno on this verse), while the other half is sprinkled upon the nation, in a most unusual departure from the norm. This blood is then referred to as the "blood of the covenant."

In various places in Tanakh, we see the forging of a covenant accompanied by a ceremony in which the partnership between the two sides finds expression. In the Covenant between the Pieces, in Abraham's time, the animals are cut in half and a smoking furnace and burning torch pass between them (Gen. 15:10). In the time of Zedekiah, mention is made of a covenant to liberate the slaves which includes the cutting of a calf in two and passing between the parts (Jer. 34:17–22). The description in the book of Exodus is certainly similar: In this ceremony the blood is divided in two, with one half sprinkled towards God, as it were (represented by the altar), and the other sprinkled upon the nation.[7] In each of these ceremonies

---

7. It is difficult to imagine how the blood was actually sprinkled over the entire nation. Ibn Ezra proposes that the "elders represented all of Israel."

Ezekiel 36:16–38

there is something that is divided in half, but while only one of the parties to the covenant passes in between the halves of the animals in the first two instances, in the third instance the blood is sprinkled over both parties to the covenant, thereby reinforcing the symbolism of the partnership between them. In light of this we can now better understand the use of the root Z-R-K in relation to the nation. As we have seen, the sprinkling of the blood is part of a sacrificial process, but here the emphasis is on reciprocity: Just as the blood of the sacrifice is sprinkled on the altar, which represents God, so it is sprinkled upon the nation – the other party to the covenant. Now it emerges that the sprinkling of a substance upon the nation within the framework of the covenant served as the model for our chapter in Ezekiel, in which clean water is sprinkled upon the people within the framework of the renewal of the bond with God.

These two covenantal ceremonies, however, are not identical. The central difference is that in Ezekiel it is water that is sprinkled, while Exodus describes a sprinkling of blood. There are many possible reasons for this difference. First, it would seem that the book of Exodus involves blood because on the practical level, the covenant in Exodus involved burnt offerings and peace offerings, and the ceremony came after the sprinkling of the blood upon the altar; this preceding step does not exist in Ezekiel. In addition, the sprinkling in the book of Exodus does not include an element of purification; that was already a necessary precondition for the sacrifices. Beyond this, however, sacrifices are not an ideal or typical means of purification. In the book of Ezekiel, the people are sprinkled with water, which is perhaps the most obvious purifying substance. There may also be a rather technical reason for the difference: the chapter in Ezekiel relates to a situation in which there is no Temple; the offering of sacrifices and the use of blood are not a relevant option.[8]

A review of the book of Ezekiel as a whole suggests another possible reason for the difference between the ceremony in Exodus and the

---

8. It is no coincidence that in a chapter in which the description of the process of restoration is extremely detailed, elements related to the Temple are absent. Their time will come later (especially in chapters 40–48), after the purification of the nation is complete. This is one of the ways in which Ezekiel "protects" the future Temple that he describes from contamination.

purification described here. In the book of Ezekiel, blood is generally representative of the deeds that lead to the Destruction of the Temple and to exile,[9] and this in found in our chapter, too: "So I poured out My wrath on them for the blood which they shed upon their land" (Ezek. 36:18). Thus, it is reasonable to posit that, in the absence of the Temple, the purification of the people will be carried out with water alone, which the prophet declares to be absolutely pure, such that the deeds of the nation – as severe as they are – cannot contaminate them.

A comparison between the ceremony of purification in Ezekiel and the forging of the covenant in Exodus shows that despite the difference with regard to the substance sprinkled over the nation, considerable similarity exists. In both instances the entire nation is present: In the book of Exodus it is the entire generation that has just left Egypt, while Ezekiel speaks of the nation that has been gathered together from all the lands (36:24). Both instances involve a covenant-forging ceremony: in the book of Exodus there is explicit use of the word "covenant," while in Ezekiel we find a different formulation which is commonly used in the context of reciprocal relations between God and the nation: "and you shall be My people, and I will be your God" (v. 28).

A Rite with Echoes of the Past

We might therefore conclude by saying that the essence of the ceremony of purification is the verse, "I will sprinkle clean water upon you, and you shall be clean: I will cleanse you from all your uncleanness and from all your fetishes" (36:25). The biblical background to this ceremony is twofold. On one hand, it recalls the ceremony whereby someone who has contracted ritual impurity is purified using the *mei nidda* (Num. 19) – such that the sins of the nation are compared to the impurity of death, and God's sprinkling of water is compared to the sprinkling of the purifying water that is performed by the priest. On the other hand, it also recalls the forging of the covenant in Exodus, at the center of which is the "ceremony of blood." In this way Ezekiel reinforces the magnitude of this cleansing ceremony and emphasizes the severity of the people's deeds by comparing their impurity to the

---

9. See Ezekiel 7:23; 9:9; 16:38; 22:2–6, 27; 33:25, and more.

Ezekiel 36:16–38

impurity contracted from contact with death – a severe form of impurity requiring a comprehensive process of purification. Simultaneously, Ezekiel emphasizes that the future purification – like the covenant at Horeb – has historical significance, and will redefine the relationship between God and His people.

Chapter 36 of Ezekiel constitutes the most detailed prophecy of restoration in the book of Ezekiel. The prophetic units that speak of restoration include common elements: God bringing the people out from among the nations; God gathering the people; the sanctification of God's name in the eyes of the nations that results from the gathering; God bringing the people back to their land; and the people's knowledge of God in the future. However, more generally, Ezekiel's prophecies lack some classic elements: salvation and flourishing, on one hand, and expressions of sorrow, reconciliation, or consolation, on the other.

In closing, we note that this prophecy is read as the *haftara* for *Parashat Para*, to which it is connected in three ways: First, is the connection between the purification process of the red heifer needed to be completed before Passover and the national purification process described here. Second, it contains linguistic similarity to the expressions of redemption that appear in Exodus (ch. 6);[10] and third, the conclusion, with its description of Jerusalem, is linked to the Return: "As Jerusalem is filled with sacrificial sheep during her festivals" (Ezek. 36:38). *Targum Yonatan* translates, "Like the holy nation, like the nation that is purified and comes to Jerusalem at the time of the Passover holiday."

---

10. The expressions of restoration share a common introduction: "Say to the House of Israel…I am the Lord" (Ezek. 36:22), and a similar conclusion: "And you shall be My people, and I will be your God, and they shall know that I am the Lord" (36:38). However, it should be noted that the expressions of restoration themselves are not identical: In Exodus 6 we find "I will free" (*vehotzeiti*; v. 6); "and I shall deliver" (*vehitzalti*; v. 6), "and I shall redeem" (*vegaalti*; v. 6), "and I will take" (*velakahti*; v. 7). In Ezekiel 36 we find, "I will take" (*velakahti*; v. 24), "gather you" (*vekibatzti*; v. 24), "I will bring" (*veheveiti*; v. 24), and "I will sprinkle" (*vezarakti*; v. 25). These differences would seem to emphasize the difference between the Exodus from Egypt and the return of the nation to its land in the future.

The Nation's Purification and Restoration

THE NATION'S RESTORATION (36:32–38)

The final verses of chapter 36 sees a recurrence of themes from previous chapters; they should be viewed as an addition and complement to them. In verses 31–32, the prophet emphasizes that the people have not changed their behavior, and therefore are not worthy of having God return them to their land on the basis of their own merit. Verses 33–35 complete the order of events in the future and prophesies that when they reach the land, God will cleanse His people of all their iniquities, whereupon the cities will be rebuilt, the desolate land will become like the Garden of Eden, and the cities that now stand in ruins will once again be fortified. In verse 36, the prophet emphasizes that the nations will thereby know that it is God who has rebuilt the ruins of His land – and this is, in fact, God's motivation for the Return. In addition, in verses 37–38 the prophet concludes the allegory of the shepherds which appeared in chapter 34 (his appeal to the leaders of the people) and the prophecy of restoration to the mountains of Israel from chapter 36.

Within this unit we discern an echo of the prophecies' organization in the book of Ezekiel, and its significance: The prophet presents the allegory of the shepherds, by appealing to the flock as God's people, only after addressing the status of the people in chapters 35–36, as we have seen. He adds the final link in the allegory of the shepherds, describing the flock (the people/sacrifices brought by the people) in the future, based on the multitudes that visited Jerusalem in the past:

> Thus said the Lord God: Moreover, in this I will respond to the House of Israel and act for their sake: I will multiply their people like sheep. As Jerusalem is filled with sacrificial sheep during her festivals, so shall the ruined cities be filled with flocks of people. And they shall know that I am the Lord. (Ezek. 36:37–38)

THE GARDEN OF EDEN

The prophet then adds another dimension to the change in the people's status, stating that the land will flourish and produce trees and fruit. It seems that it is with this message in mind that Ezekiel chooses an expression that depicts the land as giving more and better fruit than any other land – the "Garden of Eden." The Garden of Eden is familiar to us as a vision of utopia dating back to Genesis 2–3, but in the book of Ezekiel, somewhat surprisingly, the image is used mainly in prophecies concerning Tyre and Egypt. In the prophecy to Tyre, the place of the king is described – "You were in Eden, the garden of God" (28:13). In the prophecy to Egypt it appears several times in different variations. In 31:8–9 we find: "Cedars in the garden of God could not compare with it.... No tree in the garden of God was its peer in beauty.... And all the trees of Eden envied it in the garden of God." Further on in the same chapter, the prophet describes the fate of Pharaoh, king of Egypt, who descends to Sheol along with his trees of the Garden of Eden:

> And all the trees of Eden, the choicest and best of Lebanon, all that were well watered, were consoled in the lowest part of the netherworld.... Who is comparable to you in glory and greatness among the trees of Eden. And you too shall be brought down with the trees of Eden to the lowest part of the netherworld. (31:16, 18)

Now, Ezekiel completes the prophetic message on this topic. Indirectly, it emerges that in the future, the Garden of Eden will not be associated with the other nations; instead, it will be a description of the land and the dwelling place of the people of Israel. The significance of the Garden of Eden's transition from the prophecies concerning the nations to the prophecies of restoration is amplified by the fact that this description of the land is completely exposed to the view of the nations. In this way, Ezekiel sharpens the contrast between the future of the nations and the future of Israel:

> And men shall say, "That land, once desolate, has become like the Garden of Eden; and the cities, once ruined, desolate, and ravaged, are now populated and fortified." And the nations that are left around you shall know that I the Lord have rebuilt the ravaged places and replanted the desolate land. I the Lord have spoken and will act. (36:35–36)

SEEKING GOD

The shift in God's attitude towards His people in Ezekiel's prophecy, it seems, may be discerned in the conspicuous use of the root D-R-SH, with the climax of this new attitude finding expression in 36:36. If we track the appearance of this root throughout the book we find that in the past, God's relationship with His people was in crisis; the people's seeking (*derisha*) of God during the years of Destruction was responded to negatively. With regard to the future, however, there is a transformation in the use of the verb; the two contexts in which it appears in a positive sense speak of the future. In chapter 14 we find this root in verses 3, 7, and 10, all evincing the distance between God and His people. In verse 3, for instance, we read, "Shall I respond to their inquiry (*ha'idarosh idaresh*)?" Later, in chapter 20, the root appears in verses 1, 3, 31, and 40 – and once again, in each instance the context is one of distancing, of lack of concession to their requests. Verse 3 of that chapter provides a fitting example: "Have you come to inquire of Me (*halidrosh oti atem ba'im*)? As I live, I will not respond (*im idaresh*) to your inquiry – declares the Lord God." Likewise verse 31: "Shall I respond (*vaani idaresh*) to your inquiry, O House of Israel? As I live – declares the Lord God – I will not respond (*im idaresh*) to you."

The possibility of a future in which God inquires of, seeks out, or shows a positive interest in His people appears for the first time within the vision of the restoration (20:39–44): "There I will accept them, and there I will take note (*edrosh*) of your contributions" (20:40). An inquiring of a different sort, expressing concern and closeness, appears in 33:6, where God demands the meting out of justice to the observer who fails to warn His people. Thereafter, in the chapters devoted to the future restoration of the nation, God demands that justice be meted out to the leaders who do not inquire after or care about His flock: "with none to take thought (*ein doresh*) of them and none to seek them" (34:6; likewise v. 8). In contrast, verses 10–11 state that God will seek His flock and gather them to Him. The process reaches its climax in 36:37, where, for the first time in the book, we find God initiating contact with His people: "Moreover, in this I will respond (*idaresh*) to the House of Israel." This image complements the theme set down in chapter 34, where God seeks out His flock at the hands of the shepherds. However, while in that context the seeking was not oriented directly towards the people but rather towards the leaders who had been criminally negligent in their duty, here the prophet describes a direct inquiry. Thus, this verse attests to a significant change in the bond between God and His people.

Rabbi Eliezer of Beaugency draws a connection in his commentary between the end of chapter 36 and chapter 37 with its prophecy of the dry bones:

> And if one should say, "But this is a promise to those who would be living at that time. For those who had died in exile, captive and despoiled, by the sword and by fire, in sanctification of God's name, and [those] who died of old age, who had awaited consolation and deliverance all their lives, but did not see it – how are they to be consoled?" The response to this is, "The hand of the Lord was upon me." (Ezek. 37:1)

The uniqueness of Ezekiel's prophecy in chapter 37, then, arises from the fact that it addresses even the dead, announcing that there is hope for them, too – the renewal of the bond between God and His people includes them, too.

These prophecies of cleansing and of a renewed relationship with God constitute a shift in the book's tone and lead us into a detailed description of the future restoration in the final section of the book.

Chapter 22

The Dry Bones and the Future Kingdom
Ezekiel 37:1–28

The famous prophecy known as the "vision of the dry bones" reflects the nation's sense of despair following the Destruction of Jerusalem, and thereby complements the message of chapters 35–36. The prophecy is divided into two main units: the first in verses 1–14, the second in 15–28.

THE BONES IN THE VALLEY (37:1–14)

The prophecy begins with God's hand carrying Ezekiel out of his place in Babylon, bringing him "by the spirit of the Lord" and placing him in a valley. In the valley, God's glory is revealed to Ezekiel in tangible form; in fact, the valley has been mentioned previously (3:22–23; 8:4). It is difficult to know where this valley actually is – in Babylonia or in the Land of Israel; perhaps it was a place in Babylonia from which the prophet could see what was happening in the land. Radak, commenting on 3:22, explains:

> For the valley was a purer place than Tel Abib, where people lived, and it recurred time after time, to infuse him with God's providence and guidance. Furthermore, in that same valley in which [the ancient tower of] Babel had been built, God had showed His providence over His creations, for there He had mixed up their language and nullified their plan.

According to Radak, the valley is uninhabited, a place of special historical importance. Perhaps the transcendental nature of this prophecy is amplified by the fact that the location where it is conveyed cannot be identified.

The spirit of God, by means of which Ezekiel is transported, is mentioned elsewhere in the book: "Thereupon the spirit of the Lord fell upon me…. I know what comes into your mind. Many have you slain in this city; you have filled its streets with corpses" (11:5–6). The prophecy in our chapter, then, perhaps both represents the inverse of the prophecy in chapter 11 and complements it. There, the spirit of God exposed the bloodshed and the slain who lay throughout the city. In our chapter, the spirit of God returns – but to revive the slain, who have in the meantime become a pile of bones lying in the valley. In the prophecy, God observes the dry bones and asks, "Can these bones live again?" The prophet responds: "O Lord God, only You know" (37:3).

This answer seems to encapsulate Ezekiel's prophetic message throughout the book. God's status and His power stand at the center of his prophecy. The nation's past, present, and future are clarified by its relationship with God. Indeed, for the prophet it is altogether possible that not a single survivor of the nation will remain (as he himself declares in 9:8–9, and as the nation declares in 33:10), an idea climactically conveyed through the description of the meat burning in the pot, where the bones, too, are burned (24:10), and the beholder has no inkling of what will be. The prophet therefore has no distinct answer based on prior knowledge or principles such as the covenant, the merit of the forefathers, desecration of God's name, or the like. The answer will depend only on God's own decision.[1]

---

1. Rabbi Eliezer of Beaugency, commenting on Ezekiel 37:3, writes: "An artisan has an expert opinion as to whether a broken vessel can be repaired or not." See also Rabbi Joseph Kara's interpretation of this verse.

Now, the divine response addresses the bones directly:

> And He said to me, "Prophesy over these bones and say to them: O dry bones, hear the word of the Lord! Thus said the Lord God to these bones: I will cause breath to enter you and you shall live again. I will lay sinews upon you, and cover you with flesh, and form skin over you. And I will put breath into you, and you shall live again. And you shall know that I am the Lord!" (37:4–6)

The prophet has received a response to God's question. But the response in no way indicates that the future and fate of the bones are self-evident. Moreover, in the absence of divine intervention, the bones appear doomed to remain dry and dead.

Perhaps the prophecy, foretelling the nation's restoration by means of God's spirit, is meant as a contrast to what is happening at the same time in Jerusalem. This idea arises from one of Jeremiah's prophecies:

> And they have built the shrines of Topheth in the Valley of Ben-hinnom to burn their sons and daughters in fire.... Assuredly, a time is coming – declares the Lord – when men shall no longer speak of Topheth or the Valley of Ben-hinnom, but of the Valley of Slaughter; and they shall bury in Topheth until no room is left. The carcasses of this people shall be food for the birds of the sky and the beasts of the earth, with none to frighten them off.... At that time – declares the Lord – the bones of the kings of Judah, of its officers, of the priests, of the prophets, and of the inhabitants of Jerusalem shall be taken out of their graves and exposed to the sun, the moon, and all the host of heaven which they loved and served and followed, to which they turned and bowed down. They shall not be gathered for reburial; they shall become dung upon the face of the earth. And death shall be preferable to life for all that are left of this wicked folk, in all the other places to which I shall banish them – declares the Lord of Hosts. (Jer. 7:31–8:3)

The description of the unburied human bones that are strewn "upon the face of the earth" expresses more than just the great number of deaths during the years of siege and destruction. The withholding of burial dishonors the dead, and the removal of bones from their burial place likewise shows contempt.

In light of this, Ezekiel's encounter with a valley full of bones may attest to the disgrace of the people, and not necessarily to its future restoration. How will the situation develop? That depends entirely on God. Even when the realization of the prophecy becomes tangible, the prophet anxiously anticipates the spirit of God, which is slow in coming:

> And while I was prophesying, suddenly there was a sound of rattling, and the bones came together, bone to matching bone. I looked, and there were sinews on them, and flesh had grown, and skin had formed over them; but there was no breath in them. (Ezek. 37:7–8)

The comparison of the divine promise with the reality demonstrates that the essence is missing: the promise began with mention of "the breath" (v. 5); in reality, all elements but the breath are present. At this point another appeal is added to the prophecy, an appeal made directly to that breath: "Then He said to me, 'Prophesy to the breath, prophesy, O mortal! Say to the breath: Thus said the Lord God: Come, O breath, from the four winds, and breathe into these slain, that they may live again'" (v. 9).

Only after the prophet calls upon the spirit is the prophecy realized in full: "The breath entered them, and they came to life and stood up on their feet, a vast multitude" (v. 10). It seems that the gradual progression of the realization of the prophecy, finding expression in the prophet's dialogue with God, reveals something of the tension that Ezekiel feels as he waits (perhaps impatiently) for the realization of God's promise before his eyes.

Ezekiel then receives another prophecy. Here the emphasis is on the connection between the vision of the dry bones and the feeling that is prevalent amongst the nation:

The Dry Bones and the Future Kingdom

And He said to me, "O mortal, these bones are the whole House of Israel. They say, 'Our bones are dried up, our hope is gone; we are doomed.' Prophesy, therefore, and say to them: Thus said the Lord God: I am going to open your graves and lift you out of the graves, O My people, and bring you to the Land of Israel. You shall know, O My people, that I am the Lord, when I have opened your graves and lifted you out of your graves. I will put My breath into you and you shall live again, and I will set you upon your own soil. Then you shall know that I the Lord have spoken and have acted" – declares the Lord. (vv. 11–14)

A PROPHECY FOR ALL TIME

In the vision of the dry bones, as in many other prophecies in Ezekiel (ch. 16, 34, and more), the allegory and the reality that it represents are interwoven throughout. It therefore seems inappropriate to try to separate them and ask what part of this prophecy actually took place and what is solely allegory. Admittedly, there are different ways of interpreting this chapter.[2] One view is summed up in the words of Maimonides in his *Guide of the Perplexed* (II:46): "When [the prophet] says, 'and He set me down in the valley,' this only happened in the visions of God."[3] Thus, Maimonides views the entire prophecy as an allegory. However, Ḥazal offer a different view, suggesting a description of something tangible and real:

> R. Eliezer said: The dead whom Ezekiel resurrected stood up, uttered song, and immediately died. What song did they utter? "The Lord slays with righteousness and revives with mercy." R. Eliezer b. R. Yossi HaGelili, said: The dead whom Ezekiel revived went up to the Land of Israel, married wives and begat sons and daughters. R. Yehuda b. Beteira rose up and said: I am one of their descendants, and these are the tefillin which my grandfather left me [as an heirloom] from them. (Sanhedrin 92b)

---

2. See Kasher, *Yeḥezkel 25–48*, 720–22, appendix XII.
3. Translation based on Shlomo Pines, trans., *Guide of the Perplexed* (Chicago: University of Chicago Press, 1963), 404.

Ezekiel 37:1–28

Whether the description is of an actual occurrence or an allegory, it is clear that in the Jewish national consciousness, this prophecy remains timeless. An echo of this perception is found in the *Kuzari*, which connects the nation's hopes for redemption with this chapter in the book of Ezekiel.[4] For our generation, seeing the establishment and prospering of the State of Israel after the horror of the Holocaust, this consciousness of redemption bound together with the vision of dry bones is greatly amplified. We see expressions of this idea in many different places and spheres, such as in the reading of this chapter in many of the ceremonies marking Holocaust Remembrance Day, or in contemporary Hebrew poetry, such as the poem "Ezekiel" by Jacob Fichman, in which he speaks of "the dream of resurrection whose arrival you foresaw":

> Of all my nation's seers you are most wondrous in my eyes…
> How keen your locution is to me, keen is your revelation,
> How keen are the visions you raise.
> This marvelous design, in which Creation bloomed
> The dream of resurrection whose arrival you foresaw!
> This is none other than the blooming of an aching heart
> In which a vision, ripening, of delight
> A song to revive the soul of a scorched earth.
> And as one lingers before the desolation
> Having crossed the valley and its terrors
> He carries a torch under his uniform.[5]

ISRAEL'S RESTORATION (37:15–25)

In the second half of chapter 37, an additional element – unmentioned until this point – arises: the future unification of the exiles of Israel with the exiles of Judah. The prophet now speaks of the Kingdom of Israel, exiled by the Assyrian kingdom almost 150 years prior. When the time

---

4. "We are not like the dead, but rather like a sick and attenuated person whom the physicians have despaired of, and yet hopes for a miracle or an extraordinary recovery, as it is written: 'Can these bones live?' (Ezek. 37:3)."
5. Jacob Fichman, "Yeḥezkel," *Arugot: Divrei Shira UProza* (Jerusalem: Bialik, 1954), 51–52; see also Yaakov Orland's poem, "HaBika," *Shirim MeEretz Utz* (Tel Aviv: Mahbarot LeSifrut, 1963), 20–21.

The Dry Bones and the Future Kingdom

comes, he states, these exiles, too, will return to the land, along with the exiles of Judah who are in Babylonia.

This is a rather surprising prophecy. Until this point, Ezekiel has not mentioned the exiles of Israel. Moreover, the people's questioning of their status in exile, discussed earlier, arose from the fact that as, as far as we know, the exiles of Israel, unlike the exiles of Judah, did not live as a community with a distinct, independent identity. Their prevailing worldview was pagan; alongside obeying the local administration, exiled groups also showed loyalty to the local deity.[6] Therefore, this prophecy concerning the reunification of the Kingdom of Israel with the Kingdom of Judah is both a notable and a significant development.

Our prophecy is an elaboration of verse 11, in the first part of the chapter: "These bones are the whole House of Israel. They say, 'Our bones are dried up, our hope is gone; we are doomed.'" The nation did not believe that it would recover; and even the prophet is unable to answer the question, "Can these bones live again?" Ezekiel is forced to direct the question to God: "I replied, O Lord God, only You know" (v. 3). The mere presence of bones does not suffice to point to the nation's future. Human bones can be discovered many years after the person has died, when they are already entirely desiccated and devoid of vitality; their condition may make identification impossible, such that one cannot know whose bones they were.

But the state of these bones is different. Despite the very long time that has passed, the bones are identifiable: They are the bones of the House of Israel. The 150 years that have passed since the exile of the Kingdom of Israel are not proof of their annihilation. The nation receives a divine promise of divine restoration: "Prophesy…I am going to open your graves and lift you out of the graves, O My people, and bring you to the Land of Israel" (v. 12).

Like many other prophecies in the book of Ezekiel, here too both metaphor and meaning are intertwined. The prophet compares the two kingdoms to two separate pieces of wood, which in the future will again become one, and then states explicitly that the nation will once again be reunited:

---

6. This reality is supported by the text in II Kings (17:24–41) and Ezra (4:1–3).

> And you, O mortal, take a stick and write on it, "Of Judah and the Israelites associated with him;" and take another stick and write on it, "Of Joseph – the stick of Ephraim – and all the House of Israel associated with him." Bring them close to each other, so that they become one stick, joined together in your hand. (vv. 16–17)

The people, hearing the prophet's words, refuse to believe their message. Their response clearly demonstrates that the reunification of the Jewish people is most unexpected, an implausible vision. In the wake of their reaction, the prophet reinforces his words and states his message explicitly:

> And when any of your people ask you, "Won't you tell us what these actions of yours mean?" answer them, "Thus said the Lord God: I am going to take the stick of Joseph – which is in the hand of Ephraim – and of the tribes of Israel associated with him, and I will place the stick of Judah upon it and make them into one stick; they shall be joined in My hand." You shall hold up before their eyes the sticks which you have inscribed. (vv. 18–20)

Now the prophet returns to the prophecy of the nation's restoration. He integrates the idea of reunification as a single kingdom – an element that was not mentioned in his earlier prophecies of restoration: "I will make them a single nation in the land, on the hills of Israel, and one king shall be king of them all. Never again shall they be two nations, and never again shall they be divided into two kingdoms" (v. 22). The expression "into a single nation" in this verse now assumes its full significance, as referring to all parts of the nation. It should be noted that the mention of "the hills of Israel" as the place of this reunification is also significant; it complements Ezekiel's prophecy in chapter 36, which addressed the mountains of Israel.

The prophet continues:

> Nor shall they ever again defile themselves by their fetishes and their abhorrent things, and by their other transgressions. I will save them in all their settlements where they sinned, and I will cleanse them. Then they shall be My people, and I will be their God. (v. 23)

Notably, the prophet emphasizes that it is not the people who change their behavior or ceases to sin; rather, it is God who cleanses His people after bringing them out from among the nations.

ETERNAL DWELLING, LEADER, COVENANT, AND SANCTUARY (37:26–28)

Our prophetic unit concludes with verses 26–28, in which Ezekiel conveys the promise that the people's restoration, in all its various manifestations (dwelling, *nasi*, covenant, and Temple), will last forever:

> Thus they shall remain in the land which I gave to My servant Jacob and in which your fathers dwelt; they and their children and their children's children shall dwell there **forever**, with My servant David as their *nasi* **for all time.** I will make a covenant of friendship (*brit shalom*) with them – it shall be an **everlasting covenant** (*brit olam*) with them – I will establish them and multiply them, and I will place My Sanctuary among them **forever.** (vv. 25–26)

The expression "covenant of friendship" appeared previously, in chapter 34: "And I will grant them a covenant of friendship. I will banish vicious beasts from their land, and they shall live secure in the wasteland, they shall even sleep in the woodland" (34:25). In this prophecy in chapter 37, Ezekiel adds the element of eternity.

The expression "everlasting covenant" is mentioned only in a prophecy that precedes the Destruction, but which foretells the future restoration: "Nevertheless, I will remember the covenant I made with you in the days of your youth, and I will establish it with you as an everlasting covenant" (16:60). However, the prophetic context is different in each case and accordingly, the message entailed in this expression is unique to each context. In our chapter, the "everlasting covenant" symbolizes the eternal bond between the nation and its God. In chapter 16 there is an emphasis on the contrast between God's fulfillment of the covenant and the people's violation of the covenant – "for you have spurned the pact and violated the covenant" (16:59) – and this expression serves to highlight this gap.

Similarly, the promise concerning the eternal sanctuary or Temple appears for the first time in this prophecy; for this reason, it is emphasized twice in this unit: My dwelling-place also shall be over them; and I will be their God, and they shall be My people. And the nations shall know that I am the Lord that sanctify Israel, when My sanctuary shall be in the midst of them forever. (37:27–28). These verses parallel, to a certain extent, the promises that appear at the beginning of *Parashat Beḥukkotai* (Lev. 26:3–13). Even the formulation of the promises is similar in both places. Nevertheless, this similarity also serves to highlight what is unique to our prophecy – not only in relation to Ezekiel's other prophecies, but also compared to the promises in the Torah. It would seem that another significant innovation in this prophecy is that the Temple will exist forever – first through the promise that the Temple will exist in the people's midst forever, and then again through the promise that God will dwell in their midst forever.

The future Temple has not yet been mentioned at all in Ezekiel's prophecies of restoration. The only other place in which a prophecy ties the people to the Temple is in 43:9 – "and I will dwell among them forever," where the formulation emphasizes the Divine Presence rather than the physical structure in the midst of the people. This fact reflects the close connection between the Temple and the nation in the future. Or, more accurately, it reflects the fact that it is not the Temple that is at the center of the promises to the nation for the future; instead, the promise is that God Himself will dwell in the midst of His people forever. In light of this, attention should be paid to the fact that the element of eternity ("forever") is absent from the parallel verses in the book of Leviticus, as is the promise concerning the *nasi*. On the other hand, in the book of Leviticus we find a different element that does not appear in Ezekiel's prophecy – a promise of victory in war. The reason: There are no explicit wars in the future described by Ezekiel (36:35).

Compared to the rest of the book, the four promises that appear here, and that will be kept forever, are unique: the nation's existence upon its land (37:25), the covenant with God (v. 26), a unified leadership for both segments of the nation (vv. 19, 22), and the Temple that will stand forever: "And when My Sanctuary abides among them forever, the nations shall know that I the Lord do sanctify Israel" (v. 28).

The Dry Bones and the Future Kingdom

This concluding verse brings all of the motifs together and emphasizes the impact of this ideal upon other nations. It serves to emphasize the positive themes found in the prophecies after the Destruction; listeners may take some measure of comfort and optimism – which has been lacking until now. Thus, these prophecies introduce a new dimension into the book of Ezekiel.

Although this conclusion of chapter 37 sounds like a suitable platform from which to proceed to describe the vision of the future Temple (ch. 40–48), we first encounter two chapters that are devoted to the war of Gog from the land of Magog. These make no mention at all of the Temple; only afterwards does the prophet return to this subject. This transition indicates that the necessary conditions for the return of God's glory to the Temple are not yet in place. It is these conditions that are addressed by the next two chapters.

Chapter 23
Gog from the Land of Magog
Ezekiel 38:1–39:29

Chapters 38 and 39 comprise a unit that describes God's war against "Gog of the land of Magog." Along with Gog's downfall and the manner in which God wages war against him, the prophet also describes his special strength and the sanctification of God's name that results from his defeat. This prophecy complements the other restoration prophecies in the book discussed in previous chapters. Thus far, the prophecy has climaxed with the nation's return to its land and its purification from sin. Now we discover that the process remains unfinished. The nation's restoration occurs hand in hand with the strengthening of God's status in the world. But God's status is only fully cemented after His war against Gog from the land of Magog – a war that ends with the promise that God will not hide His face from His people.

This prophecy deals with the role of God, who distinguishes between good and evil and between past and future (similar to Isaiah

Ezekiel 38:1–39:29

34–37 and Zechariah 9–14[1]). At the center of the prophecy is God's judgment against the nations that have rebelled against Him, a necessary stage on the road to Israel's restoration. The uniqueness of this prophecy in Ezekiel, compared to the above-mentioned prophets, lies in its scope, the explicit naming of the aggressors, and the timing of the war specified in the prophecy: *after* the nation's return to its land.

THE DESCRIPTION OF GOD'S WAR WITH GOG (38:1–39:10)

Chapters 38 and 39 share many common motifs, but there is a clear division between them. Chapter 38 deals primarily with Gog's might and strength, while chapter 39 centers on his anticipated downfall. At the beginning of chapter 38, God commands Ezekiel to prophesy to "Gog of the land of Magog, the chief prince of Meshech and Tubal" (v. 2). Over the course of this prophecy we learn of the military preparations of the army of Gog. Gog arrives in the land at the head of an army that includes other nationalities, but he and his army are actually led by divine guidance:

> I will turn you around and put hooks in your jaws, and lead you out with all your army, horses, and horsemen, all of them clothed in splendor, a vast assembly, all of them with bucklers and shields, wielding swords. Among them shall be Persia, Nubia, and Put, everyone with shield and helmet; Gomer and all its cohorts, Beth-togarmah [in] the remotest parts of the north and all its cohorts – the many peoples with you. Be ready, prepare yourselves, you and all the battalions mustered about you, and hold yourself in reserve for them.[2] (vv. 4–7)

---

1. These prophecies, too, are related to the Day of God that is mentioned by other prophets, too, including Isaiah 13; Jeremiah 30; Joel 4; Micah 4; Zechariah 12, 14; Daniel 11; Psalms 2, 83.
2. The commentators are divided concerning the meaning of the closing words of the verse – "*vehayita lahem lemishmar.*" Rashi understands it in the literal sense – that Gog protects his army and ensures its welfare and safety, while Radak maintains that the army protects him, since a king needs protection and bodyguards.

Gog from the Land of Magog

The war takes place after Israel has returned to its land; this is stated explicitly. Thus, these chapters in the book follow chronologically after chapters 34–37, which address the process of return:

> After a long time you shall be summoned; in the distant future you shall march against the land [of a people] restored from the sword, gathered from the midst of many peoples – against the mountains of Israel, which have long lain desolate – [a people] liberated from the nations, and now all dwelling secure. (v. 8)

Although the arrival of Gog is described as a divine initiative, God's response indicates that Gog plans a quick military campaign aimed at taking spoils and grabbing prey before the people are able to fortify themselves in the cities to which they have returned to live:

> Thus said the Lord God: On that day, a thought will occur to you, and you will conceive a wicked design. You will say, "I will invade a land of open towns, I will fall upon a tranquil people living secure, all of them living in unwalled towns and lacking bars and gates, in order to take spoil and seize plunder" – to turn your hand against repopulated wastes, and against a people gathered from among nations, acquiring livestock and possessions, living at the center of the earth. (vv. 10–12)

What ends up happening is quite different. In fact, it is the opposite: "Therefore prophesy, O mortal, and say to Gog: Thus said the Lord God: ... I will bring you to My land, that the nations may know Me when, before their eyes, I manifest My holiness through you, O Gog!" (vv. 14–16).

We then learn that God's war against Gog is the realization of prophecies that came to other prophets, too (perhaps this refers to Jeremiah, who also spoke of a nation that would come from the north): "Thus said the Lord God: Why, you are the one I spoke of in ancient days through My servants, the prophets of Israel, who prophesied for years in those days that I would bring you against them!" (Ezek. 38:17).

Now the prophet moves on to a description of the punishment meted out to Gog, including many elements pertaining to the end of days:

> On that day, when Gog sets foot on the soil of Israel – declares the Lord God – My raging anger shall flare up. For I have decreed in My indignation and in My blazing wrath: On that day, a terrible earthquake shall befall the Land of Israel. The fish of the sea, the birds of the sky, the beasts of the field, all creeping things that move on the ground, and every human being on earth shall quake before Me. Mountains shall be overthrown, cliffs shall topple, and every wall shall crumble to the ground. I will then summon the sword against him throughout My mountains – declares the Lord God – and every man's sword shall be turned against his brother. I will punish him with pestilence and with bloodshed; and I will pour torrential rain, hailstones, and sulfurous fire upon him and his hordes and the many peoples with him. (vv. 18–22)

This prophecy contains an element of renewal like that of the Creation. The similarity between the description of the animals in these verses and their description in Genesis 7:21–22 supports this. The elements of this prophecy that pertain to the end of days thus point to a renewal of the whole order of Creation at the end of days, a trend that is further reinforced in chapters 40–48.

The purpose of the prophecy as a whole is emphasized in the final verse of this chapter: "Thus will I manifest My greatness and My holiness, and make Myself known in the sight of many nations. And they shall know that I am the Lord" (v. 23). This verse underlines the aim of God's war against Gog, as well as its result – knowledge of God among the nations. This prophecy, then, is a response to the desecration of God's name represented by the nation's exile from its land and the Destruction of the Temple, as we shall see below.[3]

In chapter 39, the prophet addresses Gog again, setting forth his punishment:

---

[3]. The placement of these verses at the end of the prophecy fits a common trend we have noted in the book of Ezekiel: The conclusion of the prophecy contains an addition in which the main message takes a significant turn.

> I will turn you around and drive you on, and I will take you from the far north and lead you toward the mountains of Israel. I will strike your bow from your left hand and I will loosen the arrows from your right hand. You shall fall on the mountains of Israel, you and all your battalions and the peoples who are with you; and I will give you as food to carrion birds of every sort and to the beasts of the field, as you lie in the open field. For I have spoken – declares the Lord God. And I will send a fire against Magog and against those who dwell secure in the coastlands. And they shall know that I am the Lord. (39:2–6)

The description of Gog's fallen as food for the birds and beasts of the field is clarified fully at the end of the chapter, where we find its fulfillment. Now, for the first time, the prophet foretells the actions of the inhabitants of the cities of Israel, who are not involved as combatants in the war between Gog and God. All they are able to do is gather up the weapons (which will serve for the coming years as an accessible source of combustible material) and to benefit from the spoils left from Gog's army:

> Then the inhabitants of the cities of Israel will go out and make fires and feed them with the weapons – shields and bucklers, bows and arrows, clubs and spears; they shall use them as fuel for seven years. They will not gather firewood in the fields or cut any in the forests, but will use the weapons as fuel for their fires. They will despoil those who despoiled them and plunder those who plundered them – declares the Lord God. (vv. 9–10)

THE LAND'S PURIFICATION (39:11–29)

The prophet now describes the burial of Gog and all his company, which is carried out in order to purify the land.

The First Stage: The Burial of the Dead

> On that day I will assign to Gog a burial site there in Israel – the Valley of the Travelers, east of the Sea. It shall block the path of travelers, for there Gog and all his multitude will be buried. It

Ezekiel 38:1–39:29

> shall be called the Valley of Gog's Multitude. The House of Israel shall spend seven months burying them, in order to cleanse the land; all the people of the land shall bury them. The day I manifest My glory shall bring renown to them – declares the Lord God. And they shall appoint men to serve permanently, to traverse the land and bury any invaders who remain above ground, in order to cleanse it. The search shall go on for a period of seven months. As those who traverse the country make their rounds, any one of them who sees a human bone shall erect a marker beside it, until the buriers have interred them in the Valley of Gog's Multitude. There shall also be a city named Multitude. And thus the land shall be cleansed. (vv. 11–16)

Thus far, the book has made no mention of the purification of the land or of Jerusalem. This, evidently, is because it is impossible to purify the land without its inhabitants undergoing purification as well – just as it was the people who caused the land to become defiled in the first place. Following this line of thought, it might even be possible for the people's purification to lead to the land's purification automatically, without any specific process taking place.

But chapter 39 describes, for the first time, the actions necessary for the purification of the land (v. 12). So while we might have assumed that the people's purification would also lead to that of the land, there is, in fact, a precondition: removal of the causes of defilement.

The purification of the land entails several stages:

1. God allots Gog a specific burial place in Israel.
2. The bodies of Gog and of all his multitudes are buried there.
3. From now on this burial place is known as "the Valley of Hamon-Gog (Gog's Multitude)."
4. The burial campaign, following which the land will be restored to its purity, lasts seven months, undertaken by "the people of the land."
5. Rangers pass through the land, after these seven months, burying any bones that might remain.
6. The rangers mark every place where human bones remain, until these too are brought for burial in the Valley of Hamon-Gog.

Gog from the Land of Magog

In order to purify the land after Gog and his army are defeated, it becomes necessary to bury the many casualties. What, then, has caused the defilement of the land mentioned in these verses? The great number of corpses strewn over the land seems to be what makes the purification necessary; it is their presence that has defiled the land. The impurity of a corpse is mentioned explicitly in Ezekiel 9:7, and accords with the Torah's teaching that physical contact with bones, or their presence together with a person within a tent, cause the person to become ritually impure (Num. 19).

The fact that the corpses of Gog and his soldiers are lying about with no burial place – as required by the law in Deuteronomy (21:23) – causes the defilement of the land. The removal of the corpses will purify it. Therefore, Ezekiel describes here how over a period of seven months the House of Israel will bury all the dead, and thereby purify the land. In addition, the valley in which the corpses will be buried – the "Valley of the Travelers" – will henceforth be known as the "Valley of Hamon-Gog." This name may allude to the past sins that were committed in the Valley of Ben-hinnom, known as a location where children were passed through fire (Jer. 2:23; II Chr. 27:3). On a deeper level, then, the prophet may be intimating that the passing of children through fire – which had been common in the land – is what caused its defilement (see also Lev. 18:21–30).

There are two parts to the purification of the land through the burial of the dead. On one hand, there is a technical component: The bones are gathered up, removing the defiling elements; bodies are prevented from remaining unburied, allowing the land to be purified. But on another level, this is a ceremony of purification specifically bound up with the wickedness of Gog. During this ceremony, the ground swallows up Gog and thereby rids itself of his defilement (39:14), in a manner that recalls the Torah's statement about a murderer: "and the land can have no expiation for blood that is shed on it, except by the blood of him who shed it" (Num. 35:33). The land is cleansed only when the murderer is properly punished, and the blood, or bones, of those who sinned upon the land are then buried.

Thus, in addition to purifying the land from the casualties of war, this ceremony also purifies the land from the sins of the past.

The similarity between the purification of the land through burial of the dead in Ezekiel and the purification of the person who is ritually

Ezekiel 38:1–39:29

impure through contact with the dead serves as further evidence of this theory, as we see in the law of the red heifer (Num. 19:11–22). Several points of comparison exist:

1. The purification process for someone who is ritually impure as a result of coming into contact with a corpse lasts seven days (Numbers 19:1, referred to also in Ezekiel 44:26: "After he has become clean, seven days shall be counted off for him"); the duration of the burial campaign in order to cleanse the land is seven months.

2. During the purification process, the impure person undergoes a cleansing on two occasions (on the third day and on the seventh day). Correspondingly, the burial of the dead is not concluded by means of a one-time act; rather, another round of inspection is necessary in order to ascertain that everything requiring burial has indeed been buried.

3. Anyone who comes into contact with a human bone (for example), is impure for seven days (Num. 19:16); correspondingly, Ezekiel emphasizes the need to bury human bones: "As those who traverse the country make their rounds, any one of them who sees a human bone shall erect a marker beside it, until the buriers have interred them in the Valley of Gog's Multitude" (39:15).[4]

The Second Stage: Removal of Possible Worship Sites

The next prophecy describes a banquet that the God of Israel prepares from the flesh of the mighty and the blood of the princes following the burial, a banquet intended – surprisingly enough – for the birds and the animals. This banquet will demonstrate God's judgment to all the nations:

> And you, O mortal, say to every winged bird and to all the wild beasts: Thus said the Lord God: Assemble, come and gather from all around for the sacrificial feast that I am preparing for you – a

---

4. It should be pointed out that the expression "*etzem adam*" (human bone) in this exact form is found only in the two sources discussed here. A variation of this expression, in the plural – "*atzamot adam*" – is found in three places in the book of Kings.

great sacrificial feast – upon the mountains of Israel, and eat flesh and drink blood. You shall eat the flesh of warriors and drink the blood of the princes of the earth: rams, lambs, he-goats, and bulls – fatlings of Bashan all of them. You shall eat fat to satiety and drink your fill of blood from the sacrificial feast that I have prepared for you. And you shall sate yourselves at My table with horses, charioteers, warriors, and all fighting men – declares the Lord God. (39:17–20)

This prophecy complements the purification of the land. Although burying the dead bodies stops those bodies from causing impurity, the burials cannot stop the graves from becoming a pilgrimage site. According to pagan belief, a human grave symbolizes a place where the dead have a continued presence; burial places often served as pilgrimage sites, receiving offerings that included food. At times, burial places also served to signify ownership over some territorial unit. In these verses, the dead themselves become flesh for consumption. Those who consume them – the birds and the beast of the field – could have been sacrificed as offerings to the dead (in the pagan context); here the situation is reversed: They themselves eat the flesh and drink the blood of God's enemies. By means of these two stages, one following consecutively after another, Ezekiel prepares the ground for the appearance of God's glory to the nations.[5] Perhaps these verses might even be regarded as a prophecy of restoration for Israel, since Jeremiah's prophecies before the Destruction include a parallel punishment directed against the nation:

> Assuredly, a time is coming – declares the Lord – when men shall no longer speak of Topheth or the Valley of Ben-hinnom, but of the Valley of Slaughter; and they shall bury in Topheth until no room is left. The carcasses of this people shall be food for the birds of the sky and the beasts of the earth, with none to frighten them off. (Jer. 7:32–33)

---

5. See Francesca Stavrakopoulou, "Gog's Grave and the Use and Abuse of Corpses in Ezekiel 39:11–20," *Journal of Biblical Literature* 129, no. 1 (2010): 67–84.

Ezekiel 38:1–39:29

The Final Stage: The Nations Will Know God

Ezekiel now describes the purpose of the process: "Thus will I manifest My glory among the nations, and all the nations shall see the judgment that I executed and the power that I wielded against them. From that time on, the House of Israel shall know that I the Lord am their God" (39:21–22).

In his description, the prophet hints at the fundamental difference between the nations' attitudes towards their deities and Israel's approach to God:

> And the nations shall know that the House of Israel were exiled only for their iniquity, because they trespassed against Me, so that I hid My face from them and delivered them into the hands of their adversaries, and they all fell by the sword. When I hid My face from them, I dealt with them according to their uncleanness and their transgressions. (vv. 23–24)

Note the prophet's emphasis: God exiled His people because of their sins, and because He chose to hide His face. In the pagan world, by contrast, the harm inflicted on a particular nation was proof of the weakness of their god; the suffering was not interpreted as a punishment or as the hiding of a divine face. The sharply contrasting Jewish view appears at the end of a prophecy that discusses the removal of pagan centers of worship.

Ezekiel's prophecy at the conclusion of the unit contains the purpose of all of his prophecies. The following verses serve as a conclusion not only for chapters 38–39, but also for all Ezekiel's restoration prophecies:

> Assuredly, thus said the Lord God: I will now restore the fortunes of Jacob and have mercy on the whole House of Israel; and I will be zealous for My holy name. They will bear their shame and all their trespasses that they committed against Me, when they dwell in their land secure and untroubled, when I have brought them back from among the peoples and gathered them out of the lands of their enemies and have manifested My holiness through them

in the sight of many nations. They shall know that I the Lord am their God when, having exiled them among the nations, I gather them back into their land and leave none of them behind. I will never again hide My face from them, for I will pour out My spirit upon the House of Israel – declares the Lord God. (vv. 25–29)

God's "holy name" is a central motif in this prophecy (39:7, 25). In several places in these chapters, the purpose of God's war against Gog is mentioned, each time with additional depth and elaboration.[6] First the prophet states that at the time of this war God will bring the nation to its land, and thereby become known amongst the nations: "I will bring you to My land, that the nations may know Me when, before their eyes, I manifest My holiness through you, O Gog!" (38:16). Later, the prophet emphasizes that not only will God's name become known among the nations, but His name will also be magnified and sanctified – so much so that many nations will recognize Him: "Thus will I manifest My greatness and My holiness, and make Myself known in the sight of many nations. And they shall know that I am the Lord" (38:23). Finally, the prophet mentions, for the first time, that God's holy name must become known among the nations because it was desecrated earlier. This "making known" will make the nations aware that God is the Holy One of Israel: "I will make My holy name known among My people Israel, and never again will I let My holy name be profaned. And the nations shall know that I the Lord am holy in Israel" (39:7).

The repeated emphasis on God's name having been desecrated begins only from the middle of the prophecy (rather than from the beginning). This is not coincidental. Moreover, the aim of the war against Gog is exposed gradually, with each verse adding to our understanding of its ramifications. So it is only with the third appearance of the expression "making known" that the text notes that God's holy name will be made known amongst Israel, that it will no longer be desecrated, and that the nations will know that God is the Holy One in Israel. This final aim is the loftiest, bringing the nations to the pinnacle of their understanding of God and His bond with His people.

---

6. As Moskowitz notes, *Sefer Yeḥezkel*, 311.

Ezekiel 38:1–39:29

The prophecy then sums up the aim of God's war against Gog and its outcomes, regarding both the nations and the House of Israel, along with the nation's knowledge that God is holy in Israel:[7] "Thus will I manifest My glory among the nations, and all the nations shall see the judgment that I executed and the power that I wielded against them" (39:21).

The manifestation of God's glory among the nations, after they have witnessed His judgment being executed (in His war against Gog), accords with the distancing of God's glory from the Temple (ch. 8–11) as well as with its return in the vision of the future Temple (43:1–5). Manifestation of God's glory is part of the process of the nation's recognition of God: "From that time on, the House of Israel shall know that I the Lord am their God" (39:22).

This knowledge prepares the ground for the final stage in the description of the purpose of God's war against Gog: "I will now restore the fortunes of Jacob and I will have mercy on the whole House of Israel; and I will be zealous for My holy name" (Ezek. 39:25).

This verse is exceptional in three respects:

1. The expression "the fortunes of Jacob" appears only here and in Psalms (85:2),[8] although the use of the verb SH-V-B (to return, bring back) together with the word *shevut* (captivity) is common, with varying meanings; it also appears elsewhere in Ezekiel (16:53; 29:14).[9]

2. The root R-H-M (to have mercy for or compassion upon,) appears nowhere else in the book of Ezekiel.

3. This is the only place where the expression "My holy name" appears in the book of Ezekiel without any description of it having been defiled or desecrated.

---

7. These verses follow on from another prophetic unit (vv. 11–24) that laid the groundwork for God's glory being manifest among the nations and His spirit being poured upon the House of Israel.
8. According to *ketiv*, the written scribal tradition.
9. Another element making this phrase unusual is the use of the appellation "Jacob." In the book of Ezekiel, it appears only twice; in comparison, Isaiah uses "Jacob" no less than thirty-nine times, while Jeremiah uses it ten times.

This verse, then, is a summary of God's purpose in His war against Gog: first, the returning of "the fortunes of Jacob" to its land expresses the ingathering of the twelve tribes to their land. Perhaps this unique expression is used to convey that the people's return to the land comes about by virtue of its having been connected to God ever since the days of Jacob as the Chosen People, rather than as a result of the nation's deeds or behavior.

In addition, after many prophecies in which the prophet emphasizes that the motive for returning the people to its land is solely God's wish to sanctify His name among the nations, he now introduces an unusually reconciliatory note: "I will have mercy on the whole House of Israel" (39:25). In contrast to the harsh attitude of the prophet, the bond between God and His people is ultimately also influenced by the divine attribute of mercy.[10] Moreover, since this verse makes no mention of desecration of God's holy name, there is also no mention of His name being sanctified in the eyes of the nations. It seems that instead of sanctification, the time has now come for "zealousness" for His holy name. This zealousness explains the need for God's war against Gog, and its consequences, as well as the ingathering of the nation of Israel from among all the nations, despite its sins. At the end of this zealousness God will pour His spirit upon the nation: "I will never again hide My face from them, for I will pour out My spirit upon the House of Israel – declares the Lord God" (v. 29).[11]

Despite the unique nature of these chapters, they sum up themes that have been addressed in various contexts in earlier prophecies. For example, this prophecy contains no mention of any actions carried out by the people, because the nation's restoration will not come by virtue

---

10. In addition to the fact that the word "*raḥamim*" (mercy) appears nowhere else in the book of Ezekiel, we also noted above that other expressions of consolation always appear in a negative context – with one other exception, in 36:21: "I had pity (*ve'eḥmol*) for My holy name." In both of these instances the prophet notes that the motive for God's defense of His holy name is *ḥemla*, expressing the uniqueness of the bond between God and His people, and the idea that God is prompted here not only by the need to perform justice, but also by His compassion.
11. For a more detailed analysis on this, see Tova Ganzel, "The Descriptions of the Restoration of Israel in Ezekiel," *Vetus Testamentum* 60 (2010): 197–211.

of their actions. Likewise, the war against Gog is waged not by Israel, but rather by God alone. These chapters position God at the center in other ways, too: the main message running through the prophecy is the nations' recognition of God's glory (39:21), and thereafter the Jewish people's recognition of its God (v. 22) and return to its land (v. 29).[12]

GOG AND MAGOG THROUGHOUT THE GENERATIONS[13]

These chapters of Ezekiel are part of the nation's historical consciousness. Throughout the generations, this prophecy has been cited as describing the events that will take place directly before, or during, or directly after the coming of the Messiah. Maimonides writes:

> The simple interpretation of the prophets' words appear to imply that the war of Gog and Magog will take place at the beginning of the Messianic age. Before the war of Gog and Magog, a prophet will arise to inspire Israel to be upright and prepare their hearts.... All these and similar matters cannot be definitely known by man until they occur for these matters are undefined in the prophets' words. (*Mishneh Torah, Hilkhot Melakhim UMilkhamot* 12:2)[14]

Throughout the generations, Jews have anticipated the realization of this prophecy. Ḥazal teach: "The Holy One, blessed be He, sought to make [King] Hezekiah the Messiah, and to make Sennacherib and his armies – Gog and Magog, but since he [Hezekiah] did not utter praise, it was concealed" (Ruth Rabba 7:3).

Thus, our sages draw a connection between the war against Sennacherib and Ezekiel's prophecy, asserting that that war could have represented the historical actualization of the prophecy about Gog and Magog, even though it took place many years before Ezekiel received this prophecy. Likewise, many years later, in the fifteenth century

---

12. For a detailed discussion of this, see Tova Ganzel, "The Prophecies of Joel: A Bridge between Ezekiel and Haggai," *Journal of Hebrew Scriptures* 11 (2011): 1–22.
13. For more on the name "Gog and Magog" and location, see Kasher, *Yeḥezkel 25–48*, 764–769, appendix XIV.
14. Translation taken from Eliyahu Touger, trans., *Mishneh Torah: A New Translation with Commentaries and Notes* (New York: Moznaim, 1991–2008).

commentary of Abrabanel on these chapters, Ezekiel's prophecy concerning Gog and Magog is interpreted as a prophecy "concerning the Christians, the children of Edom," who are destined to come to the Land of Israel (it is possible that the Crusades, the last of which took place two hundred years before Abrabanel's time, served as the context for this view). Moreover, Abrabanel, who was expelled from Spain by the Christians, interprets the events described in these chapters as God's vengeance on the Christians for their deeds, rejecting the Christian interpretation, which attributes the events to their faith.[15] It is no coincidence that these chapters are at the center of Ezekiel's prophecies dealing with God's revenge on the nations. In the Jewish historical consciousness, they represent a climactic description of divine retribution. For example, we find in the Talmud:

> R. Shimon b. Pazi said in the name of R. Yehoshua b. Levi in Bar Kappara's name: He who observes [the practice of] three festive meals on Shabbat is saved from three evils: the travails of the Messiah, the retribution of Gehinnom, and the wars of Gog and Magog.... "The wars of Gog and Magog:" "day" is written here [Ex. 16:25]; whilst there it is written "in that day when Gog shall come" [Ezek. 38:18]. (Shabbat 118a)

We also read: "R. Yohanan said in the name of R. Shimon bar Yohai: A bad son in a man's house is worse than the war of Gog and Magog" (Berakhot 7b).

Thus, Ezekiel's prophecy left an indelible impression on Jewish national consciousness. The echoes of the expression which became a concept in its own right – "Gog and Magog" – stand out prominently in the words of our sages, commentators, and even philosophers and poets.

With this, Ezekiels's prophecies of restoration draw to a close and his prophecies concerning the future Temple begin.

---

15. It is interesting to compare Abrabanel's view of these chapters with the interpretation of Malbim, whose commentary reflects the events of the nineteenth century.

Ezekiel 38:1–39:29

APPENDIX: MOTIFS IN EZEKIEL'S PROPHECIES OF RESTORATION

With the end of all of the Ezekiel's restoration prophecies in chapter 39, and before we move on to the book's final group of prophecies, we pause to review the motifs that are repeated throughout the prophecies of restoration – and how they diverge from our expectations.

Novel Messages in the Prophecies of Restoration

The common themes treated by Ezekiel exist throughout all of his prophecies, but the prophecies also contain special elements, unique to each prophecy within its context. Below, we take a closer look at what elements or messages are new to each of the restoration prophecies.

Chapters 11, 16, and 20 lay out the prophecies of restoration that preceded the Destruction. In none of these chapters does the prophet call upon the people to change their ways in order to prevent the imminent disaster.

The unique message that appears in 11:14–21 is that the people's ingathering in the land in the future is not the result of any change in the people's behavior, but rather the result of God's wish to sanctify His name in the eyes of the nations. The change will be effected by God replacing their "heart of stone" with a new heart (v. 19). This serves to reinforce the prophet's message to the exiles that despite their sins, it is specifically from them that the future of the nation will sprout, and not from those remaining in the land.

In chapter 16 (vv. 59–63), we find another prophecy of restoration; this one is different from all the others (and therefore is not included in the chart below). At the end of the chapter, most of which is devoted to highlighting the scope of the nation's sins and their severity, the prophet suddenly makes a sharp turn (in a manner that is entirely unique, and occurs nowhere else in the book) and speaks of a process of atonement: "When I have forgiven you for all that you did – declares the Lord God" (16:63). So despite the very severe rebuke given to the nation, this harsh chapter also ends on an optimistic note.

The third prophecy of restoration is found in 20:33–44, and consists of two parts (20:33–39, 40–44). This prophecy, too, ends with the message that despite the nation's "corrupt acts" (*alilot nishḥatot*) – a unique expression conveying the severity of their sins – God will bring them to their land.

Each of the prophecies of restoration that come after the Destruction (ch. 34, 36, 37, 39) also contain a unique message. In chapter 34's prophecy, which concludes in verses 25–30, for the first time, Ezekiel does not speak of the past or of the shepherds who did not carry out their task as they should have; instead, the prophetic message might be summarized as God's blessing to His people (34:31).

The unique idea of the prophecy of restoration in chapter 36 lies in the ceremony of purification, which we saw above. Here, too, the prophecy ends with an optimistic message that had not appeared up until now: the resettlement of the cities with "flocks of people" (36:38).

The prophetic message in chapter 37 contains Ezekiel's first mention of the reunification of the two kingdoms and of the Divine Presence that will dwell in the nation's midst forever.

Finally, the end of chapter 39, too, illuminates elements that are unparalleled in the book. The main ideas we see here are the return to the Land of Israel, compassion, and God's zealousness for His people. It seems that these concluding verses of this part of the book of Ezekiel represent a deliberate change of direction in Ezekiel's prophetic message at the conclusion of his prophecies.

In addition to these prophecies, we find one more prophecy of restoration that is interwoven with Ezekiel's prophecy to Tyre (28:25–26). This prophecy, too, contains a unique message: the reference to the nation as "My servant Jacob" (v. 25), as well as the contrast between God's actions towards His people and those towards the other nations, both stated in one verse: "And they [Israel] shall dwell on it in security. They shall build houses and plant vineyards, and shall dwell on it in security when I have meted out punishment to all those about them who despise them" (v. 26).

Recurring Motifs in Ezekiels' Prophecies of Restoration

While each prophecy carries its own individual message, there are words that recur in all of the prophecies.

Ezekiel 38:1–39:29

Chapter							
Pre-Destruction Prophecies							
11:17–19			I will gather (*vekibatzti*) you from the peoples	And assemble (*ve'asafti*) you out of the countries	And I will give (*venatati*) you the Land of Israel	And I will give (*venatati*) them a heart of flesh	
20:34–37		I will bring you out (*vehotzeiti*) from the peoples	And gather (*vekibatzti*) you from the lands	And I will bring (*veheveiti*) you into the wilderness of the peoples	I will enter into judgement with you… (*venishpateti etkhem*) And I will make you pass… (*vihe'evarti etkhem*)		
20:41–44		When I bring (*behotzi'i*) you out from the peoples	And gather (*vekibatzi*) you from the lands	And I will be sanctified (*venikdashti*) through you in the sight of the nations	When I have brought (*behavi'i*) you to the Land of Israel	There you will recall… (*uzekhartem*) you shall know (*viyedatem*)	
Prophecies concerning the Nations							
28:25–26			When I have gathered (*bekabtzi*) the House of Israel from the peoples	and have shown Myself holy (*venikdashti*) through them in the sight of the nations			And they shall dwell (*veyashvu*)… And they shall know (*veyadu*)

Gog from the Land of Magog

Chapter							
Post-Destruction Prophecies							
34:13, 22, 30		I will take them out (*vehotzeitim*) from the peoples	And gather them (*vekibatztim*) from the countries	And I will bring them (*vehaviotim*) to their own land			And I will rescue... (*vehoshati*) they shall know... (*veyadu*)
36:23–29	I will sanctify (*vekidashti*) My great name... And the nations shall know that I am the Lord	I will take (*velakahti*) you from among the nations	And gather (*vekibatzti*) you from all countries	And I will bring (*veheveiti*) you back to your own land	I will sprinkle clean water upon you (*vezarakti aleikhem mayim tehorim*)	And I will give (*venatati*) you a new heart	Then you shall dwell... (*viyshavtem*) And when I have delivered (*vehoshaati*) And they shall know (*uzekhartem*)
37:21, 23, 25, 28		I am going to take (*loke'ah*) the Israelite people from among the nations	And gather (*vekibatzti*) them from every quarter	And bring (*veheveiti*) them into their own land	I will save... (*vehoshaati*) And I will cleanse (*vetiharti*) And they shall remain (*veyashvu*)	And when My Sanctuary abides among them forever, the nations shall know that I the Lord do sanctify Israel.	
39:25–28	and will have mercy on the whole House of Israel (*verihamti*) And I will be zealous for My holy name (*vekineti leshem kodshi*)	When I have brought (*beshovevi*) them back from among the peoples	And gathered (*vekibatzi*) them out of the lands of their enemies	And have manifested My holiness (*venikdashti*) through them in the sight of many nations.	I gather (*vekinastim*) them back into their land		they shall know

Ezekiel, Jeremiah, and Isaiah

We have seen that each of Ezekiel's restoration prophecies has its own unique message or elements, and we have looked at themes that are common to Ezekiel's prophecies of restoration. Some of these themes also serve to set his prophecies apart from Jeremiah's prophecies of consolation and Isaiah's prophecies of redemption.

Inasmuch as we have noted the unique characteristics of Ezekiel's prophecies, so might we characterize the unique components of the parallel prophecies in the book of Jeremiah (found primarily in chapters 30–33).[16] His prophecies include a call to repentance, a process whose reward is assured: a return to Zion, a worthy leadership, fertility in the land. In addition, his prophecies focus on the centrality of the Ark of God's Covenant and the role of Jerusalem as God's Throne, and they describe the nation's prayer and supplication to God, with God responding to the prayer and bringing them back to the land.

Jeremiah's calls to repentance took place in the period that preceded Ezekiel's prophecy. During the era of Jeremiah's prophecy, it still seemed that it might be possible to avert the Destruction, if only the people would change their behavior. Generally speaking, those of Jeremiah's prophecies that are distinguishable from Ezekiel's include many positive motifs: return and repentance, compassion, relief, love, joy, consolation, and forgiveness. Indeed, Jeremiah's prophecies for the future seem to aim to comfort the people, and they therefore contain words of consolation over the Destruction of Jerusalem – an element absent from the book of Ezekiel and from the other chapters in the book of Jeremiah.

At the same time, Jeremiah's prophecies lack certain other central elements found only in Ezekiel's restoration prophecies. For instance, in Ezekiel we find a more detailed description of the return of the people to the land; some central details of this process are absent from Jeremiah's accounts. Similarly missing are the ceremony of purification of the people by God, the future sanctification of God's name, the pouring of God's spirit upon the people, atonement, and the promise of the eternal Temple.

---

16. Also in Jeremiah 3:14–18; 16:14–15; 23:3–8; 24:4–7; 29:10–14; 46:27–28; 50:34.

It should also be noted that the salvation and deliverance that characterize many of Isaiah's prophecies of redemption are largely absent from both Ezekiel and Jeremiah. The reason for this, ostensibly, is that the prophetic response to the tragedy of exile and Destruction is the promise of future restoration. This promise is an encouraging and reassuring one, but ultimately it cannot turn back time and prevent the Destruction and exile. The prophets who lived through the period of the Destruction could not be as consoling. In contrast, many chapters of Isaiah contain messages of redemption – but that was because the Destruction of the Temple did not happen in his time.

Chapter 24

The Temple with God's Glory in Its Midst

Ezekiel 40:1–43:27

The final nine chapters of the book of Ezekiel comprise a vision of the future Temple, one that is rich in detail, setting out the dimensions of the building, the various sacrifices, land inheritances, and more. Our focus will be more thematic, focusing less on details.

THE PROPHECY'S SETTING (40:1–4)

The last part of the book of Ezekiel begins by noting the date: "In the twenty-fifth year of our exile, the fourteenth year after the city had fallen, at the beginning of the year, the tenth day of the month..." (40:1). Besides the chronological date (apparently, the tenth of Nisan in the year 573 BCE), this introduction also indicates the significant dates of that period which serve as markers for counting years: the exile of Jehoiachin and the Destruction. In fact, this is the only prophecy which Ezekiel dates in relation to the Destruction. Until now Ezekiel has counted years based on the exile of Jehoiachin (see, for example, 1:2;

8:1; 24:1; and others), which attests to its significance as a turning point by which to date events. Now, fourteen years after the Destruction of Jerusalem, the grave ramifications of this catastrophe are seeping into the consciousness of the exiles in Babylonia. Most had been exiled with Jehoiachin prior to the Destruction, and were therefore largely cut off from what was happening in the Land of Israel. Now, perhaps with new exiles joining their communities in Babylonia, they begin to internalize the significance of the Destruction.

It is no coincidence that Ezekiel's prophecy about the future Temple comes now, once the nation has become accustomed to the reality of life in exile. They have no active Jewish center in the Land of Israel (following the descent of the remnant to Egypt, which appears to have occurred just a few years after the Destruction). In their new reality, the exiles are left uncertain about their future and their status. This is reflected in the prophecies of Ezekiel and, even more so, in the messages of the prophets of the Return to Zion, Haggai, Zechariah, and Malachi.

This prophecy is something of a lone voice in a period of scant prophetic activity, making it a prophecy of great importance. (The next date to be noted in a prophecy is the Edict of Cyrus, during the period of the Return, some thirty-five years after this prophecy by Ezekiel, and Haggai and Zechariah were active only some sixteen years after that declaration.[1]) In fact, this prophecy by Ezekiel, uttered in the Land of Israel, is the last one by which we can assess the state of the exiles in Babylonia at this time.[2] The importance of the date is emphasized by the prophet himself: "On that very day the hand of the Lord came upon me, and He brought me there" (40:1).

The prophet is brought back to the Land of Israel: "He brought me, in visions of God, to the Land of Israel, and He set me down on a very high mountain on which there seemed to be the outline of a city on the south" (v. 2). The description of the place where he is set

---

1. The end of the book of Jeremiah (52:31–34) deals with the fate of Jehoiachin in Babylonia, in the year 561 BCE, about twelve years after this prophecy by Ezekiel – the one exception to this rule.
2. The only prophecy in the book of Ezekiel that is dated later than this is the prophecy to Egypt (29:17), which we have discussed previously, but there are no other prophecies in the Bible explicitly dated later than that.

The Temple with God's Glory in Its Midst

down – "a very high mountain" – is certainly interesting. The verse gives no indication whether Ezekiel is referring to somewhere within the boundaries of the city of Jerusalem or whether he refers to the entire Land of Israel west of the Jordan. Perhaps he is describing the place gradually, such that only at the end does he indicate the precise location: "Land of Israel," "a very high mountain," "the outline of a city," "on the south." But is the city Jerusalem? This question is left unanswered. The question is even intensified in the following chapters, which make no explicit mention of the city's name.

Immediately upon arrival in the city, the prophet sees a man whose job is to measure, using a thread of flax and a measuring reed (the accepted instruments for this task in the Ancient Near East):

> He brought me over to it, and there, standing at the gate, was a man whose appearance was the appearance of copper. In his hand were a cord of linen and a measuring rod. The man spoke to me: "Mortal, look with your eyes and listen attentively and note well everything I am going to show you – for you have been brought here in order to be shown – and report everything you see to the House of Israel." (vv. 3–4)

God brings the prophet to the place where the land surveyor awaits him and emphasizes the importance of conveying the upcoming vision to all of Israel. The root R-A-H (to see, look, show, appear) is repeated five times over the course of these two verses, along with a mention of eyes. This emphasis is apparently meant to convey the importance of passing on the vision precisely as the prophet has seen it.

THE BUILDING PLAN (40:5–42:20)

From chapter 40, verse 5 until the end of chapter 42, the prophet describes the Temple's plan.[3] The verses present a multitude of

---

3. On the face of it, the description seems so detailed that one has the impression that a model Temple could be built on the basis of its dimensions. However, upon closer inspection it emerges that a number of essential details are omitted. Many sketches have attempted to make sense of the plan as set forth in these chapters, and we shall

difficulties.[4] It is not the nation that will build the Temple – this is the message that the verses seem to collectively convey. Therefore, no plan according to which the construction might proceed is necessary. Perhaps the opacity of the verses and the futility of trying to base the construction on them is deliberate. Their aim might be to rule out the possibility of anyone initiating the Temple's reconstruction on the basis of this prophecy at any stage, now or in the future.[5] It is nonetheless important to the prophet to convey the vision of the building of the Temple in a very tangible and convincing way, while also remaining vague enough to prevent premature efforts. So the detailed description carries a dual – and indeed internally contradictory – message: On one hand, the Temple is presented as something concrete and real; on the other, it cannot actually be built (at least at this stage).[6]

At first the prophet outlines the dimensions of the wall surrounding the Temple and of the eastern gate (40:5–16). An interesting detail, difficult to understand in this description, concerns the windows referred to as *ḥalonot atumot* (v. 16). This phrase might mean that they are fake windows, framed and set in relief but actually filled with stone. Perhaps this is because one is forbidden to look in on the Sanctuary. The windows exist, but are in reality "opaque." Symbolically, this expresses the

---

not elaborate on them here. The interested reader might refer, for example, to *Daat Mikra* on Ezekiel; Moskowitz, *Sefer Yeḥezkel*, 319–49; Cohen, *Yeḥezkel*, 322–28; and modern commentaries on the book of Ezekiel.

4. See the commentary of Yehiel Moskowitz in his introduction to these chapters (*Sefer Yeḥezkel*, 317–24), where he lists the various exegetical proposals for solving these difficulties, and then highlights the exegetical problems that remain.
5. This idea offers a clear answer to the question that has troubled many scholars – why the Second Temple was not built in accordance with Ezekiel's vision. The builders simply had no technical way of doing so, even had they wanted to (in addition to the many other challenges facing them, as attested to in the prophecies of Haggai, Zechariah, and Malachi). Moreover, it may be that the prophetic message of these chapters in Ezekiel is that it is not the nation that will build the Temple based on this model – or, at least, that that was the way in which his prophetic message was understood. Perhaps the expectation of a Temple that would be built by God and would fit the description in these chapters added to the difficulties facing the returnees to the land when they commenced building the Second Temple.
6. See Tova Ganzel and Shalom E. Holtz, "Ezekiel's Temple in Babylonian Context," *Vetus Testamentum* 64 (2014): 211–26.

The Temple with God's Glory in Its Midst

special protection for the Temple at the points of potential weakness, such as the windows.[7]

The prophet then describes the dimensions of the outer courtyard and the gates (the northern gate, the southern gate, and the inner court gate; vv. 17–37). The end of chapter 40 includes a description of the burnt offering, the sin offering, and the guilt offering upon tables at the entry to the northern gate, as well as the chambers of the priests who "perform the duties of the Temple" and "perform the duties of the altar" (vv. 38–46). These priests are henceforth referred to as "the descendants of Zadok, who alone of the descendants of Levi may approach the Lord to minister to Him" (vv. 46); we will discuss their special status below. Here, too, within the framework of the dimensions of the house, there is a clear tendency towards protecting the Sanctuary, much as we saw with the windows. For this reason the priests are "priests who perform the duties" – sometimes translated as "keepers of the charge of the house" – and therefore their lineage is carefully guarded.

In verse 48, the prophet moves on to a description of the inner plan of the Temple. He first describes the porch (*ulam*, vv. 48–49), followed by the *heikhal*, the Holy of Holies, the inner chamber, and the decorations on the walls (41:1–26). In the midst of this description the prophet notes the wooden altar and the table (v. 22). In chapter 42, the prophet is brought to the outer courtyard, where he describes the chambers in between the outer courtyard and the inner one (42:1–14). In verses 13–14 he notes the holy chambers and their function:

> The northern chambers and the southern chambers by the vacant space are the consecrated chambers in which the priests who have access to the Lord shall eat the most holy offerings. There they shall deposit the most holy offerings – the meal offerings, the

---

7. Dr. Guy Stiebel explains the verse in I Kings, "He made windows for the House, recessed and latticed (*shekufot atumot*)" (I Kings 6:4), as being derived from the idea of a *mashkof*, a lintel, protecting the entrance. See Guy D. Stiebel, "Lehotzi Ora LaOlam: Adrikhalut Simlit shel Mivnei Pulḥan," *Eretz Israel* 28 (2007): 219–34. I have adopted the same interpretation for the verse in Ezekiel.

> sin offerings, and the guilt offerings, for the place is consecrated. When the priests enter, they shall not proceed from the consecrated place to the outer court without first leaving here the vestments in which they minister; for the [vestments] are consecrated. Before proceeding to the area open to the people, they shall put on other garments.

The chambers are meant to be places where the priests can eat the sacrificial meat and change their garments. Emphasized here, too, is the gap: the distance between the priests (and their garments) on one hand, and the people, on the other. The people are not involved with the sacrifices in these verses, nor do they even see the priests in the garments in which they minister. Symbolically, this image carries a harsh message about the distancing of the people from the future Temple – a message reiterated and impressed more deeply in the chapters that follow. Ezekiel concludes this section of the Temple tour with a description of the perimeter of the Temple Mount and the wall around the Temple (vv. 15–20).

THE RETURN OF GOD'S GLORY TO THE TEMPLE (43:1–9)

The prophet describes the return of God's glory to the Temple (we touched on these verses earlier, when discussing the journeys of God's glory in the book of Ezekiel):

> Then he led me to a gate, the gate that faced east. And there, coming from the east with a roar like the roar of mighty waters, was the presence of the God of Israel, and the earth was lit up by His presence. Like the appearance of the vision which I had seen, like the vision that I had seen when I came to destroy the city, and the visions were like the vision I had seen by the Chebar River Forthwith, I fell on my face. (Ezek. 43:1–3)

Here we will note a few points that complement our earlier discussion. As at the beginning of chapter 40, the prophet makes repeated use of the root R-A-H (to see, appearance, vision). However, while previously what the prophet saw was the plan of the Temple, here the same root points to a vision of God's glory.[8] In addition, as in chapter 1, here too the vision is full of sound and light. God's glory is revealed not in silent modesty, but with great power. The "roar of mighty waters" to which God's voice is compared will turn out to represent the bond between God and His people in chapter 47. This image serves as a sort of "compensation" for the nation's lack of participation in offering sacrifices – unlike the situation at the time of the Temple built by Solomon. Now the prophet emphasizes once again the return of God's glory to the Temple: "The presence of the Lord entered the Temple by the gate that faced eastward. A spirit carried me into the inner court, and lo, the presence of the Lord filled the Temple" (vv. 4–5).

These verses create an exalted sense of God's complete presence. The transition to the next four verses is therefore sharp and unexpected:

> And I heard speech addressed to me from the Temple, though [the] man was standing beside me. It said to me: O mortal, this is the place of My throne and the place for the soles of My feet, where I will dwell in the midst of the people Israel forever. The House of Israel and their kings must not again defile My holy name by their harlotry and by the corpses of their kings at their death. When they placed their threshold next to My threshold and their doorposts next to My doorposts with only a wall between Me and them, they would defile My holy name by the abominations that they committed, and I consumed them in My anger. Therefore, let them put their harlotry and the corpses of their kings far from Me, and I will dwell among them forever. (vv. 6–9)

The sudden fall from such lofty exaltation to such depths seems to reflect the fact that one of the conditions for the return of God's glory to the Temple is that "the House of Israel and their kings must not again defile My holy name." The aim of this prophecy is to highlight the cause of the Temple's defilement, in the years in which God's glory left the Temple

---

8. In addition, the appearances of the root here serve to contrast and complement its use in chapter 8 where it characterizes the idolaters, who do not see God.

and the edifice was destroyed, since this prophecy belongs to the vision of the future Temple (ch. 40–48) and not to the chapters of rebuke (ch. 2–24). Unlike the concept of "profaning (*ḥillul*) of God," which, in the book of Ezekiel, always refers to God's status in the eyes of the other nations, the "defiling (*tuma*) of God's name" arises from the actions of Israel – actions whose gravity causes a more profound desecration of God's name than any outward apparent damage to His standing. Therefore, the prophet repeats the main reason for God's glory having left the Temple twice in verses 7–8: The House of Israel, through its evil actions, caused God's holy name to be defiled.

> The House of Israel and their kings must not again defile My holy name by their harlotry and by the corpses of their kings at their death. When they placed their threshold next to My threshold and their doorposts next to My doorposts with only a wall between Me and them.

These verses describe the burial of the kings close to the Temple. According to the Rashi, Radak, and Rabbi Eliezer of Beaugency, the kings were actually buried in the Temple itself. This interpretation amplifies the severity of the actions.[9] Such burial would bring severe impurity upon those in proximity to the burial site; beyond this, it would represent a defiant challenge to God's supremacy over the mortal kings. Symbolically, burial of the kings in the Temple is an expression of the kings' view of themselves as worthy of resting near the holiest place, next to God, while they themselves perform actions that are considered harlotry (*zenut*). In the book of Ezekiel this expression is used as a general reference to the worst type of idolatry. The cessation of such activity is a necessary condition for God dwelling in the nation's midst forever. In the verses that follow, Ezekiel demands shame as a condition for giving over the

---

9. However, in the final chapters of II Kings, which discuss the sins of the kings during this period, no mention is made of burial of the kings in the Temple, although the idolatry introduced into the Temple is explicitly noted (II Kings 21:4–7; 23:6–7). Where explicit mention is made of burial of kings, the location is the garden of Uzza (II Kings 21:18, 26) or the city of David.

plan of the Temple to the people: they must "be ashamed of their iniquities" (v. 10) and "ashamed of all they have done" (v. 11). Although these are chapters devoted to the vision of the future Temple, following the chapters of restoration, the prophet nevertheless emphasizes once again the severity of the sins that brought about the Destruction of the First Temple. The conclusion of this prophecy represents the end of the rebuke to the nation in the book of Ezekiel. Now, a study of the prophecies leaves us longing for a vision of the future without any painful reminder of the events of the past.

MORE CONCEALMENT THAN REVELATION (43:10–44:31)

> [Now] you, O mortal, describe the Temple to the House of Israel, and let them measure its design. But let them be ashamed of their iniquities: When they are ashamed of all they have done, make known to them the plan of the Temple and its layout, its exits and entrances – its entire plan, and all the laws and instructions pertaining to its entire plan. Write it down before their eyes, that they may faithfully follow its entire plan and all its laws. Such are the instructions for the Temple on top of the mountain: the entire area of its enclosure shall be most holy. Thus far the instructions for the Temple. (43:10–12)

The prophet now comes back to the plan of the Temple after recalling, towards the beginning of chapter 43 (vv. 7–9) the past sins of idolatry. The command to the prophet to make known the plan for the Temple, to set it down in writing before them and present it in all its detail, serves to make it tangible and concrete. But surprisingly enough, there is also no explicit mention here of the location of the Temple, which is conveyed with the rather vague expression, "on top of the mountain" (which recalls Ezekiel 40:2, where Ezekiel speaks of "a very high mountain").

The description of the Temple and the city, like the details of the future Temple itself, has some concrete and precise elements, but at the very same time, lacks some very central details. The reader is left with a sense of being "in the dark." This feeling follows us as, in the coming chapters, Ezekiel reconstructs the place of the nation and its status, the

Ezekiel 40:1–43:27

role of the prophets, the Levites, the priests, and the *nasi*, and the degree to which these are connected to the future Temple. This Temple will be different from its predecessor in that it exists in the midst of a people that has been reorganized, with new laws, laws that the text leaves somewhat vague and unclear.

THE PLACE OF THE NATION IN THE VISION OF THE FUTURE TEMPLE

In these chapters, as in other passages prior to the vision of the future Temple, the nation's place in the Temple is limited; there is no general invitation for the people to take an active part in either its establishment or in the divine service. The minimal involvement of the people in this vision of the future Temple is indicated by the small number of verses in which Ezekiel speaks of the people when discussing the future Temple (ch. 40–48). As we have seen, Ezekiel is charged with informing the people of the plan for the Temple with all its details, so that the people will keep the plan of the Temple and its activities (40:4 and here, 43:10). We have also seen that the people are mentioned with reference to their former sins having caused the defilement of God's holy name (43:7–11), and the emphasis on the need to distance these sinners from the future Temple (44:5–9). The only verses in which the people's place in the Temple is mentioned are those which describe the people when the priests go out to them in the outer courtyard (44:19). Moreover, the prophet emphasizes that the place of the offering of sacrifices is in the inner courtyard, which is separated from the people (46:20). The closest place that the people are able to reach is "the gate of the inner court which faces east" (46:1), which is opened only on Shabbat and Rosh Ḥodesh, and the people prostrate themselves outside of this gate while it is open (46:3). In addition, the people are responsible for funding the communal sacrifices that are offered in the Temple – but once again, the actual sacrifice is carried out without their presence (45:13–17).

Given the above, the impression arising from Ezekiel's prophecy is that the Temple is not a spiritual center for the entire nation. The Temple serves the priests and Levites, who perform their service within it as representatives of the people. The only roles that are given to the people are the auxiliary functions: funding of the sacrifices, prostration,

The Temple with God's Glory in Its Midst

and a partial view of the divine service. Another significant dimension showing the distancing of the people from the Temple is that they (who caused the Temple's defilement in the past) are now only to be found in the outer courtyard. This is in contrast to the picture arising from the plain text in the book of Leviticus, which suggests that a lay Israelite may approach the sacrificial altar. This distancing seems to be aimed at protecting the Temple from elements that may lead to its defilement, thereby causing its destruction. In this way, Ezekiel's prophecy of an eternal dwelling, an eternal *nasi*, an eternal covenant, and an eternal Temple can be fulfilled.

PURIFICATION CEREMONIES FOR THE ALTAR AND THE TEMPLE (43:13–27)

Ezekiel's prophecies, as we have noted, seek to counter the factors that led to the Destruction of the First Temple. His prophecies now emphasize the need to protect the Temple from impurity on a permanent basis; they therefore prohibit the people from entering the Temple and limit the people's involvement in its activities.[10] Admittedly, one might offer the opposite interpretation: From now on, God will rest His presence on his people even when there is no entry into the Temple: "I will never again hide My face from them, for I have poured out My spirit upon the House of Israel – declares the Lord God" (39:29).

The people's lack of inclusion in the sacrificial service and entry into the Temple is a function of their higher spiritual level, which is not limited to the Temple. This process accords with Ezekiel's words in chapter 36: "And I will give you a new heart and put a new spirit into you: I will remove the heart of stone from your body and give you a heart of flesh; and I will put My spirit into you" (36:26–27).

The next prophecy is devoted to the ceremony of purification of the altar; appended to it is a prophecy about purification and atonement of the Temple found in chapter 45. The commentators debate whether

---

10. The location of the ceremonies in Ezekiel's prophecies as compared to the location in Leviticus 16 is another example of the distancing of the people from the Temple: Ezekel describes the ceremony as taking place in the courtyard, while in Leviticus it takes place within the Sanctuary.

Ezekiel 40:1–43:27

the descriptions of the offering of sacrifices in these chapters in Ezekiel refer to a one-time ceremony of inauguration of the Temple – like the inauguration of the *Mishkan* – or whether they are meant to be performed each year.[11] These verses are difficult to explain. This is also reflected in the Talmudic statement (Menahot 45a) that Elijah will solve these difficulties in the future. Indeed, the plain language of the verses makes it difficult to determine this question one way or the other, but it seems that the verses devoted to the purification and atonement of the Temple (45:18–20) describe a one-time ceremony, representing a continuation of the purification of the altar in our chapter (43:18–27). This is the conclusion drawn in the Talmud:

> Thus saith the Lord God, In the first month, on the first day of the month thou shalt take a young bullock without blemish, and thou shalt offer it as a sin offering in the sanctuary. A sin offering? But surely it is a burnt offering? – R. Yohanan said, This passage will be interpreted by Elijah in the future. R. Ashi said, [It refers to] the special consecration offering [to be] offered in the time of Ezra just as it was offered in the time of Moses. There has also been taught [a *baraita*] to the same effect: R. Judah says, This passage will be interpreted by Elijah in the future. But R. Jose said to him, [It refers to] the consecration offering [to be] offered in the time of Ezra just as it was offered in the time of Moses. He replied, May your mind be at ease for you have set mine at ease. (Menahot 45a)

In other words, just as chapter 43 contained a description of the ceremony of inauguration of the altar, so, too, chapter 45 contains a description of the ceremony of inauguration of the Temple. The purification of the altar and the atonement of the Temple in Ezekiel's prophecy will be performed as one-time acts. We should therefore understand the atonement purging the Temple of "uncleanness caused by unwitting or

---

11. I discuss this question in more detail in my article, "Haftarat Tetzaveh, Yehezkel 43:6–27," in *Maftirin BeNavi: Iyyunim BeHaftarot UVeDivrei HaNevi'im*, ed. Aharon Eldar (Jerusalem: HaSokhnut HaYehudit, 2010), 341–43.

The Temple with God's Glory in Its Midst

ignorant persons" (45:20) as describing the purification of the Temple and the altar from impure contact which has adhered to it up until the inauguration, rather than from the impurity of the nation's sins (which Ezekiel mentions also in 45:7–9 preceding this prophecy). If these are indeed one-time events, and these chapters in Ezekiel are arranged in chronological order, then Ezekiel describes first a ceremony of inauguration of the altar (ch. 43), followed next by a description of the entry of God's glory into the House and the tithes given to the priests (ch. 44), and finally the *nasi*'s role and the inauguration of the Temple (ch. 45).

Chapter 25

Temple Functionaries
Ezekiel 44:1–31[1]

A SEALED TEMPLE (44:1–9)

> Then he led me back to the outer gate of the Sanctuary that faced eastward; it was shut. And the Lord said to me: This gate is to be kept shut and is not to be opened! No one shall enter by it because the Lord, the God of Israel, has entered by it; therefore it shall remain shut. (44:1–2)

These verses show the process we have seen so far gaining steam. Perhaps the clearest expression of the Temple's isolation from the people is the emphasis on the gate through which God entered: It now remains shut. In fact, even the *nasi*, who must be able to reach the Temple, will do so indirectly, without passing through the gate: "Only the *nasi* may sit in it and eat bread before the Lord, since he is a *nasi*; he shall enter by way of the vestibule of the gate, and shall depart by the same way" (v. 3).

---

1. A detailed comparison of these sections with Numbers 15–18 and various places in the book of Leviticus can be found in Kasher's commentary, *Yeḥezkel 25–48*, 844–47; the comparison and the questions that arise will not be addressed here.

Ezekiel 44:1–31

Among the various details pertaining to the structure of the Temple, the prophet suddenly perceives God's presence within it:

> Then he led me, by way of the north gate, to the front of the Temple. I looked, and lo! the presence of the Lord filled the Temple of the Lord; and I fell upon my face. Then the Lord said to me: O mortal, mark well, look closely and listen carefully to everything that I tell you regarding all the laws of the Temple of the Lord and all the instructions regarding it. Note well who may enter the Temple and all who must be excluded from the Sanctuary. And say to the rebellious House of Israel: Thus said the Lord God: Too long, O House of Israel, have you committed all your abominations, admitting aliens, uncircumcised of spirit and uncircumcised of flesh, to be in My Sanctuary and profane My very Temple, when you offer up My food – the fat and the blood. You have broken My covenant with all your abominations. You have not discharged the duties concerning My sacred offerings, but have appointed them to discharge the duties of My Sanctuary for you. (vv. 4–8)

Much like the beginning of chapter 43, the prophecy once again emphasizes the need to convey the details of the plan to the people. But this time there is an additional prophetic message about distancing strangers. This Temple of Ezekiel is not a magnet, an international center; rather, in light of the sins of the past, it has no place for strangers: "Thus said the Lord God: Let no alien, uncircumcised in spirit and flesh, enter My Sanctuary – no alien whatsoever among the people of Israel" (v. 9).

LEVITES AND PRIESTS (44:10–46:24)

The prophecy goes one step further: Even the faithfulness of the office-bearers who served in the Temple in the past must be reexamined. Ezekiel blames the Levites for having misled the people (vv. 10–11) and ministering to those visiting the Temple while engaged in serving idols:

> Because they served the House of Israel in the presence of their fetishes and made them stumble into guilt, therefore – declares the Lord God – I have sworn concerning them that they shall suffer their punishment: They shall not approach Me to serve Me as priests, to come near any of My sacred offerings, the most holy things. They shall bear their shame for the abominations that they committed. (vv. 12–13)

Despite their status and their role, the Levites did not take responsibility for the people's behavior. So while they will serve in the Temple, they will not share in the authority bestowed on the priests: "I will make them watchmen of the Temple, to perform all its chores, everything that needs to be done in it" (v. 14).

In contrast, Ezekiel entrusts the priests with a range of tasks: offering sacrifices, instructing the people, sitting in judgment, and guarding the Torah. Why does Ezekiel transfer all the leadership functions to the priests? Moreover, why does his description of the priests' service center not on the Temple, but rather on instruction? It appears that there were also priests who misused their position. In times of crisis, the role of the priests is to teach the ways of Torah as well as serve in the Temple. Instead, the priests did what is described by Ezekiel as follows:

> Her priests have violated My teaching: they have profaned what is sacred to Me, they have not distinguished between the sacred and the profane, they have not taught the difference between the unclean and the clean, and they have closed their eyes to My sabbaths. I am profaned in their midst. (22:26)

The priests who neglected their role and failed to instruct the people during their difficult time – even if they did not actually mislead them – will not be given a role in the future Temple. (These priests appear to be the descendants of Itamar.) Those priests who are descendants of Zadok, who demonstrated faithfulness to the House of David and followed God's ways, even in times of crisis, will indeed merit to minister in the Temple: "But the levitical priests descended from Zadok, who maintained the service of My Sanctuary when the people of Israel went astray from Me – they shall approach Me to minister to Me" (44:15).[2]

With the Temple service performed by a smaller team of priests, the expectation is that it will be performed with greater skill and more punctilious attention to the laws of ritual purity. In this way, the future Temple will be protected from the defilement that brought about the destruction of its predecessor in Ezekiel's time. For this reason, Ezekiel emphasizes that the most important function of the priests in the future – as in the past and the present – is instructing the people to follow the ways of God; this is even more essential than offering sacrifices. What caused the Destruction of the Temple was not a lack of sacrifices, but rather a lack of basic understanding among the people about what the service of God entails, what it means to have an exclusive commitment to Him and His Torah. This priestly role is amplified and emphasized by Ezekiel over and above the ritual roles involved in the Temple service. Later in the chapter, after listing instructions concerning the clothing to be worn by the priests (vv. 17–19), the prohibitions against shaving their hair (v. 20) and drinking wine (v. 21), and the limitations on whom they are permitted to marry (v. 22), the prophet states once again:

> They shall declare to My people what is sacred and what is profane, and inform them what is clean and what is unclean. In lawsuits, too, it is they who shall act as judges; they shall decide them in accordance with My rules. They shall preserve My teachings and

---

2. At the same time, the selection of Zadok's descendants has a historical basis. In his commentary on Ezekiel 40:46, Radak notes that Zadok – the first High Priest to serve in the Temple built by Solomon – was a descendant of Pinḥas, who was given a promise of eternal priesthood, while the curse upon Eli doomed the descendants of Itamar. For the actions of the priests from the House of Zadok, see II Samuel 15–16; 19:12; 20:25; I Kings 1:8; 4:2; I Chronicles 15:11; 16:39; 18:16; 29:22. The preference shown to the House of Zadok is clearly apparent in II Samuel 15:24–29, and was institutionalized at the time of Adonijah's rebellion against David, when Abiathar joined Adonijah, while Zadok remained faithful to David. Immediately upon ascending the throne, Solomon chose Zadok as High Priest and removed Abiathar from service. During the period of Hezekiah, too, the priest was a descendant of the House of Zadok (II Chr. 31:10), and later on Ezra's lineage is traced to Zadok son of Ahitub (Ezra 7:2).

My laws regarding all My fixed occasions; and they shall maintain the sanctity of My sabbaths. (vv. 23–24)

Rabbi Eliezer of Beaugency writes in his commentary on Ezekiel 40:45:

> "The priests who perform the duties of the Temple" – but they will not perform the sacrificial service, but rather will perform the service of the Levites, to be singers…these are the priests who are not of the seed of Zadok the priest (see 48:11). In the future they will be disqualified from the sacrificial service, but will be singers and gatekeepers like the Levites, because they "have violated My teaching" (see 22:26), and they became like priests for idolatry. They led the children of Israel astray, and distanced themselves from the Holy One, blessed be He; therefore, they, too, will be distanced.

KING AND PROPHET

In addition to the changes that we have seen, Ezekiel's prophecy reveals a fundamental change with regard to the leadership of the nation: In this Temple, there will be no role for kings of Israel. In place of a king, in the future, there will be a *nasi*, whose functions will be to mediate between God and His people by means of his seat of power, which is in the Temple precinct; to offer sacrifices, and more (ch. 46). The place of the prophets is likewise left empty, because in the past some of them caused the people to become defiled:

> And if a prophet is seduced and does speak a word [to such a man], it was I the Lord who seduced that prophet; I will stretch out My hand against him and destroy him from among My people Israel… that the House of Israel may never again stray from Me and defile itself with all its transgressions. (14:9–11).

So for these prophets, too, there is no room in Ezekiel's vision of the future Temple:

> My hand will be against the prophets who prophesy falsehood and utter lying divination. They shall not remain in the assembly of My people, they shall not be inscribed in the lists of the House of Israel, and they shall not come back to the Land of Israel. Thus shall you know that I am the Lord God. (13:9)

Thus, Ezekiel foretells that the prophets will have no portion and no role in the future leadership. This would seem to explain why the terms "prophets," "prophecy," and "vision" appear in the book of Ezekiel only up to chapter 39, and not in chapters 40–48.[3] Ezekiel's avoidance of any use of the root N-B-A (prophecy) in these chapters seems to reinforce the sense that prophecy in its present form will have no place in the future.

The closing prophecy before the chapters devoted to the vision of the future Temple may suggest a hint of a substitute for the connection between God and His people that is effected through prophecy in the First Temple period: "I will never again hide My face from them, for I have poured out My spirit upon the House of Israel – declares the Lord God" (39:29). This "pouring of the spirit" upon the entire nation, according to the prophet Joel, ultimately transforms the entire nation into prophets: "After that, I will pour out My spirit on all flesh; Your sons and daughters shall prophesy; Your old men shall dream dreams, And your young men shall see visions" (Joel 3:1).

We have seen in Ezekiel's prophecy that the changes in this Temple include not only the outer structure of the edifice, but also fundamental difference in who enters it. This change relates both to the measure of access afforded the people, but also the division of roles among the various leaders of the nation, and the degree to which they are connected to the Temple.

Now the connection between Ezekiel's prophecy of rebuke and the vision of the future Temple becomes clearer: The actions of the people and their leaders in the years prior to the Destruction are what led to the

---

3. Notably, even the word "prophecy," which appears frequently in chapters 1–39 to emphasize Ezekiel's divine mission to Israel or to other nations, appears nowhere in the last nine chapters.

(limited) extent of their involvement in and access to the future Temple as described by the prophet. Once again, despite the level of detail in the description of the roles of the various officials, we cannot translate these descriptions into practice because some critical details are missing: Does the lack of mention of any High Priest in Ezekiel's prophecy indicate that this office no longer exists? If so, how are we to understand this? Will this future Temple have an area that is designated "the Holy of Holies" (41:4), which no one ever enters? Here, too, we remain in the dark. Perhaps this ambiguity is meant to further reinforce our hypothesis that the absence of some critical details is intentional. It is meant to rule out any possibility of the people attempting, out of longing for the Temple, to initiate its establishment, along the lines of this prophetic vision, before the proper time arrives.

Chapter 26
A New Place for God
Ezekiel 45:1–48:35

The book's final chapters introduce a number of new topics: first, the allocation of inheritances, which will be different from what is familiar to the people; second, directives about sacrifices and Temple rites; and, finally, a new way of connecting with God.

THE ALLOCATION OF INHERITANCES (45:1–15)

The beginning of chapter 45 deals with the division of the land among the tribes of Israel. But the division here is fundamentally different from the division that is familiar to us, the one dating to the period when the land was originally settled. The most conspicuous difference is the allocation of an inheritance to the priests, "the ministrants of the Sanctuary who are qualified to minister to the Lord" (45:4), the Levites, "the servants of the Temple" (v. 5), and the *nasi*, so that "My *nasi* shall no more defraud My people" (v. 8). This new division apparently serves two different purposes. First, the placement of the Levite inheritance between the inheritance of the other tribes and the Temple is meant to prevent the Temple from being defiled. In addition, this new arrangement will prevent the office-bearers from being dependent, to some extent, on the people – a situation which in the past (during the period of the Judges and during the First Temple period) led to misuse of the leaders' power.

Aside from discussing the allocation of the land's portions, the prophet emphasizes the need for a regime of judgment and justice (vv. 9–10) to prevent oppression of the people on the part of the *nasi*. Thereafter, the prophet moves on to other subjects, and chapters 45–46 include attention to the laws of sacrifices, the role of the prophet, and the place where the meat of the sacrifices is cooked.

"ITS WORDS CONTRADICT WORDS OF THE TORAH" (45:16–46:18)

Ezekiel is the only prophet whose prophecies also include laws meant for the people. There are some significant discrepancies between the laws that he sets down (in chapters 40–48) and the laws of the Torah. This leads to the obvious question raised by our sages:

> R. Judah said in the name of Rav, that man is to be remembered for good, and Hanina b. Hezekiah is his name; for were it not for him the book of Ezekiel would have been suppressed, since its sayings contradicted the words of the Torah. What did he do? He took up with him three hundred barrels of oil and remained there in the upper chamber until he had explained away everything. (Menaḥot 45a)[1]

Differences between the sacrifices set forth in chapters 45–46 in the book of Ezekiel and those described in chapters 28–29 in Numbers abound. First, Ezekiel lays out the sacrifices offered on festivals:

1. In Ezekiel, a bullock is offered as a sin offering on the fourteenth of Nisan (45:21–22), but there is no mention of any such sacrifice in Numbers. According to Ezekiel, on the Festival of Matzot, seven bullocks are offered, along with seven rams and a meal offering of an ephah and a hin of oil, as well as a goat kid as a sin offering (45:22–25). In Numbers,

---

1. See also Shabbat 13b and Ḥagiga 13a with slight changes.

in contrast, we find two bullocks and one ram, and an accompanying meal offering consisting of three tenth-measures of fine flour for the bullocks and two tenth-measures of fine flour for the ram, along with seven lambs and the goat kid as a sin offering (Num. 28:16–22).

2. On Sukkot, according to Ezekiel, seven bullocks are offered along with seven rams and a meal offering of an ephah and a hin of oil (as on the Festival of Matzot), and a goat kid as a sin offering (45:25). But in the book of Numbers we find a descending number of bullocks offered each day, starting with thirteen on the first day and ending with seven on the last day; the meal offering for each bullock is three tenth-measures; there are two rams which each have a meal offering of two tenth-measures; there are fourteen lambs with an accompanying meal offering of a tenth-measure for each; and a goat kid is brought as a sin offering with no accompanying meal offering.

3. The book of Numbers enumerates the sacrifices to be brought at other times: Shavuot, Rosh HaShana, Yom Kippur, and Shemini Atzeret. Ezekiel mentions none of these. Each of these holidays lasts for a single day, and perhaps the book of Ezekiel does not mention any of them because Ezekiel's prophecy makes no change in any of them. However, this may be a deliberate omission – implying no future commemoration of these holidays if the Temple is built in keeping with the plan that Ezekiel presents, in accordance with God's will.

The rest of the chapter deals with the sacrifices of Shabbat and Rosh Ḥodesh.[2] Here, too, there are discrepancies between the sacrifices set forth in Ezekiel's prophecy and those stipulated in the book of Numbers.

1. According to Ezekiel, on Shabbat six lambs are offered along with a meal offering "as much as he wishes," and oil, as well as ram with an ephah measure as its accompanying meal offering (46:4–5). According

---

2. It is for this reason that this chapter is read as the *haftara* for Shabbat Rosh Ḥodesh.

to the book of Numbers, the offering for Shabbat is two lambs whose meal offering consists of two tenth-measures and a libation offering (Num. 28:9–10).

2. On Rosh Ḥodesh, according to Ezekiel, the offering is a bullock and a ram, with a meal offering of an ephah and oil, as well as six lambs whose meal offering is "as much as he can afford" (Ezek. 46:6–7). The book of Numbers, on the other hand, mentions two bullocks whose meal offering is six tenth-measures and oil, a single ram whose meal offering is two tenth-measures and oil, and seven lambs whose meal offering is seven tenth-measures and libations of wine (Num. 28:11–15). In addition, there are other differences concerning the additional meal offerings for the free-will sacrifice (see Num. 15:4–10; Ezek. 46:11).

Many commentators have noted the differences between the sacrifices as prescribed in the Torah and those described by Ezekiel. For instance, Radak notes in his commentary on Ezekiel (46:4): "This is not the sacrifice that is written in the Torah – neither for Shabbat nor for Yom Tov. The sacrifices will follow a new format." See also Rashi (on 46:4), who explains the differences in relation to the number of lambs offered on Shabbat and the number of bullocks offered on Rosh Ḥodesh (46:6), as well as the commentary of Rabbi Eliezer of Beaugency (on 45:14, 25; 46:5; and elsewhere). Below we shall attempt to propose a different partial explanation for the differences.

It is difficult to characterize all the differences between the sacrifices set down in the Torah and those we encounter in Ezekiel's prophecy. Perhaps the reason for the differences in Ezekiel lies in the historical background to his prophecies, which included the Destruction of the Temple and exile. Accordingly, the changes to the sacrifices listed in Ezekiel should be viewed as part of the broader totality of change we discussed earlier, including a new order of leadership. All share an aim: preventing a repeat of the catastrophic departure of the Divine Presence and the subsequent Destruction of the Temple.

THE FUTURE TEMPLE (47:1–48:35)

We have noted a number of other changes in Ezekiel's vision of the future Temple; the purpose of these, too, is to maintain the sanctity of

A New Place for God

the Temple and ensure that God's presence will remain there forever. We have already discussed the extension of the courtyards surrounding the Temple and the strict security placed at their gates; the special windows; the limitations as to the priests who are worthy of serving in the Temple; restrictions on the *nasi*'s access to specific areas within the Temple precinct; and the decreased involvement of the people in offering sacrifices. These changes are designed to prevent those who are ritually impure from approaching. In addition, the geographic location of the Temple appears to undergo changes. The designation of the place where Ezekiel sees the temple vision as "a very high mountain" leaves the question of whether this building was within the bounds of Jerusalem without a definitive answer.[3] The Temple, then, may be removed from the city; its distance from the population center would likewise be aimed at protecting it from the possibility of defilement.

Our chapters note that the changes extend from the Temple itself to Jerusalem and to the other parts of the country: the city becomes shared by all the tribes of Israel, and the land is divided among the tribes in an egalitarian manner (47:13–48:35). This redivision of the inheritances will help to reduce antagonism among the tribes, and perhaps help to prevent oppression and theft, since these, too, were among the reasons for God's departure from the Temple in the past. The book of Ezekiel ends with the words, "And the name of the city from that day on shall be, 'The Lord is there'" (48:35). The new name given to Jerusalem expresses the constant presence of God within it. In light of our discussion in previous chapters, these words reflect the essence of the prophecy as a whole – it has presented Jerusalem and the Temple's new form, which will facilitate the eternal Divine Presence in the city.[4]

The Temple described by Ezekiel contains no hint of an ark, cherubim, a table for showbread, or a candelabrum; all that is mentioned is

---

3. For the argument that the city about which Ezekiel prophesies is not Jerusalem and that the Temple is not found there, see the survey in Ben-Yashar, "HaMerkava BeSefer Yeḥezkel," 22ff (see introduction, n. 11).
4. See Moshe Greenberg, "The Design and Themes of Ezekiel's Program of Restoration," *Interpretation* 38 (1984): 181–208. Greenberg's article notes some elements that are meant to protect the sanctity of the Temple in the future; it served as a basis for our discussion, and we have expanded on his list here.

an altar of wood. Perhaps, one may posit, the absence of the holy vessels from Ezekiel's vision does not necessarily imply their absence from the Temple. But it is possible that they are absent from the text because they will indeed not exist in the future Temple. If so, this change might also be meant to preserve the sanctity of the Temple. The absence of any holy vessels means less involvement on the part of the Temple's various office-bearers, lessening the chance of defilement.

It thus seems that the changes in the future Temple – the distancing of the people, the new format of priestly leadership, the *nasi*, the vessels, the location – are a prophetic response to the Temple's destruction. In Ezekiel's time the people did not observe God's word in accordance with Moses' Torah, and, as a result, the worst possible scenario became reality: The Temple was destroyed and the nation was exiled from the land. In response, the Temple that appears in Ezekiel's vision is safeguarded from any future destruction. In various different ways, Ezekiel envisions a protected Temple whose existence is assured forever, and a city whose entire purpose is to have God's presence in its midst. It may well be that our prayers for the Third Temple are that it be rebuilt following Ezekiel's new plan, which ensures the eternal presence of God among his people. This, in fact, may have been Hanina b. Hezekiah's intention when he toiled to ensure that the book of Ezekiel was not buried and forgotten.

HEALING WATERS (47:1–12)

In the midst of the book's final chapters, a brief passage in chapter 47 offers a surprising turning point in the vision of the future Temple. The prophet speaks here neither of the structure nor of the order of service, but rather describes a wondrous stream that emerges from the entrance to God's House and flows all the way to the Arabah:

> He led me back to the entrance of the Temple, and I found that water was issuing from below the platform of the Temple – eastward, since the Temple faced east – but the water was running out at the south of the altar, under the south wall of the Temple. Then he led me out by way of the northern gate and led me around to the outside of the outer gate that faces in the

direction of the east; and I found that water was gushing from [under] the south wall. (47:1–2)

At first, the water level is low. But then it rises until it becomes a raging river, impossible to cross:

> As the man went on eastward with a measuring line in his hand, he measured off a thousand cubits and led me across the water; the water was ankle deep. Then he measured off another thousand and led me across the water; the water was knee deep. He measured off a further thousand and led me across the water; the water was up to the waist. When he measured yet another thousand, it was a stream I could not cross; for the water had swollen into a stream that could not be crossed except by swimming. (vv. 3–5)

The prophetic description of Ezekiel's encounter with the stream pulls the reader in to a more personal, nuanced description: We identify with the image presented. This is a shift in tone from the awe-inspiring and imposing descriptions of the plans of the Temple.

The prophet is commanded to sit on the banks of the stream and to observe its wonders:

> "Do you see, O mortal?" he said to me; and he led me back to the bank of the stream. As I came back, I saw trees in great profusion on both banks of the stream. "This water," he told me, "runs out to the eastern region, and flows into the Arabah; and when it comes into the sea, into the sea of foul waters, the water will become wholesome. Every living creature that swarms will be able to live wherever this stream goes; the fish will be very abundant once these waters have reached there. It will be wholesome, and everything will live wherever this stream goes. Fishermen shall stand beside it all the way from Ein Gedi to Ein Eglaim; it shall be a place for drying nets; and the fish will be of various kinds [and] most plentiful, like the fish of the Great Sea. But its swamps and marshes shall not become wholesome; they will serve to [supply] salt. All kinds of trees for food will grow up on both banks of the

stream. Their leaves will not wither nor their fruit fail; they will yield new fruit every month, because the water for them flows from the Temple. Their fruit will serve for food and their leaves for healing." (vv. 6–12)

Ezekiel's sitting at the bank of the stream – unlike his tour inside the plan of the Temple or his falling upon his face when he experiences the divine vision – conveys a feeling of calm and tranquility and, most of all, humanity. It is an encounter between the divine and the human that is not inside the Temple, a place that inspires awe and fear. But the properties of this stream are nonetheless unique and wondrous: All who take refuge in it are healed; the salty water of the Dead Sea is sweetened; the fishermen are promised an abundance of fish; the trees growing on the banks not only do not wither, but will bear fruit throughout the year, and their leaves have medicinal properties.

Owing to the wonders of this stream and the trees on its banks, many scholars treat this chapter as a complement to the Garden of Eden, or even the days of Creation.[5] But this description also has special significance in the context of the book of Ezekiel. The profusion of trees and the encounter with the different forms of life do not occur in a place used for idolatry. Rather, this is a place of encounter with the divine. This appears to be part of the profound healing that the nation undergoes.

If we regard this description as the climax – although not the conclusion – of the book of Ezekiel as a whole, we find an important complement to a theme we have described throughout the chapters of restoration. Although Ezekiel has distanced the people from anything connected to the Temple, now he also expresses the creation of a divine connection with the people that has never existed before.

The language used to describe Ezekiel's encounter with the river (47:2) is similar to the language of his tour of the future Temple (42:2). There are additional parallels between the Temple and the river: the measuring of the level of the water (47:3–5) recalls the measuring of

---

5. For elaboration, see Lea Mazor, "Masa Naḥal HaPla'im min HaMikdash el HaYam (Yeḥezkel 47:1–12): Siluk HaTohu UBeria Ḥadasha," in *Gan BeEden MiKedem*, ed. Rachel Elior (Jerusalem: Magnes, 2010), 81–104.

the plan of the building (40:6, 8, 9, and others); the addressing of the prophet with the words, "Do you see, O mortal" (47:6) is similar to God addressing Ezekiel when He shows him the deeds of the people in the Temple (8:12, 15, and others); it also accords with God's appeal to Ezekiel to see the plan of the Temple (40:4).

The wondrous river that appears at the end of the book is evidently a way of bringing the Sanctuary into the very midst of the people, through connecting with the miraculous abundance and healing forces of the river, powers not found in the usual course of nature.

This connection between God and the people through the water that emerges from the Sanctuary has special significance coming at the end of the book of Ezekiel, where the ceremony of purification of the whole people is performed using "clean waters" (36:25). In order to heal the people, the prophet foresees a fissure in the regular order of nature. Beyond purification – a necessary condition for the people's restoration in the future – there will also be possible forms of healing that pass through the Sanctuary, but that do not require the people to approach. If so, this resolves a series of questions that have remained unanswered: If, as the words of the prophet thus far suggest, the nation persists in its sinful ways, and their purification is the result of God's will alone, then surely there is no atonement for the deeds of the past. In addition, does the distancing of the people from the Temple mean that the connection between them and God is severed? Will the final impression of the nation's actions in the Temple be forever remembered as those deeds that caused the Destruction and the exile to Babylon – since, in the future, the conclusions will already have been drawn and the people will be kept away from the Temple?

Now we see that the healing properties of the river in fact have the wondrous ability to repair the flaws that caused the Destruction. The distancing of the people from the Temple turns out to be a physical measure that does not reflect spiritual distancing: God connects the people to the Temple by means of the river that flows from the very midst of the House, notwithstanding the geographical distance.

Ultimately the bond between God and His people is not only renewed unilaterally; the entire nation is part of the process as it is nourished, by the river from the Temple, more directly than ever before.

Perhaps an echo of this can be found in the prophecy of Zechariah, which post-dated that of Ezekiel:

> In that day, fresh water shall flow from Jerusalem, part of it to the Eastern Sea and part to the Western Sea, throughout the summer and winter. And the Lord shall be king over all the earth; in that day there shall be one Lord with one name. (Zech. 14:8–9)

The river connecting the Temple and the people is an image that remains with the reader. In a book full of blood and destruction, a book so severe that it even prophesies God hiding His face from His people, we are comforted in the knowledge that in the future, He will seek a connection with His people.

Conclusion

A Unique Prophet, a Unique Prophecy

Ezekiel is a singular prophet in many ways, and his book is a fascinating collection of prophecies that reflect his time and place.

First, Ezekiel's prophecies are not wielded as threats but rather descriptions of a Destruction that is a fait accompli, something the people are not willing to accept. He uses a variety of forms to illustrate his points, including symbolic acts, language that echoes predictions in the Torah, and parables that often interweave allegory and reality.

Moreover, Ezekiel is the first to prophesy in exile, serving to demonstrate that the people's future may, in fact, be outside of the land. This prediction – especially in light of the nation's fairly recent chronicles, in which tribes were lost to history after being exiled – is a hard one for both the exiles and the remnant in Jerusalem to accept. It signals a shift in the nation's very infrastructure. The prophet's message about individual responsibility reflects the new state of affairs; no longer is the nation judged as a unit. The new ideas prepare the nation for an existence outside of its homeland.

Ezekiel refers constantly to the nations that surround Israel – both in direct prophecies that relate to them and in his frequent mention of

Conclusion

the way in which they view Israel. The Destruction of the Temple and the return to the land are all forced on the nation by God, and they are meant to reverberate for the nations around it, proving first the nation's unworthiness and then God's supremacy.

Woven throughout the book are descriptions of God's glory moving from place to place. We follow God's glory as it departs the Temple – demonstrating the finality of the prophecies of Destruction – and then read Ezekiel's words of restoration, with the return of the Divine Presence to the future Temple. But this new Temple is a different one, protected from defilement and destruction. With the distancing of the people from the Sanctuary and the new forms of leadership, the Temple is safeguarded against the missteps of the past and can thus house the Divine Presence eternally. In the final chapters, Ezekiel provides a measure of restoration: The people, though physically removed from the Temple, will be drawn close to God in other ways, symbolized by the waters that run from the Temple outward.

Having completed the book, we are left with a lingering question as to the relationship between the prophet and his prophecy. Who is Ezekiel, the man? Where do his qualities, his thoughts, and his sorrow find expression? When are his words the words of God alone? We are familiar with our sages' teaching that "no two prophets prophesy in the identical phraseology" (Sanhedrin 89a). Does the absence of love, compassion, and sorrow in this book express a different dimension of God's connection with His people? What is the relationship between the prophecies of Jeremiah and Isaiah and those of Ezekiel? Should we strive to arrive at a harmonious understanding of these prophetic messages, which seem so different from one another? Or are they perhaps meant to be studied as different facets of God?

The question becomes even more pressing with the chapters describing the future Temple. Was there hope that the Second Temple would be built on this model? And after the Destruction of the Second Temple, is the model presented by Ezekiel in these chapters still relevant and achievable? Do we hope or pray for its implementation? And how?

Ezekiel's prophetic messages present the connection between God and His people, as well as the anticipated restoration of the nation, in a unique light. Sometimes it seems that the work of Ezekiel, the seer, is not yet complete.

Bibliography

Abraham, Kathleen. "An Inheritance Division among Judeans in Babylonia from the Early Persian Period," in *New Seals and Inscriptions, Hebrew, Idumean and Cuneiform.* (*Hebrew Bible Monographs 8*), ed. Meir Lubetski, 206–21. Sheffield: Sheffield Phoenix Press, 2007.

———. "The Reconstruction of Jewish Communities in the Persian Empire: The Al-Yahudu Clay Tablets," in *Light and Shadows – The Catalog – The Story of Iran and the Jews*, ed. H. Segev and A. Schor, 264–68. Tel Aviv: Beit Hatfutsot, 2001.

Ahituv, Shmuel. *Assufat Ketuvot Ivriyot MiYemei Bayit Rishon VeReshit Yemei Bayit Sheni*, 172. Jerusalem: Bialik, 1992.

———. *Echoes from the Past: Hebrew and Cognate Inscriptions from the Biblical Period*, 92, 126–33. Jerusalem: Carta, 2008.

Arnold, Bill T. *Who Were the Babylonians?*, 91–99. Atlanta: Society of Biblical Literature, 2004.

Assis, Elie. "Why Edom? On the Hostility Towards Jacob's Brother in Prophetic Sources," *Vetus Testamentum* 55 (2005): 1–20.

———. *Identity in Conflict: The Struggle between Esau and Jacob, Edom and Israel*. Winona Lake, IN: Eisenbrauns, 2016.

Ben-Yashar, Menachem. "HaMerkava BeSefer Yeḥezkel VeMikdash Me'at," *Iyunei Mikra VeParshanut* 4 (1997): 9–28.

Ben-Zeev, Yehuda Lieb. *Mavo el Mikra'ei Kodesh*. Vienna, 1810.

Block, D. I. *The Book of Ezekiel Chapter 1–24, NICOT*, 349-50. Cambridge: William B. Eerdmans, 1997.

Braslavy, Joseph. "Sofo shel Paro: HaTanim HaGadol LeOr Pulhan HaTanim BeMitzrayim (Yeḥezkel 29:32)," *Beit Mikra* 18, no. 2 (1973): 143–49.

Breuer, Mordechai. "The Prophecy of Isaiah," in *Pirkei Mo'adot*, 457–75. Jerusalem: Horev, 1986.

Brin, Gershon ed., *Yeḥezkel*, Olam HaTanakh. Tel Aviv: Revivim, 1993.

Brin, Gershon. *Iyunim BeSefer Yeḥezkel*, 80–105. Tel Aviv: Hakibbutz Hameuchad, 1975.

Buber, Salomon ed., *Midrash Eikha Rabba al pi Ktav Yad BeOtzar HaSefarim Romi*, 29. Hildesheim: Olms, 1967.

Bustenay, Oded. *Galut Yisrael ViYehuda BeAshur UBeBavel. (Mei'ot 8–6 Lifnei HaSfira)*. Haifa: Pardes, 2010.

Chavalas, Mark William, ed. *The Ancient Near East: Historical Sources in Translation*, 387–88. Malden, MA: Blackwell, 2006.

Cogan, Mordechai. *Ovadiah, Mikra LeYisrael*, 8-10. Tel Aviv/Jerusalem: Am Oved, 1993.

Cohen, Menachem ed., *Mikraot Gedolot "HaKeter": Sefer Yeḥezkel*. Jerusalem: Bar-Ilan University Press, 2000.

Elitzur, Yehuda "Yisrael BeMidbar HaAmim (Yeḥezkel 20:32–38)," in *Iyunim BeSefer Yeḥezkel*, ed. Yitzkhak Avishur, 43-66. Jerusalem: Kiryat Sefer, 1982.

Epstein, Isidore ed., *The Babylonian Talmud*. London: Soncino Press, 1961.

Feliks, Yehuda. *Nature and Man in the Bible*, 144–47. London: Soncino, 1981.

———. *Teva VaAretz BaTanakh: Prakim BeEkologia Mikrait*, 217–18. Jerusalem: Reuven Mass, 1992.

Fichman, Jacob. "Yeḥezkel," *Arugot: Divrei Shira UProza*, 51–52. Jerusalem: Bialik, 1954.

Ganzel, Tova and Shalom E. Holtz, "Ezekiel's Temple in Babylonian Context," *Vetus Testamentum* 64 (2014): 211–26.

Ganzel, Tova. "Haftarat Tetzaveh, Yeḥezkel 43:6–27," in *Maftirin BeNavi: Iyyunim BeHaftarot UVeDivrei HaNevi'im*, ed. Aharon Eldar, 341–43. Jerusalem: HaSokhnut HaYehudit, 2010.

———. "The Descriptions of the Restoration of Israel in Ezekiel," *Vetus Testamentum* 60 (2010): 197–211.

———. "The Prophecies of Joel: A Bridge between Ezekiel and Haggai," *Journal of Hebrew Scriptures* 11 (2011): 1–22.

Bibliography

Glassner, Jean-Jacques. *Mesopotamian Chronicles*, 226–35. Atlanta: Society of Biblical Literature, 2004.

Goldberg, Ilana. "HaItzuv HaOmanuti shel HaKina al Melekh Tzor," *Tarbiz* 58, no. 2 (1989): 277–81.

Greenberg, Moshe. "HaMuva'ot BeSefer Yeḥezkel KeReka LaNevuot," *Beit Mikra* 17, no. 3 (1972): 273–78.

Greenberg, Moshe. "The Design and Themes of Ezekiel's Program of Restoration," *Interpretation* 38 (1984): 181–208.

———. "Yeḥezkel 20 VeHaGalut HaRuhanit," in *Oz LeDavid: Kovetz Mehkarim BeTanakh, Mugash LeDavid Ben-Gurion BeMele'at Lo Shivim VeSheva Shanim*, ed. Yehezkel Kaufmann et al., 433–42. Jerusalem: HaḤevra LeḤeker HaMikra BeYisrael, 1964.

———. *Ezekiel 1–20*, The Anchor Bible Dictionary. Garden City, NY: Doubleday, 1983.

———. *Ezekiel 21–37*, The Anchor Bible, 628. Garden City, NY: Doubleday, 1983.

Grossman, Avraham. *Ḥakhmei Tzarfat HaRishonim*, 289. Jerusalem: Magnes, 2001.

Grossman, Yonatan. "'Kefel Keri'a Mivni' BeYeḥezkel 33–48," *Beit Mikra* 49, no. 2 (2004): 194–224.

HaKohen, Shmuel "Eser Masa'ot Nasa Shekhina," *Sinai* 88, no. 3–4 (1981): 104–19.

Hirschfeld, Hartwig trans. *The Kuzari (Kitab al Khazari): An Argument for the Faith of Israel*. New York: Schocken, 1964.

Hoffman, Yair. "LiShe'elat HaMivneh VeHaMashma'ut shel Yeḥezkel Perek 20," *Beit Mikra* 20, no. 4 (1975): 473–89.

Horowitz, H. Saul and Israel Abraham Rabin, eds., *Mekhilta DeRabbi Ishmael*, 135. Jerusalem: Bamburger at Wahrman, 1970.

Jursa, Michael. "Nabû-Sarrussu-Ukin, Rab Sa-Resi, and 'Nebusarkesim' (Jer. 39:3)," *Nouvelles Assyriologiques Brèves et Utilitaires* 5 (2008): 9–10.

Kaddari, Menachem Zvi. *Milon HaIvrit HaMikrait*, 1066. Ramat Gan: Bar-Ilan University Press, 5766.

Kahn, Danel. "Yehuda bein Bavel LeMitzrayim (594–586 BCE)," *Shnaton LeḤeker HaMikra VeHaMizrah HaKadum* 17 (2007): 147–59.

Kasher, Rimon. "Parashat HaElem BeSefer Yeḥezkel (unit 3:22–27)," *Beit Mikra* 43, 3–4 (2008): 227–44.

———. *Yeḥezkel 1–24*, Mikra LeYisrael. Tel Aviv: Am Oved/Magnes, 2004.

———. *Yeḥezkel 25–48*, Mikra LeYisrael. Tel Aviv: Am Oved/Magnes, 2004.

Katzenstein, H. Jacob. *The History of Tyre: From the Beginning of the Second Millennium B.C.E. until the Fall of the Neo-Babylonian Empire in 538 C.E.* Beer Sheva: Ben-Gurion University of the Negev Press, 1997.

Kimche, Dov, *Bein HaShittin shel HaTanakh,* 51-53. Jerusalem: Ahiasaf, 1941.

Koryat-Aharon, Ettie. "Mamlekhet HaIr Megiddo," *Moreshet Derekh*, November 2001: 95.

Licht, Jacob. *Megillat HaSerakhim MiMegillot Midbar Yehuda*, 78–79. Jerusalem: Bialik, 1996.

Lurie, Benzion. "Shafan – Sofer HaMelekh," *Beit Mikra* 34, no. 3 (1989): 261–64.

Mazor, Lea. "Masa Nahal HaPla'im min HaMikdash el HaYam (Yeḥezkel 47:1–12): Siluk HaTohu UBeria Hadasha," in *Gan BeEden Mi-Kedem*, ed. Rachel Elior, 81-104. Jerusalem: Magnes, 2010.

Milgrom, Jacob. *Leviticus, 23–27.* The Anchor Yale Bible Commentaries. New York: Doubleday, 2000.

Moskowitz, Yehiel Zvi. *Sefer Yeḥezkel, Daat Mikra.* Jerusalem: Mosad HaRav Kook, 1985.

Nebenzahl, Rav Avigdor. "HaShaar HaPoneh Kadim Yihyeh Sagur – Lama?" *Sinai* 123–124 (2000): 369.

Orland, Yaakov. "HaBika," *Shirim MeEretz Utz*, 20–21. Tel Aviv: Mahbarot LeSifrut, 1963.

Pearce, Laurie E. and Cornelia Wunsch, *Documents of Judean Exiles and West Semites in Babylonia in the Collection of David Sofer*, CUSAS 28. Bethesda: CDL: Press, 2014.

Pines, Shlomo trans., *Guide of the Perplexed.* Chicago: University of Chicago Press, 1963.

Polak, Frank. *HaSippur BaMikra*, 91–97. Jerusalem: Bialik, 1994.

Rendtorff, Rolf. "Hazon HaHakdasha shel Yeḥezkel tokh Hashvaa LeHazonot Makbilim BaMikra (Prakim 1–3)," in *Iyyunim BeSefer Yeḥezkel*, ed. Yitzhak Avishur, 89–108. Jerusalem: Kiryat Sefer, 1982.

Rivlin, A. E. "Mashal HaGefen VeHaEsh: Mivneh, Miktzav, VeDiktzia BeShirat Yeḥezkel," *Beit Mikra* 20, no. 4 (1975): 562–66.

Rosen-Zvi, Ishay. "'VeAsita Otkha KaAsher Asita:' Mabat Nosaf al Anishat HaNo'afot BeYeḥezkel 16 Ve- 23," *Beit Mikra* 50, no. 2 (2005): 163–93.

Rosenberg, A. J. *Judaica Books of the Prophets: A New English Translation of the Text and Rashi*. New York: Judaica Press.

Schwartz, Baruch J. "Mah Bein Munaḥ LeMetafora? Nasa Avon/Pesha/ Het BaMikra," *Tarbiz* 63 (1994): 149–71.

———. *Torat HaKedusha*, 219. Jerusalem: Magnes, 1999.

Stavrakopoulou, Francesca. "Gog's Grave and the Use and Abuse of Corpses in Ezekiel 39:11–20," *Journal of Biblical Literature* 129, no. 1 (2010): 67–84.

Stiebel, Guy D. "Lehotzi Ora LaOlam: Adrikhalut Simlit shel Mivnei Pulhan," *Eretz Israel* 28 (2007): 219–34.

Tadmor, Hayim. *Ashur, Bavel ViYehuda: Mehkarim BeToldot HaMizrah HaKadum*, 95–121. Jerusalem: Bialik, 2006.

Tanakh: The Holy Scriptures. Philadelphia: Jewish Publication Society, 1917.

Touger, Eliyahu, trans., *Mishneh Torah: A New Translation with Commentaries and Notes*, New York: Moznaim, 1991–2008.

Weiss, Meir. "Al Shlosha...Ve'al Arba'a," *Tarbiz* 36 (1966): 307–18.

Yeivin, Shmuel. "Tokh Kedei Keria BeSefer Yeḥezkel," *Beit Mikra* 18, no. 2 (1973): 164–75.

Zadok, Ran "Judeans in Babylonia – Updating the Dossier," in *Encounters by the Rivers of Babylon: Scholarly Conversations between Jews, Iranians and Babylonians in Antiquity*, ed. Uri Gabbay and Shai Secunda, 109–29. TSAJ 160. Tübingen: Mohr Siebeck, 2014.

———. "The Jews in Babylonia During the Chaldean and Achaemenian Periods According to the Babylonian Sources," *Studies in the History of the Jewish People and the Land of Israel* 3. Haifa: University of Haifa, 1979.

Zadok, Ran. *Geographical Names According to New-and Late-Babylonian Texts.* Wiesbaden: L. Reichert, 1985.
Zadok, Ran. *The Earliest Diaspora: Israelites and Judeans in Pre-Hellenistic Mesopotamia.* Tel Aviv: Tel Aviv University, 2002.
Zakovitch, Yair. *Mavo LeParshanut Penim Mikra'it.* Even Yehuda: Rekhes, 1992.

Other books in the Maggid Studies in Tanakh series:

Genesis: From Creation to Covenant
Zvi Grumet

Joshua: The Challenge of the Promised Land
Michael Hattin

Judges: The Perils of Possession
Michael Hattin

I Kings: Torn in Two
Alex Israel

II Kings: In a Whirlwind
Alex Israel

Isaiah: Prophet of Righteousness and Justice
Yoel Bin-Nun and Binyamin Lau

Jeremiah: The Fate of a Prophet
Binyamin Lau

Jonah: The Reluctant Prophet
Erica Brown

Nahum, Habakkuk, and Zephaniah
Yaakov Beasley

Haggai, Zechariah, and Malachi: Prophecy in an Age of Uncertainty
Hayyim Angel

Ruth: From Alienation to Monarchy
Yael Ziegler

Eikha: Faith in a Turbulent World (forthcoming)
Yael Ziegler

Esther: Power, Fate, and Fragility in Exile
Erica Brown

Nehemiah: Statesman and Sage
Dov S. Zakheim

The fonts used in this book are from the Arno family

Maggid Books
The best of contemporary Jewish thought from
Koren Publishers Jerusalem Ltd.